W9-CKS-152

ALCOHOLISM

Property of Nurse's
Station

Westbrook
Community
Hospital

ALCOHOLISM
A Practical Treatment Guide

Edited by

Stanley E. Gitlow, M.D.
Clinical Professor of Medicine
Mount Sinai School of Medicine
City University of New York
Chairman, Committee on Alcoholism
Medical Society of the State of New York
Former President, American Medical Society
  on Alcoholism
Panel on Alcoholism, American Medical Association
New York, New York

Herbert S. Peyser, M.D.
Visiting Consultant Psychiatrist
Smithers Alcoholism Center
St. Luke's-Roosevelt Hospital
Chairman, Committee on Mental Health
Medical Society of the State of New York
Associate Attending Psychiatrist
Mount Sinai Hospital
Assistant Clinical Professor of Psychiatry
Mount Sinai School of Medicine
New York, New York

 Grune & Stratton, Inc.
(Harcourt Brace Jovanovich, Publishers)
Orlando   San Diego   New York
London   Toronto   Montreal   Sydney   Tokyo

Library of Congress Cataloging in Publication Data

Main entry under title:

Alcoholism, a practical treatment guide.
   Includes bibliography and index.
   1. Alcoholism. I. Gitlow, Stanley E. II. Pey-
ser, Herbert S. [DNLM: 1. Alcoholism—Therapy.
WM274.3 A355]
RC565.A4452   616.86'1   79-28228
ISBN 0-8089-1227-5

© 1980 by Grune & Stratton, Inc. All rights reserved. No
part of this publication may be reproduced or transmitted
in any form or by any means, electronic or mechanical,
including photocopy, recording, or any information storage and retrieval system, without permission in writing
from the publisher.

Grune & Stratton, Inc.
Orlando, Florida 32887

Distributed in the United Kingdom by
Grune & Stratton, Ltd.
24/28 Oval Road, London NW 1

Library of Congress Catalog Number 79-28228
International Standard Book Number 0-8089-1227-5
Printed in the United States of America

84 85 86 87   10 9 8 7 6 5

This text is dedicated to those whose suffering enlightens the healer.

Contents

Preface

This volume is intended to assist the practitioner in detecting and treating one of the most common illnesses currently challenging the art of medicine. Despite the often noted difficulties of treating the alcoholic, specific lay and professional efforts have succeeded in attaining impressive recoveries. What follows is a distillation of experiences of some of the foremost practitioners of this art. As a pragmatic guide, it avoids detailed references to scientific studies. No attempt is made to achieve the status of a reference text, of which there are currently many fine examples.

Throughout this text, the masculine gender has been used to refer to the patient with alcoholism, and the consort has been assumed to be feminine. Rather than a sexist bias, this reflects only a desire to achieve a convenient style. The reader should bear in mind that at least 30 percent of the alcoholics are women (see Chapter 9).

The editors wish to express their gratitude to the individual contributors whose experience and expert knowledge permitted the formulation of such a treatment guide. Lucy Robe offered great assistance in achieving a useful format, and Shirley Miller worked hard and long in transcribing material that could at times only be kindly described as disorganized.

If this text helps the clinically oriented practitioner to bring relief and recovery to some of those patients suffering from alcoholism, all of our efforts will be rewarded.

Stanley E. Gitlow, M.D.
Herbert S. Peyser, M.D.

Contributors

Richard Baum, M.D.
Associate Professor of Medicine
Department of Medicine
University of Maryland School of Medicine
Veterans Administration Hospital
Baltimore, Maryland

LeClair Bissell, M.D.
Former Chief of Smithers Alcoholism Center
New York, New York
President
Edgehill/Newport, Inc.
Newport, Rhode Island

Marvin A. Block, M.D.
Emeritus Associate Professor of Clinical Medicine
State University of New York at Buffalo Medical School
Senior Physician, Buffalo General Hospital
Chairman, Committee on Alcoholism of the Council on Mental
  Health of the American Medical Association, 1953–1963
Buffalo, New York

Marvin D. Feit, Ph.D.
Assistant Professor
University of Tennessee School of Social Work
Assistant Clinical Professor
Department of Psychiatry
University of Tennessee Center for the Health Sciences
Memphis, Tennessee

Robert D. Fink, M.D.
Superintendant
Memphis Mental Health Institute
Clinical Associate Professor of Psychiatry
University of Tennessee Center for the Health Sciences
Memphis, Tennessee

Vernell Fox, M.D.
Medical Director of Alcoholism Treatment Service
Pomona Valley Community Hospital
Pomona, California
Associate Clinical Professor of Psychiatry
University of California at Los Angeles
Los Angeles, California

Stanley E. Gitlow, M.D.
Clinical Professor of Medicine
Mount Sinai School of Medicine
City University of New York
Chairman, Committee on Alcoholism
Medical Society of the State of New York
Former President, American Medical Society
*   on Alcoholism*
Panel on Alcoholism, American Medical Association
New York, New York

Lynne Hennecke
Chairwoman, Alcoholism Task Force
Women in Crisis
Doctoral Candidate
Teachers College
Columbia University
New York, New York

Frank L. Iber, M.D.
Professor of Medicine
Chief, Gastroenterology Division
University of Maryland School of Medicine
Veterans Administration Hospital
Baltimore, Maryland

James A. Knight, M.D.
Professor of Psychiatry
Louisiana State University School of Medicine
New Orleans, Louisiana

David H. Knott, M.D., Ph.D.
Medical Director
Alcohol and Drug Dependence Clinic
State of Tennessee Department of Mental Health and Mental
*   Retardation*
Memphis Mental Health Institute
Memphis, Tennessee

Jack C. Morgan, M.D.
Clinical Instructor in Psychiatry
Department of Psychiatry
University of Tennessee Center for the Health Sciences
Memphis, Tennessee

Robert D. O'Connor, M.D., F.A.C.P.
Medical Director
Chit Chat Farms and Caron Hospital
Galen Hall Road
Wernersville, Pennsylvania

Herbert S. Peyser, M.D.
Visiting Consultant Psychiatrist
Smithers Alcoholism Center
St. Luke's-Roosevelt Hospital
Chairman, Committee on Mental Health
Medical Society of the State of New York
Associate Attending Psychiatrist
Mount Sinai Hospital
Assistant Clinical Professor of Psychiatry
Mount Sinai School of Medicine
New York, New York

Joseph A. Pursch, M.D.
Chief, Alcohol Rehabilitation Service
Naval Regional Medical Center
Long Beach, California

Frank A. Seixas, M.D.
Former Medical Director
National Council on Alcoholism
Clinical Associate Professor, Public Health
Cornell University Medical College
New York, New York

Gerald D. Shulman, M.A.
Director of Development
Health Institutes
Wernersville, Pennsylvania

Joseph J. Zuska, M.D.
Director
Alcoholism Recovery Services
St. Joseph Hospital
Orange, California

ALCOHOLISM

Stanley E. Gitlow

1
An Overview

The practicing physician, steering his personal course through life, suffers at least the common adversities that beset people forced to cope with the overwhelming forces which tend to swamp their frail vessels. This is so despite the physician's own reputation, and perhaps even an intimate need, for being able to control the frightening events which modify one's course prior to the final harbor. While attempting to exercise such precarious and fragile control, the physician encounters patients who fail to respond to assistance as well as those who, through noncompliance, appear to aid and abet their natural enemies. These enemies, infection, trauma, and neoplasia, even appear to be courted by lifestyles at variance with the medical optimum. Sadly, the physician, who might well embrace the medical discipline for the purpose of sharpening an ability to control such unpleasant fates, is thrust face to face with those very patients who thwart his desire to control disease and delay death.

This circumstance might explain in part the reticence with which today's physician approaches any chronic and recurrent illness. The special reticence with which the medical community has approached alcoholism, however, demands a greater endeavor for its understanding. Hospitals treat the medical complications of alcoholism but almost routinely fail to possess even a rudimentary treatment program for alcoholism itself. The term

1

ALCOHOLISM
ISBN 0-8089-1227-5

Copyright © 1980 by Grune & Stratton
All rights of reproduction in any form reserved.

alcoholism is rarely applied as a discharge diagnosis from an acute medical care facility to those very patients for whom the control of alcoholism represents a primary requirement for the adequate treatment of their hepatic cirrhosis, primary myocardial disease, or tuberculosis. Even those physicians working in hospitals with alcoholism treatment programs fail to refer such patients for appropriate care. Why? Can it be that in contradistinction to the other chronic illnesses, alcoholism makes specific and special demands upon the physician since drug therapy plays so small and insignificant a role in its care? Is it simpler to label these patients as "untreatable" rather than invest the time and personal involvement required in order to achieve therapeutic success? Was alcoholism the subject when we were taught "for every problem there is an answer—quick, easy, and wrong?" Does alcoholism, through its societal and moral implications, somehow awaken discomfort, perhaps even fear, within the physician? Or is it simply that we were taught so blessed little in our medical training that we can only approach this patient with a sense of foreboding, frustration, and futility?

The callous and uncaring attitude masquerading as "scientific" by the primary care physician has failed to convince the now cynical lay public of our motives. Those of us with many years of clinical experience do not require consumer advocates to convince us of the serious errors inherent in medical school curricula which result from "power plays" by departmental chairmen without regard for the health needs of the public. Exposure to the patient with alcoholism during the first eight weeks of medical school revealed that the student's preoccupation was with such issues as "why does a person drink," "what is this person's life like," "how does his family relate to the problem," and "how does he feel," rather than the fourth-year student's fixation with the SGOT and even less important esoterica.* It takes us four long, hard years to eradicate the student's humanism, all the while missing an enormous opportunity of allowing him to care for and empathize with the millions suffering from this common but treatable illness. Not only does alcoholism offer overwhelming numbers for the developing physician, but here he can study the intricate

---

*Experience with course on "Perspectives in Medicine" at Mount Sinai School of Medicine.

interrelationships of somatic complications, psychic and societal impacts upon disease, paramedical roles in disease treatment and prevention, and the import of his own attitude upon the outcome of treatment efforts.

This text has been planned in answer to the need for a simple and straightforward method by which the physician may conceptualize alcoholism, the patient's suffering from it, and those therapeutic modalities which experienced therapists have used for its treatment. Though perhaps succumbing to the stylistic problems inherent in multiple authorship, the book capitalizes on this circumstance by reflecting viewpoints of many of the experienced and authoritative experts in this country today.

At this juncture, the disease concept of alcoholism will be briefly examined in order to permit the student of medicine to approach this illness within that rational framework of study commonly applied to other human ailments.

DISEASE CONCEPT OF ALCOHOLISM

Alcoholism is a disease characterized by the repetitive and compulsive ingestion of any sedative drug, ethanol representing but one of this group, in such a way as to result in interference with some aspect of the patient's life, be it health, marital status, career, interpersonal relationships, or other required societal adaptations. (As with any other illness, alcoholism represents a dysfunction or maladaptation to the requirements of everyday life.)The key aspect of the definition rests in the recurrent return to the use of a soporific *despite* the subject's definitive best interest. No mention need be made concerning the specific volume of alcohol consumed nor the frequency with which such consumption takes place. Indeed, there are patients with this illness who ingest nothing stronger than beer, and there are those whose alcoholic intake is limited to but once or twice per year. Many, if not most patients with this disease, make substantive efforts to control the frequency or volume of their drinking, thereby achieving the status of what is commonly called "a periodic." The essence of the diagnosis rests in their need to control their drinking as opposed to their inability to do so. Normal subjects do not need to control their drinking any more than patients with alcoholism need to control their intake of carrots, beets, or cauliflower.

Unfortunately, inadequate clinical experience has led to some semantic abominations which lie-in-wait to entrap the unwary student. Our federal legislators notwithstanding, just what is "alcohol abuse?" Does it include repetitive injury to the individual's life? If so, the name is alcoholism, and if not, we need no special term. Similarly, the DSM-III, our standard reference work for psychiatric nomenclature, refers to "alcohol dependence (alcoholism)," without apparent appreciation that the disease known as alcoholism does not *equal* alcohol addiction (dependence) for a number of reasons: (1) one may have alcoholism but no longer drink; (2) the term "dependence" signifies that discontinuation of a drug results in objective physiologic derangements which may, at least in part, be relieved by the drug's readministration. In that sense, the elevated psychomotor activity (agitation) which follows the sedative action of ethanol represents the addictive phenomenon; it can be relieved by further sedative ingestion (only to reappear, even worse, later). It has been clearly established by clinical pharmacology, as well as by animal studies, that such evidence of addiction to sedative drugs starts and can be demonstrated objectively with as little as a single modest (social or therapeutic) dose. We must therefore conclude that despite the quantitative differences in the degree and frequency of ethanol addiction in the social drinker versus the alcoholic, "alcohol dependence" is nonetheless not synonymous with "alcoholism."

The student of medicine might well consider alcoholism within that framework of disease which permits some variation in its expression without necessarily resulting in overwhelming diagnostic difficulty. Thus, instead of labeling typhoid fever as alpha, beta, or gamma in type, we simply accept that in any typhoid epidemic there will be patients whose disease results in minimal dysfunction, enormous and prolonged disability, numerous complications, or even death despite the best of medical care. Similarly, lupus erythematosus may at times run a reasonably benign course involving only certain tissues, whereas in other patients it may involve other tissues and result in a rapidly progressive and downhill picture.

The term "disease" signifies only the absence of comfort, but more detailed definitions demand that the ailment be specific or particular and that it possess characteristic symptoms or causes. Thus a "symptom" is a phenomenon of disease, and the ultimate decision regarding classification of any illness as a disease rests upon whether or not the signs and symptoms commonly associated with it suffice to describe a specific entity. Any morbid entity can only be so evaluated by determining whether or not its associated symptoms, signs, etiology, distribution, complications, prognosis, and therapy are similar among the majority of patients so as to warrant the term disease as opposed to symptom. Differing social, ethnic, and racial factors result in variability in the expression of many illnesses, a circumstance which does not ordinarily detract from the use of the term disease. Those who have worked with patients suffering from alcoholism have had little question but that the histories, symptoms, and signs of this illness form a recognizable pattern. Indeed, there is little or no difference of opinion concerning this illness during its period characterized by substantive addiction. Rather, the nosological problem arises with the patient who has successfully completed detoxification. Even then, however, the student of this disease sees patterns of behavior that remain remarkably consistent and result in therapeutic and prognostic issues possessing similar consistency. The complications of this illness, though varied, are nonetheless similarly reproducible.

Perhaps the circumstance that has caused greatest misunderstanding, namely the nature of the premorbid personality of the patient suffering from alcoholism, may be viewed best from the vantage point of the fullblown clinical illness. Though the alcoholic's illness may begin from quite diverse psychological origins, once the disease of alcoholism has been grafted upon this personality structure, it dominates the clinical picture and eventually becomes the major determinant in both choice and efficacy of therapy. Thus, a patient's neurosis, character disorder, sociopathy, or affective disorder—each posing singular and somewhat specific problems—all present a clinical picture and therapeutic needs of great similarity once alcoholism has appeared.

It is hoped that we have passed the era in which functional disorders of the brain, whether of demonstrated biochemical nature such as phenylpyruvic oligophrenia or of unknown etiology such as schizophrenia or alcoholism, required the use of a term lesser or other than disease simply because 19th century pathologists had difficulty observing a defect in the gross anatomy of the organ.

Application of such a term permits the dignity and right to obtain medical attention. It fixes the responsibility of the clinical care of the alcoholic and for research into the nature of the alcoholic's suffering upon physicians, their paramedical and basic science partners. Finally, it is in the best interest of our patients since it is associated with the lowest rate of recidivism.

ALCOHOL ADDICTION

As a "lumper" rather than a "divider" of medical entities, it was natural to coin the term "sedativism" a few decades ago when it became apparent to this writer that, to most of his patients with alcoholism, it mattered little whether they ingested ethanol or any of the other somnifacient medications listed in Appendix A of this text. In fact, it seemed that chloralism, bromism, barbism, or paraldism would have been the logical name of this entity had these other sedatives simply appeared prior to alcohol. The soporific drugs act upon the brain in an almost identical manner. They elicit short-term, large amplitude sedation, followed by long-term, low amplitude agitation (Fig. 1-1). The exact temporal relationships of these asynchronous effects vary with the soporific in question, just as the rate of absorption and catabolism of the various drugs also vary. Approximately twofold tolerance can be achieved to the various soporific drugs, and when such tolerance has been achieved to any one drug of this group, it is simultaneously present for the remaining. Thus, patients with alcoholism reveal cross addiction and cross tolerance among all of the agents that are classified as somnifacients (see Appendix A). It is not unusual to hear patients describe Librium as just "the very driest of martinis." Fully fifty percent of the alcoholic patients in my own community have had addictive problems with one or another of the solid sedative compounds. The Seconal addict, though missing the malodorous breath, florid facies, protuberant abdomen, and some of the other organic complications of alcoholism,

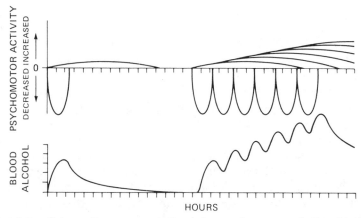

Fig. 1-1. Schematic representation of asynchronous relationship between short-term, large amplitude sedative effect of ethanol and its long-term, low amplitude agitating effect (left). Repeated doses of ethanol result in summation of its agitating effect (right). [Reprinted by permission from Gitlow SE: Alcoholism: A disease, in Bourne PG, Fox R (eds): *Alcoholism: Progress in Research and Treatment.* New York, Academic Press, 1973.]

nonetheless presents a clinical picture and a therapeutic problem almost precisely the same as those of the patient whose only soporific has been alcohol. This circumstance is stressed at this point in order to prevent the physician from offering the patient assistance out of the frying pan of alcohol use and into the fire of solid sedatives. Rarely does a therapeutic response result from the outpatient administration of tranquilizers or other sedatives to the actively drinking alcoholic, despite the patient's deep conviction and desire to learn what medical techniques the physician might offer to enable him to continue drinking in his usual manner.

The major tolerance to sedative drugs results from central nervous system adaptation; that is, a new balance is set up between the agitation remaining from yesterday's sedatives and the sedation resulting from today's sedatives. When the latter is discontinued, the agitation appears in full and the patient is said to be suffering from a withdrawal syndrome. Clinically unimportant variations in tolerance may be seen among individuals, ethnic groups, and following enzyme induction after administration of

those substances catabolized by the hepatic Microsomal Ethanol
Oxidizing System (MEOS). Another critical variation in tolerance
appears to result from increasing age. Thus, most older patients
with this illness will grudgingly confess that less alcohol is required to achieve a desired state and that this condition is both
shorter and followed by a more prolonged and disagreeable agitation than had been noted previously. This phenomenon appears to
parallel the ability of the central nervous system to tolerate other
untoward incidents as well. The boxer at age 40 cannot tolerate
head trauma as well as the boxer at age 20. Superficially, this
appears to be distinct from whatever central nervous system injury the drug itself might have produced on a chronic basis, since
teetotallers or modest drinkers can also detect this change with
age.

The sedative effect of alcohol rarely persists longer than 2–5
hours, agitation appearing coincident with the peak blood levels
of this drug (usually at the end of the second hour after its oral
administration). The term "withdrawal syndrome" is in that
sense a misnomer. Thus, the same blood ethanol levels on the
uplimb and downlimb of the blood concentration curve are associated with sedation on the one hand and agitation on the other.
Whereas the sedative effect of ethanol is of short duration but
large amplitude, the agitation following it is more subtle (lower
amplitude) and of much greater duration. These diphasic and
asynchronous psychomotor effects occur with each of the soporific
drugs, though precise amplitude and duration of each effect may
be specific to the individual agent. Though alcohol ingestion results in a varying psychological response, this desired effect is
always concomitant with the sedative effect of the drug. It may be
casually observed that no one imbibes for the effect noticed the
morning after. It is more than a little intriguing that the agitating actions of these compounds which make up the so-called withdrawal syndrome bear no relationship whatever to the rate of
excretion or degradation of the soporific substance. Thus, the
temporal and sequential relationships between sedation and agitation in the human and the mouse are precisely the same despite
the fact that the rodent catabolizes alcohol tenfold faster. Apparently the pharmacologic effect is specific to neural tissue rather
than the metabolism of the drug. An analogy may be made to
head trauma with a hammer: the speed with which the hammer is

removed from the scalp bears little relationship to the extent or duration of the CNS dysfunction. The phenomena associated with the agitation can be temporarily controlled by the sedative action of any of the soporific drugs, but each would add its own agitation to the eventual problem. The withdrawal syndrome would appear most mild in that youthful subject who drank the smallest amount for the shortest period of time and who was otherwise in good health. As the quantity and duration of sedative administration increases, the severity of this syndrome similarly increases from simple tremulousness, insomnia, palpitation, diaphoresis, and a vague sense of foreboding to the extreme of amnesia, hallucinations, and delirium tremens. At all levels of this syndrome, there is an increased tendency to grand mal seizures.

So much then for a brief description of the addiction to alcohol, a circumstance that can be reproduced in any normal volunteer. What must be kept in mind, however, is that such an addictive state in a volunteer is far from the disease called alcoholism. It is unlikely that any volunteer who once had experienced acute alcoholic hallucinosis or delirium tremens replete with seizure activity would be likely to re-volunteer for a similar experience. On the other hand, the patient with alcoholism "volunteers" over and over and over again, somehow unable to learn that each time alcohol ingestion begins, the state is set for repetition of the enormous discomfort and personal danger associated with the withdrawal syndrome. Some psychoanalysts may well believe that this "inability to learn" stems from some purely functional quirk of the personality structure. It is so simple to assume that temptation affects us all and that we must all control our appetites equally. Moral turpitude would then seem the essential ingredient in alcoholism. How pompous and self-indulgent a conclusion when some, perhaps most, of us require so little control. Is it not equally possible that *excessive need* represents the problem rather than *deficient resistance?* One is reminded of the congenitally obese rodents who fail to control their abnormally large appetites until given nalorphine to counteract their excessive endorphin synthesis. Similarly the genetic data of Goodwin, Shukit, and others should give us pause to consider the possible organicity of this disorder. Though it is tempting at the present time to embrace either a medical, a psychiatric, or a societal model for alcoholism, should we not use all of these in order to maintain an open mind today concerning the nature of this disease which few understand and nobody knows?

THE DIAGNOSIS OF ALCOHOLISM

It has long been obvious that in the teaching of medicine no one learned the characteristics of a disease without the opportunity of intimate clinical contact. Since most of those patients with alcoholism with whom a young physician has contact have not recovered from the illness, and since denial and deception represent so great a part of its expression, little can be learned about alcoholism from such patients. It is therefore essential that in order to sharpen one's diagnostic skills as well as to conceptualize a clinical picture of the illness adequate enough to permit the later development of a dialogue with such a patient, young physicians or students must attend at least a dozen open meetings of Alcoholics Anonymous. With but rare exception could they obtain as much clinical material through a visit to some other "epidemic." The diagnosis of alcoholism first requires, then, a clinical awareness of the nature of the illness. Second, a high degree of suspicion should be maintained whenever a patient presents multifactorial dysfunctional elements within his life. These patients can be likened to the Little Abner cartoon character who possessed his own personal raincloud which followed him wherever he went. Marriage, career, health—all seem destined to fall into a disrepair beyond this patient's ability to change. Yes, one may legitimately hypothesize that some other personality problem might be responsible for such dysfunction, but in today's society, alcoholism still represents the bet to beat. More specifically, the tremulous, flushed, diaphoretic patient who appears thyrotoxic but who tests negatively is most likely alcoholic. So, too, is the patient who arrives for a physical examination one morning replete with alcohol on the breath; the patient with multiple burns especially on the fingers and chest; the patient with protuberant abdomen, thin legs, dilated venules over the nose and malar eminences, and unhealthy gingeval tissues; the patient whose peptic disease, hypertension, or tuberculosis seems impossible to control consistently; the patient with adult onset

generalized seizure activity; the patient with otherwise unexplained hepatomegaly or hepatic dysfunction; the adult patient
with bilateral parotid enlargement; the patient with conversion
and psychosomatic symptoms including headache, gastrointestinal dysfunction, muscle spasm, fatigue, and palpitations; the patient with decreased attention span, diminished ability to concentrate, and reduced memory for recent events who also notices
secondary insomnia and agitation. All of these represent clues for
the alert physician, but none are as rewarding as a carefully
taken history in which intimate personal behavior and relationships are examined in a warm and friendly fashion. The ultimate
diagnosis of alcoholism in such circumstances requires a sympathetic confrontation, revealing to the patient those very circumstances discovered while taking the history. One might be
unable to establish a definitive diagnosis at the moment of initial
contact with the patient, but a relationship should be established
which would eventually permit an intimate and candid discussion. The physician must be trustworthy, credible, and nonjudgmental in order to achieve such a relationship. Rather than
reflect on how big a liar the patient is, bear in mind that his
denial of the problem remains proportionate to a sense of
hopelessness in dealing with a compulsion, the nature of which he
cannot understand and the magnitude of which has invariably
dominated an ability to cope rationally with the problems of life.
This is not the only illness associated with denial. Very few years
ago, a brilliant colleague of mine who taught clinical internal
medicine for many decades expired after failing to detect his colonic carcinoma despite a change in bowel habits and blood in his
stools.

   Those patients who seek your good office for reasons apparently unrelated to their sedative ingestion but whose real diagnosis is alcoholism reflect the size of their denial by the magnitude of the problems or symptoms which they are attempting to
ignore or blame on unrelated circumstances. The physician can
thereby gauge the fear with which the patient approaches the
possible need to stop drinking. Most patients are usually quite
convinced that you should leave their drinking alone and simply
deal with their symptoms. Should you do that, you assist in the
eventual destruction of your patient. Should you alternatively
attempt to correlate his alcohol ingestion and somatic difficulties,

you may alienate and, despite all the tact you can muster, lose further contact with the patient. A prolonged opportunity for your patient to ventilate, interspersed with sympathetic and understanding comments of your honest concern may, however, serve as a bridge over which you may be able to carry your most unwelcome and frightening message. Should you fail in this confrontation, this patient and this particular illness will not be the first to leave your good office in order to find an easier-to-accept opinion from a colleague. It is hoped that your colleague will also be honest, knowledgable, and tactful, but it may be many years before this patient will confront you with gratitude for the role which you played in his recovery.

TREATMENT OF ALCOHOLISM

Having established a diagnosis of alcoholism, what next? Treatment of all illnesses is aimed at improved function. This is true in dealing with a broken limb or with congestive heart failure. It is also true for alcoholism. We have heard much about abstinence representing an aim in the treatment of this disease. This is an error. Abstinence is not an aim but rather a means to an end. The end is simply that of improved function. For the patient with alcoholism, this aim cannot be consistently attained without abstinence, the reasons for which are threefold:

1. *To diminish the elevated psychomotor activity associated with alcohol ingestion.* Classically, the alcoholic prefers the minimally sedated state. In fact, it is not unusual to hear such a patient claim that it was only after the first drink that he felt "normal,—like everyone else, for the first time." If the patient's normal psychomotor state is almost untenable, if a moderately sedated condition is more agreeable, and if each and every sedative drug eventually results in prolonged agitation, how then will this patient adjust to the continued or intermittent use of soporific drugs? The pharmacology of these agents serves to explain the reason for the A.A. view of "one is never enough but always too much." The clinically naive consider that this so-called medical model of alcoholism

requires uncontrollable drinking to follow any single ingestion of alcohol or other sedative. This is simply not true.
Rather, the alcoholic can never be certain which initial drink
will eventually result in loss of control and substantive self-
destructive behavior. The issue then is that any rational and
healthy person who could not anticipate which drink would
lead to eventual injury would avoid drinking in the first
place. The alcoholic is unable to accomplish this consistently.
Use of the soporific results in the variable agitation described
earlier; it represents the "hook" of the addiction and as such
is enormously uncomfortable for the alcoholic.

2. *To control organic pathology.* Almost every complication of
   alcoholism requires abstinence for a maximal rate of improvement. In almost every instance, medical therapy in the
   presence of active drinking fails to achieve a satisfactory recovery. Similarly, a minimal therapeutic effort is usually followed by maximal recovery when abstinence is achieved.
   Hence, the physician, from no matter what discipline, should
   focus firmly on the requirement to achieve abstinence since
   this and this alone appears to achieve the greatest likelihood
   for recovery from the organic complications of this illness.

3. *For psychotherapy.* It is as impossible to develop insight for
   the actively drinking alcoholic as it is to perform psychotherapy on one of the active contenders in the midst of a prize
   fight. Just as the internist must realize that the organic dysfunction associated with the withdrawal syndrome has a concomitant defect in cognitive function, so, too, must the psychiatrist realize that sedative drugs modify brain function in
   such a manner as to markedly interfere with the development of insight. I am reminded of the patient who quipped
   "It's hard to learn to navigate from the deck of a sinking
   ship." Numerous alcoholics, including alcoholic physicians
   and psychiatrists, have volunteered their experiences relevant to the impossibility of achieving psychotherapeutic results during the use of alcohol. In fact, the development of
   insight during psychotherapy tends to be quantal in nature
   rather than a continuum. The patient need only drink periodically, at those times during which insight might otherwise
   develop, for the psychotherapeutic effort to be largely can-
   celled.

Thus, abstinence becomes our means to the aim of improved function. Therapy itself is roughly divided into three parts: achieving motivation, detoxification, and definitive care. These tend to blend together just as establishing the diagnosis and confronting the patient will very often blend with the act of motivating the patient. During the period of detoxification, the able physician is setting the stage for the patient's definitive course.

Accomplishing any of these three elements of treatment requires the willingness on the part of the physician to treat both the patient and the disease. This willingness can be determined by asking three questions:

1. *Does the physician believe that he has something to offer?* Every physician, with perhaps the singular exception of the pathologist, treats the alcoholic. Unhappily, the majority are probably unaware of the diagnosis their patients present. But whether it is the pediatrician who treats the abused child of the alcoholic parent, the obstetrician who delivers the infant disabled by the fetal alcohol syndrome, the surgeon who operates on the mangled trauma victim destined for D.T.s, or the ENT surgeon who resects the laryngal cancer, each, directly or indirectly, is treating the alcoholic. Thus, every physician should have something to offer. In truth, however, only the physicians who feel they can help, help. For this, they must have acquired personal experience with recoveries achieved by other patients who had suffered equally or greater from their alcoholism.

2. *Can the physician give the necessary time?* The diagnosis and confrontation of the alcoholic requires at least an hour and sometimes a number of separate hours of intimate contact with the patient. Motivating the patient can usually be accomplished during that period. Under the best of circumstances, most physicians should be able to accomplish this much: making the diagnosis, confronting the patient, and motivating the treatment. The patient's further care through detoxification and definitive therapy may well tax the physician too much and require areas of expertise which he might not possess. The chapters that follow go into considerable detail concerning the methods for referral of such a patient.

3. *Can the physician identify with the patient?* There is some
   reason to believe that when the ratio of patients to physicians
   is too great, when the patient's appearance or other qualifica-
   tions differ too greatly from that of the physician, or when the
   patient elicits personal fear or possibly frustration in the
   physician, the quality of medical care suffers. This is true in
   epidemics, major disasters, and circumstances wherein the
   physician may differ greatly from the patient in religion,
   race, and ethnic origin. The problem of "over identification"
   also must be noted, since a physician might well require, for
   himself, a patient's recovery. The physician's personal drinking habits, as well as his attitude toward drugs and
   chemotherapy in general, may well determine the ability to
   treat an alcoholic. It is of more than casual interest that,
   until a few years ago, a training psychoanalyst would
   examine in detail the physician-patient's attitude toward
   love, money, sex, family, etc., but almost uniformly fail to
   evaluate attitudes toward the use of social-psychoactive
   drugs—despite the estimated ten percent incidence of alcoholism and other drug addiction among physicians.

Having determined the willingness of the physician to treat
the alcoholic, how can he motivate the patient to enter into
treatment? At the outset, it should be apparent that the need to
be motivated may be estimated from the characteristics of the
patient's initial presentation. For instance, if the patient comes to
the physician's office primarily because drinking has resulted in a
loss of control of his life and those aspects of it which he most
values (home, job, and health), it implies that major steps towards
recovery have been taken: the patient recognizes that alcohol
and/or other sedative ingestion plays a major role in the illness,
that he is powerless in controlling it, and therefore requires professional assistance in combating it. The patient has quite apparently, though perhaps temporarily, abandoned some of his denial
and may possess, with little effort on your part, that motivation
necessary to initiate rehabilitation. If, on the other hand, the
patient seeks your assistance primarily because someone else
demands that he speak to you concerning his drinking, there is
still active denial. His appearance to your office implies suspicion
that he might indeed have a drinking problem, and it also permits

immediate discussion of those personal events in his life which
led to the displeasure and concern of a "significant other." His
appearance also implies that he continues to possess circumstances in his life which maintain substantive meaningful-
ness to him—otherwise no coercion would be possible.

Finally, the patient may seek your assistance for a reason
which seems to him to be unrelated to alcohol use. Whether physical (headaches, gastrointestinal disturbances, hypertension) or
emotional (marital discord, anxiety over job, insomnia, or agitation), the patient fails to formulate any connection between the
drinking and the problem. The immensity of the denial can best
be estimated by the magnitude of the symptom which is ignored
or blamed on unrelated circumstances. The physician can thereby
gauge the fear which the patient has concerning the possible need
for giving up alcohol. In approaching this most difficult problem,
the physician must bear in mind that the patient has attempted
to relinquish his particular method of dealing with life's problems
by substituting some alternative scheme for coping,—to no avail.
Hence his conviction that you should leave his drinking alone and
simply deal with his symptoms. Foremost, he would prefer that
you exert all of your professional skill in developing a plan
whereby he can continue to drink without further difficulty. If
you are unwilling or unable to accomplish this, the patient is at
least certain that: (1) having lived with himself for innumerable
years, he is much more cognizant of his personal problems than
you could possibly be; and (2) he knows a great deal more about
drinking than you possibly could. Sometime during the interview,
it will be incumbent upon you to disabuse him of this concept.
With great tact and allowing ample opportunity for the patient to
describe his problems, you may intersperse sympathetic and understanding comments of your concern for his pain and suffering.
Your generally supportive and sympathetic attitude may lead to
the formation of that fragile relationship which would permit
development of courage for a therapeutic effort.

What specific techniques may the physician use?

1. Reflect to the patient those critical factors by which alcohol is
    adversely affecting the patient's preferred self-image. The
    patient who claims a desire to continue an intimate relation-
    ship with his wife and children, but whose drinking has seri-

ously compromised an ability to fulfill this; the patient whose financial and career needs are in jeopardy, but who continues to drink despite warnings from his superiors; the patient whose career and intimate personal pleasures are dependent upon sound cognitive function, but whose continued use of soporific drugs damages the central nervous system—all of these require a sympathetic confrontation concerning the exact role played by continued drug (ethanol) use.

2. Offer the dignity of the disease concept of alcoholism. Numerous studies have revealed an inverse relationship between acceptance of the disease concept and recidivism. Physicians who fail to appreciate or understand this view would do well to embrace it if only for the benefit to their patients.

3. Offer hope. The despairing patient must have restored belief in his recovery. This circumstance must be supported by the physician's previous experiences with treatment of this disease, or a personal exposure to the recovered members of A.A.

4. Impress the patient with your personal knowledgability concerning this illness. Obviously, the patient's faith in your diagnosis and therapy, as well as in the hope which you hold out for his recovery, is totally dependent upon his faith in your expertise and general knowledge of the illness. Quite apparently this knowledgability is unlikely to result from that degree of clinical contact and instruction offered by the majority of medical schools today. Visits to Alcoholics Anonymous meetings, alcoholism treatment centers, and rehabilitation facilities will be necessary in order to gain a conversant and even facile level of awareness by means of which the patient may be reassured.

5. Educate the patient about the nature of alcoholism. It is imperative that the patient realize how little he knows about his own illness. In describing the compulsion to drink, the author has often used the analogy of a bullfight wherein the determination to resist drinking is likened to locking horns with the bull. The lack of success inherent in such a circumstance is easily imagined, but the singular act of learning the nature of the bull—how and when it charges, and how it moves its horns—enables the patient with a cape to make the bull look remarkably like a jackass. Considerable time must

be spent with the patient pointing out the pharmacology and pathophysiology of sedative ingestion in order to verify the likelihood that knowledge and understanding might lead to recovery. The patient will often be confused about a more recent loss of tolerance, unaware that tolerance to sedatives decreases with age. He will have noted but not understood the relationship of ethanol's sedation to its inevitable agitation. He may have recognized but never openly admitted to himself that his drinking resulted in memory defects and loss of ability to concentrate. Now is the moment for the patient to see the dead end of that alley down which he has been progressing.

6. While offering sympathy for the patient's suffering, present a specific method for therapy. Although flexibility might marginally increase the number of patients who can fit into any therapeutic scheme, it is quite critical that the physician remain unyielding in the application of those therapeutic methods which he knows by experience are vital for recovery.

7. Exert leverage when available and necessary. Confrontation in and of itself will often represent as much leverage as the patient may require for the initiation of therapy. On the other hand, some patients require somewhat more of a crisis and, for them, loss of a job, a consort, or a professional license might offer that leverage which is required to initiate the meaningful treatment regimen. The subtleties inherent in applying such leverage at the appropriate moment require great clinical judgment and are discussed at greater length in the chapters that follow.

8. Relieve pain during detoxification. Your willingness to appreciate the patient's physical and psychic discomfort during detoxification increases the patient's belief in your personal interest. Such an intimate relationship may go far toward motivating this patient to continue in a program for rehabilitation following the treatment of his withdrawal syndrome.

Having motivated the patient to comply with your therapeutic suggestion, your concept of his treatment requirements necessitates that you define the degree of his illness and resources, and that you set a legitimate therapeutic goal. Does the patient require acute hospital care for the treatment of the withdrawal syndrome, for the organic complications of alcoholism, or for physical protection from excessive sedative use? Do the patient's resources still include intimate relationships, emotional stability, and private finances? Is his status such that one might legitimately aim at nothing less than complete recovery, or has there been enough physical and mental damage so that a therapeutic compromise must be anticipated?

Having defined these circumstances, the physician can more rationally determine the need for in-hospital detoxification, the potential length of time for treatment of the withdrawal syndrome, and the need for long-term care and rehabilitation. Relapses (slips), though possible at any time in the course of treatment of the alcoholic, tend more frequently to occur shortly after discharge from an inpatient facility (within one month of initial treatment), approximately three to four months after initiation of treatment, and again about 10−11 months after beginning such therapy. Recidivism diminishes appreciably if consistent sobriety has been maintained within an active therapeutic program for 24 months. A small but definite relapse rate continues indefinitely thereafter. Clinical improvement in cognitive function appears to be greatest during the first few months of abstinence but increases progressively to an asymptote at approximately 24 months. It is remarkable that the functional improvement in career and interpersonal relationships of the alcoholic bears such a specific temporal relationship to recovery from brain injuries following stroke, trauma, and infection. Should it appear to the physician that the patient does not have the personal resources, strength, and support mechanisms which would permit an early return from an acute care facility to his usual environment, then a prolonged stay at a rehabilitation facility offers both the education and duration of abstinence which might make definitive recovery more likely. These factors usually become clear to the physician immediately prior to or during detoxification. The patient who has stopped drinking himself or has been discharged from a treatment facility now requires definitive assistance in combatting the illness within the confines of his own environment. The major precept to be followed by the physician at this juncture is to avoid the Timothy Leary concept of "Better Living Through Chemistry." The care of the patient at this stage in treatment should be without the use of drugs, with the major

exception of Antabuse (Appendix D). The use of any solid sedatives or tranquilizers at this stage in the patient's care will markedly increase the likelihood of relapse. More appropriately, one
should offer a directive, confrontative, and supportive type of
therapy, the principle aim of which is to break the patient's isolation. Extensive clinical contact has substantiated the author's
belief that isolation is pathognomonic of this illness and that
therapy is successful only in proportion to its ability to change
this specific circumstance. The physician's relationship with the
patient may often be the initial opportunity for the patient to
relate to another human being on a deep and intimate level. As
noted by Dr. Kenneth Williams, the isolation may have started
with the anomie experienced in the patient's childhood, though it
is often increased with the failure to achieve a satisfactory sexual
identification during adolescence (note Chapter 9), and finally
some results from the aberrant use of alcohol in a society in which
90 percent of its members are not forced to drink covertly or
excessively. The physician's successful relationship with the patient may enable him to eventually formulate relationships with
others. This often requires a peer group with whom the alcoholic
may identify. Alcoholics Anonymous offers such peer group support as well as educational and other mechanisms for on-going
recovery. It is not uncommon for the family members of the alcoholic to require similar support and treatment. Long-term sobriety and recovery of the patient's health, career, and interpersonal relationships often result in marked improvement in self-
esteem; this in and of itself supports continued therapeutic success. Successful interference with the problem of isolation and
inadequate self-esteem may be more difficult in the socioeconomically deprived or female patient (Chapters 9 and 10).

About two percent of the patients under treatment for alcoholism will also need treatment for a complicating major
psychiatric problem, such as schizophrenia or a bipolar affective
disorder. Such a diagnosis requires a period of asbolute abstinence from soporific drugs in order to make a bona fide evaluation
of the patient. Some of the patients with premorbid personality
deficits can be treated without recourse to psychotropic drugs.
The use of tricyclic antidepressants, lithium, or phenothiazines
should be eschewed when possible, since they markedly complicate the care of the alcoholic. On the other hand, those few pa-

tients for whom such drug therapy is imperative must be individually supported in order to avoid alienation from such support mechanisms as Alcoholics Anonymous.

The chapters that follow are complete with numerous details which will serve to shed light on many of those issues to which I have alluded. An old Talmudic quip notes that "for the man who doesn't know where he's going, any road will take him there." Though the past three decades have often emphasized the wisdom of that ancient scholar, it has become progressively clear that those physicians who have worked extensively with patients suffering from alcoholism are in far greater agreement about the nature of the illness and its treatment than the pertinent scientific literature would suggest. I can only trust that this text will encourage *all* physicians to detect and confront the patient with alcoholism and *some* physicians to join us in the treatment of these seriously ill patients. Not only will the patients benefit, but the physicians will experience extraordinary rewards.

REFERENCES

Boston Collaborative Drug Surveillance Program. Clinical Depression of the Central Nervous System Due to Diazepam and Chlordiazepoxide in Relation to Cigarette Smoking and Age. *N Eng J Med* 288: 277–280, 1973

Castleden CM, George CF, Marcer D, Hallett C: Increased sensitivity to nitrazepam in old age. *Br Med J* 1: 10–12, 1977

Chappel JN: Attitudinal barriers to physician involvement with drug abuse. *JAMA* 224: 1011–1013, 1973

Gitlow SE: Alcoholism: A disease, in Bourne PG, Fox R (eds): *Alcoholism: Progress in Research and Treatment*. New York, Academic Press, 1973

Goodwin DW: *Is Alcoholism Hereditary?* New York, Oxford University Press, 1976

Hamerman D: Primary care—is it here to stay? The implications for medical education. *Bull NY Acad Med* 55: 540–550, 1979

Macy Foundation. Medical Education and Drug Abuse: Report of a Macy Conference. Josiah Macy Jr. Foundation. Report of a joint conference on instruction in the problem of drug abuse. New York, William F. Fell Co, 1973

Main TF: The ailment. *Med Psychol* 30: 129–145, 1957

McQuarrie DG, Fingl E: Effects of single doses and chronic administration of ethanol on experimental seizures in mice. *J. Pharmacol Exp Ther* 124: 264, 1958

Pace N: The Cornell medical student's field trip through the world of alcoholism, in Seixas FA (ed): *Currents in Alcoholism.* New York, Grune and Stratton, 1977, vol 2, pp 233–242

Reidenberg MM, Levy M, Warner H, Coutinho CB, et al: Relationship between diazepam dose, plasma level, age, and central nervous system depression. *Clin Pharm Ther* 23: 371–374, 1978

Schukit MA, Goodwin DS, Winokur G: A study of alcoholism in half siblings. *Amer J Psychiatry* 128: 1132, 1972

Spalt L: Alcoholism: Evidence of an X-linked recessive genetic characteristic. *JAMA* 241: 2543–2544, 1979

LeClair Bissell

2
Diagnosis and Recognition

Virtually every physician who treats older adolescent or adult patients is already seeing people with serious drinking problems. If asked, however, whether or not he is treating any alcoholics, the doctor will frequently say no. Since only a relatively small number of physicians report that they see alcoholics, and since alcoholism is not a particularly difficult diagnosis to make, one is forced to question why this situation exists. There is little reason to believe that alcoholics seek treatment only from the minority of physicians quick to recognize them. They do in fact distribute themselves rather impartially among us.

WHY DOCTORS AVOID DIAGNOSIS

While it has been claimed that the physician does not want to look into the drinking habits of patients because of a reluctance to examine his own, and while this may at times be true, I think that for most of us the difficulty lies elsewhere. Doctor and patient are often products of the same culture, a culture that has groomed us from childhood to believe that alcoholism is not really an illness but is instead a sign of weakness. We then feel that we are not making a diagnosis of a disease but are accusing the

23

ALCOHOLISM
ISBN 0-8089-1227-5

Copyright © 1980 by Grune & Stratton
All rights of reproduction in any form reserved.

patient of something. We are embarrassed and a little bit afraid of how our patients will react. They may get angry or defensive and certainly will not greet the diagnosis with delight, not only because they then have to face the need to learn to live without their accustomed drinking but also that they must accept an illness that still carries with it a degree of social stigma.

To make the diagnosis of alcoholism, then, is going to involve the physician in what he fears may well be an uncomfortable and awkward discussion with a patient, who, most likely, is going to deny its accuracy and is going to insist that the real problem is something else altogether, usually some difficulty—real or imagined—that lies beyond the ability of either of them to control.

Physicians face an additional problem. Like anyone else, they like to feel competent, to know what they are expected to do and how to do it. They are told that alcoholism is a disease and not a symptom of something else and that they are expected to know how to treat it. Since they may well have received less than an hour of education about alcoholism in their formal medical training and since they may have been taught little or nothing about what to say to an alcoholic when actually faced with one, they will then have to rely on what they have observed their colleagues doing with their alcoholics. This kind of role model teaching usually has been a demonstration of denial that alcoholism exists, an attitude that even if it does exist little or nothing can be done about it, and, in any case, that it is up to the patient somehow to find the motivation to change and devise a cure.

THE ALTERNATIVE DIAGNOSIS

The physician's role, then, is usually seen as limited to dealing with the late medical complications of drinking, with perhaps a warning to patients that alcohol is hurting their bodies and, if they continue to drink, will doubtless do increasing harm. Social consequences of the drinking behavior may be left to others or totally ignored. That patients may well have been attempting unsuccessfully to control their drinking and may be trying desperately to understand the predicament in which they find themselves is often not considered. That being an active alcoholic is a painful experience and that a desire to escape that pain can provide motivation toward recovery for an alcoholic, as for many another patient, may be forgotten.

Clearly, then, if to diagnose alcoholism is simply going to mean that the doctor is faced with an embarrassing confrontation with the patient, at the end of which nothing constructive will have occurred for either of them, and if, in addition, the physician is going to be left feeling inept, incompetent, and uncomfortable, the easiest way to handle the situation is to pretend that the disease isn't there at all. The patient doesn't really want to hear the diagnosis, his insurance coverage will sometimes specifically exclude reimbursement for alcoholism if it is honestly diagnosed rather than masked by a euphemism, and the doctor doesn't want to be faced with the expectation of treating an illness that he doesn't know how to treat.

COMPROMISE BY REFERRAL

A frequent compromise is to acknowledge that the patient appears to be drinking too much but to assume that he must be self-medicating for an underlying emotional problem. Recommending consultation with a psychiatrist makes the referring physician feel much better and shifts the responsibility to another physician. Many psychiatrists, however, are reluctant to diagnose or treat alcoholics for the same reasons as the rest of us.

Another compromise by referral occurs when the patient needs other forms of help: with employment, housing, planning for convalescence, or making contact with family members. The physician recommends that the patient see a social worker or clergyman. This avoids discussing the drinking problem yet offers the hope that a professional in another discipline will deal with it. If things go well, the doctor is vindicated. If things do not, at least the responsibility is shared. Meanwhile, the doctor/patient dialogue has been restricted to less threatening topics than the drinking problem.

Instead of pushing or pretending it away, we should be willing and able to diagnose alcoholism, but we must know enough about it to feel reasonably comfortable discussing it with our patients so we can convince them that this is indeed their problem.

Sensible patients, alcoholic or otherwise, will not cooperate with treatment plans for a disease they don't think they have. Our attitude toward the patient, our knowledge about the disease, and our willingness to communicate candidly with the patient represent the initial requirement for motivating recovery.

FURTHER IMPEDIMENTS TO RECOGNITION

Once physicians are willing to recognize an alcoholic and once they are able to accept that the stereotype of what an alcoholic is like may be interfering with their abilities as diagnosticians, they are almost ready to find alcoholics.

One-line definitions of alcoholism are not really very helpful. Nor are demands for simplistic statements about etiology. With alcoholism, we are dealing with a disease of complex etiology where many factors—mental, physical, genetic, and environmental—all combine in one individual to make him fall victim.

Just as there is no single etiology for this illness, neither is there any one symptom that every alcoholic has or that only an alcoholic has. Sometimes what appears to be vagueness about definition or causality is used as an excuse for avoiding the treatment of the alcoholic patient. One senses the basic discomfort attached to making this diagnosis not only in the fruitless arguments about etiology that also serve as delaying tactics but also in the long theoretical discussions that concern themselves with the difficulty in diagnosing very early, subtle, and perhaps equivocal cases of alcoholism. Since there will be no shortage of obvious alcoholic patients once we are committed to finding them, we must address our attention initially to the easy-to-identify cases and move on to the more obscure ones as experience and diagnostic acumen improve.

Alcoholism is a progressive illness that in the majority of cases takes from 5 to 20 years to develop. Not only do physicians have to guard aginst reluctance to diagnose, but they must also become aware that they have been taught by social attitudes and tradition to think of alcoholism only in terms of its late stages.

They are going to be uncertain and uncomfortable when faced with it in its early stages. They may feel vaguely guilty, as if they are becoming prudish or judgmental, a kind of culturally induced ambivalence more likely to leave them indecisive than in the face of other addictions such as cigarette smoking or opiate abuse. Meanwhile, patients are likely to minimize their drinking. The classic statement by the recovered alcoholic patient looking back on early contacts with physicians, when the diagnosis might well have been made but was missed, is, "I didn't volunteer the facts and no one really asked." Dr. Stanley Gitlow has said, "Alcoholism is the disease that keeps telling the person who has it that he doesn't." Conscious of what they're doing or not, alcoholics don't want to hear their problem discussed, and because of fear, embarrassment, or some other reason they're not at all sure they want their doctor to know.

Most of us think about alcoholics in stereotypes: usually male, middle aged, perhaps a bit shabby, certainly hedonistic and irresponsible on some level, often unemployed or in low-status jobs. The underlying assumption is that only a certain type of person becomes alcoholic. If doctors defer to this myth, they may not even consider the diagnosis in a young, attractive, wealthy, responsible career woman whose presenting complaint will include no mention of drinking, whose dress will be meticulous, and who is highly unlikely to smell of alcohol at her eleven a.m. appointment.

If alcoholics are viewed as somehow different from the rest of us, it will be doubly hard to recognize the illness in our patients, our colleagues, or in ourselves until it is far advanced.

DIAGNOSIS

Diagnosing alcoholism is basically the same as diagnosing pneumonia, except that it can be a lot more challenging. A disease may be conceptualized as a state of altered or diminished function. Although commonly related to aberrant physiology, biochemistry, or anatomy, its precise cause may be unknown. In the case of pneumonia, the infectious microorganism might be a common pharyngeal inhibitant they would not therefore repre-

sent the complete etiology in itself. The ultimate proof of diagnosis, the morbid anatomy, is obviously rarely demanded, but
instead the clinician accepts a conglomerate of subjective and
objective findings in order to establish a diagnosis sufficient to
support rational therapy. The ultimate aim in formulating any
diagnosis lies in the desire to restore function. To that end, the
recognition and treatment of the patient with alcoholism parallels all other illness. Although alcoholism, especially in its early
and uncomplicated form, may not offer the objective handle many
clinicians prefer for diagnosis—elevated blood pressure, a
pathogenic bacterium, elevated BUN, or Gaucher cells in the
bone marrow—it is nonetheless readily recognized by a rather
specific history and pattern of behavior. The accuracy and reliability of diagnosis, rarely achieving perfection in any branch of
medicine, does not differ substantially in the case of alcoholism.

The patient's denial system, representing a major and frequent impediment in the diagnosis of alcholism, is not peculiar to
this disease alone. One might but consider cancer, tuberculosis,
and venereal disease, a few others commonly minimized by suspicious patients. Fortunately, diagnosis of these illnesses is rarely
complicated by a denial system within the physician as well.

It is crucial to realize that patients will not find it easy to
give an accurate history; in fact, they may find this next to impossible. It may appear to the doctor that patients are deliberately
lying. Perhaps they are, but usually they first lie to themselves.
Therefore as they see it, they're telling their physician the simple
truth. Noting the tremendous gap between what alcoholic patients report and the reality of their situations, it may seem in-
credible to the physician that patients can be so steadfast in their
denials. If the physician is naive about alcoholism and uncertain
about the diagnosis, the patients' unruffled airs of sincerity can
often convince the unwary professional that *he* is the one who has
the problem, that he is being unfair and overly suspicious, or that
concerned friends and family are exaggerating reports of trouble.

Simply, one is looking for patients who repeatedly ingest a
sedative drug (perhaps ethanol) despite their own definitive best
interests. The diagnosis is inherent in the fact that the subject
compulsively uses sedation (ethanol) despite its interference with
job, home, health, or interpersonal relationships.

Diagnostic clues are available from history, physical examinations, and the laboratory. Certain signs will relate quite simply

to alcohol itself, either because too much of it is present in the patient or because the patient shows signs of withdrawal from physical dependence on alcohol.

Simple drunkenness and alcoholism are not the same thing. One sign may be useful, however: alcoholics often demonstrate a very high tolerance to alcohol, particularly in the early years of their drinking. A male patient will often report this significant bit of history with actual pride, saying that after the unpredictable adolescent learning-to-drink experiences, he was the one who didn't get sick, didn't get drunk, didn't have hangovers, could take a tremendous amount of alcohol, "drink them all under the table and drive them all home." And he probably could. (Later, as the disease progresses, this early high tolerance will become unpredictable and then be lost, so that he eventually gets drunk on amounts that previously didn't affect him.)

The physician should be suspicious if a very high blood alcohol level—one that would normally result in serious impairment—is noted in a patient who continues to function well. For example, a recovered alcoholic physician recalls his drinking being questioned by a senior physician after a house staff party. Full of pride, the alcoholic countered that he'd been the only doctor to report on time the following morning, make rounds, tend to all his patients, and complete his charting. "True," said the senior man, "but that takes a lot of practice. Better think about it!"

Amount Patient Drinks

Asking alcoholic patients at the start of their interviews to declare exactly how many drinks they take, or in what form, places the doctor in an unnecessary power struggle. Since this is the very line of questioning that alcoholics expect and are prepared to resist, they are unlikely to give accurate answers.

We don't need a signed confession from our patients, nor arguments we cannot win—it only puts the patients on the defensive and makes them conceal the truth from the beginning. Just as we don't need to know the number of acid-fast bacilli in a person's lungs to diagnose tuberculosis, we don't need to know how many ounces a patient drinks to diagnose alcoholism.

The amount consumed is not nearly as important as the effect it has upon the drinker, whether the drink be vodka (under

the misguided notion that vodka isn't detectable on the breath),
whiskey, wine, or beer. Many an alcoholic will insist, however,
that one "can't be an alcoholic on just beer." Look for the coexis-
tence of alcohol and trouble, not for the amount consumed or the
volume of fluid in which it is diluted.

Patterns of drinking (solitary, periodic loss of control) and
attitudes (purposeful, medicinal) about it can be revealed when
we take the patient's history. A change in style of response can
yield a good clue, such as the patient who tells you the exact
number of cigarettes smoked and cups of coffee drunk. If, however, when asked about alcohol, the same patient shifts from precise and quantitative answers to "I drink socially" or "I take a
few," this should make you wonder why.

Avoid a change in your own style of questioning when shifting from such innocuous subjects as family history to that of
ethanol ingestion. A joking tone or judgmental phrasing or inflec-
tion of your voice can close out any significant or truthful response by the patient. You may use, "Do you smoke or drink?"
followed by, "How much?" "Do you have some every day?" or
"Just on weekends or holidays?" or "More than one or two?" Inte-
grate this history with the less threatening discussion of other
substances (coffee, cigarettes, etc.).

Withdrawal Symptoms

We can assume that by the time a patient is in full-blown
delirium tremens, most physicians will know what is happening.
However, other signs indicative of physical dependence are often
overlooked or misunderstood.

A first grand mal seizure in an adult should always make us
think of alcoholism, particularly if it occurs during the 72 hours
following a marked reduction in drinking while the secondary
hyperirritability that follows the initial depressant action of alcohol is still having its effect.

Another indication is intention tremor following a drinking
bout, intensified if the patient is self-conscious. An example is the
alcoholic trying to control his hands enough to sign his name
while being watched.

Less obvious indications of alcohol withdrawal are mild
hypertension, tachycardia, slight elevations in temperature, mild

diaphoresis, and occasional atrial premature contractions. Laboratory work commonly will reveal an elevated blood glucose and a slightly subnormal BUN. If the patient also has an abnormally elevated SGOT, no matter how mild, that returns to normal almost at once after admission to a hospital (and cessation of drinking) and if, in addition, the patient diureses 1–2 kg (2–4 lb) in the first three hospital days while the initial minimal proteinuria and low BUN return to normal, this is strong evidence that alcohol in quantity has been present.

Although we have not yet done a formal study of this phenomenon, it is my impression that nearly half of the male Smithers Center Rehabilitation Unit patients have been told of hypertension or glucose intolerance and are often being medicated for these problems. After 28 days of abstinence, however, most show no evidence of hypertension (even under considerable emotional stress) or evidence of diabetes.

Personality Change

Seizures, tremors, and peripheral neuropathic and cerebellar signs are often reasons to refer alcoholics to neurologists. Less commonly, a patient's family reports a marked and sudden personality change during an evening's drinking and they wonder if this could be a form of epilepsy, especially since the patient had no previous history of this kind of behavior.

The change is usually from pleasant to extremely hostile, belligerent, even violent, or to helpless, whining, and maudlin. The behavior seems out of proportion to the amount of drinking observed by the family. In actuality, the alcoholic may be concealing the true extent of his drinking or combining alcohol ingestion with other sedatives. His own behavior is often frightening for the alcoholic, if descriptions of it are believed or if the altered behavior is remembered. The alcoholic has heard the phrase "in vino veritas" and is afraid of really being the nasty person who appears so unexpectedly.

Blackouts

Another frequent but little understood phenomenon is the "blackout." This must not in any way be confused with "passing out." The alcoholic blackout is a period of total amnesia in a drinking setting during which the drinker may or may not appear to others to be under the influence of alcohol.

Pilots have reported cross-country flights and surgeons successful operations during blackouts, yet they were not recognized by others as being impaired. The alcoholic's spouse frequently feels that the drinker remembers what happened but doesn't want to admit it. The psychiatrist assumes that the patient thought or did something guilt or anxiety provoking during the blackout and now unconsciously refuses to remember it. The neurophysiologist speculates on reduced RNA synthesis when blood alcohol levels are high.

(I wonder if blackouts are a form of chemically induced retrograde amnesia caused by belated drinking in an individual episode. Perhaps the person who did not appear drunk to family or colleagues was in fact *not* drunk at the time but can't remember because of getting very drunk later.)

Occasionally nonalcoholics experience blackouts, particularly early in their drinking when learning by trial and error what they can tolerate. Most of us, however, were we to experience such a frightening event—a real period of time in which we walk and talk and make telephone calls and do business and park the car, yet cannot remember doing so—would go at once to a physician for an explanation.

Not so alcoholics, who sense that blackouts are part of their drinking, the part of life that they don't want too closely examined. They will adapt to blackouts, learning ways to cover up their occurrences, and will continue to drink in spite of them. This willingness to tolerate repeated blackouts as part of one's method of living rarely if ever occurs in the absence of alcoholism. The diagnostic clue, then, becomes the patient's equanimity in the face of repeated blackouts.

Physical Examination

People familiar with alcoholism notice physical signs without even touching or talking to the patient. Obvious characteristics can be spotted on the street or in a social situation.

I recall a medical seminar on the treatment of the public inebriate where one of the physicians present was obviously in trouble with alcohol himself. We all discussed the disease of alcoholism in the abstract, avoiding our colleague who was so clearly very ill and sat with shaking hands, slightly bloated and plethoric facies, telltale parotid swelling and a Cushingoid look. (This facial resemblance to Cushing disease, coupled with a story of personality change, hypertension, and glucose intolerance, has inspired many an eager house officer to start collecting 24-hour urine specimens or to order ACTH stimulation tests, while instead a waiting period for the patient of three to four days without alcohol might make all of these symptoms disappear.)

One might draw attention to another look-alike, that of the thyrotoxic. The tremulous, nervous, sweating patient with mild systolic hypertension, tachycardia, and an occasional arrhythmia who fails to reveal objective measurements of hyperthyroidism may simply reflect the hyperadrenergia associated with ethanol dependence.

Examination not only of an alcoholic's face but of the skin may yield other clues. The perifollicular hemorrhages on the inner thighs of a scorbutic derelict are discussed ad nauseam, but small bruises on the alcoholic housewife are far more common. When she drinks, she bumps into doorknobs and furniture; sometimes she falls. Her bruises are not usually massive ones, but they're found in different places and in a variety of colors, depending on when they occurred.

Cigarette burns on fingers, chest, legs, or pajamas or nightgown can imply abuse of alcohol or drugs.

Physical examination will also indicate whether or not other sedatives are involved. The patient using only alcohol can usually be roused from sleep by pain or by vigorous stimulation. However, if decubitus ulcers or blistered skin from remaining too long in one position are evident, it is wise to suspect other drugs.

Severe peridontal disease is another clue. Alcoholics as a group do not neglect physical or oral hygiene. Rather, in my experience, typical alcoholics are usually clean and neat, especially on visits to the doctor. They may frequently brush their teeth to disguise their breath, just as they take extra vitamins in hopes of protecting their livers. Nonetheless, Vincent gingivitis and pyorrhea are, for reasons still not fully explained, common in alcoholics; teeth relatively free of caries are often lost while the patient is still fairly young.

Secondary Diseases

Every pathology textbook describes the physical complaints stemming from body systems damaged by long-term exposure to the small, toxic alcohol molecule itself. Although diseases secondary to chronic alcoholism were thought initially to result from malnutrition and alcohol toxicity, more and more are revealed as inducible by alcohol alone. Lieber and Rubin demonstrated that alcohol itself can cause fatty liver and proximal myopathy in normal, well-nourished, vitamin-supplemented medical students[1-3] as well as actual cirrhosis in some primates.[4]

Alcoholism should be regarded as a probable cause or concomitant factor until proven otherwise in the following: cirrhosis, fatty liver, pancreatitis, initial grand mal seizure in an adult, and peripheral neuropathy. Less obvious alcoholism-related illnesses include antibiotic-resistant tuberculosis in an adult, carcinoma of the head and neck, and lung abscesses not related to malignancies. Significant impairment of the T cell immune system by alcohol was demonstrated by Lundy et al.[5]

Casual observations of abnormal liver functions (elevated SGOT, SGPT, GGTP, etc.), abnormal serum lipid profile (Fred. type IIA, IV, etc.), elevated serum uric acid, hyperglycemia, or hyperosmolality should raise the suspicion of alcoholism, although none of these findings is diagnostic per se. Similarly, an alcohol level in a biologic aliquot should raise a diagnostic suspicion but cannot serve as proof unless it is extremely elevated in conjunction with a clinical state demonstrating tolerance. These biochemical measurements must be evaluated in conjunction with the clinical circumstances in order to establish the diagnosis of alcoholism. A blood alcohol level of 0.19 percent may establish drunkeness for purposes of motor vehicle operation but does not necessarily or absolutely make the medical diagnosis of alcoholism. Lieber and colleagues have developed a test of amino acid metabolism that may similarly indicate heavy or persistent ethanol ingestion, but it remains to be seen if it will successfully separate the chronic heavy social drinker from the alcoholic while still managing to detect the so-called "periodic" alcoholic. For more detailed laboratory data, see Appendix B, "Criteria for the Diagnosis of Alcoholism."

Detection in General Hospitals

Approximately 70 percent of all adult Americans are drinkers. Somewhere between five and ten percent of these are or will become alcoholics, with the urban dweller and those at the two extremes of the educational ladder most at risk. Alcoholics, or patients whose illness is alcohol related, occupy between 20 and 60 percent of the adult beds in acute general care hospitals. Careful studies bear this out even in hospitals not located in areas with heavy concentrations of alcoholics.

Just because alcoholism is diagnosed less in one specialty than in another does not mean that it is unusual in any group. The tendency to diagnose more alcoholism in ward areas than in private and semiprivate sections is misleading; it usually reflects physician attitudes and social expectations rather than reality.

More men that women are alcoholic (ratio of 3:1, approximately[6]), and since the disease is most common after the age of 30 years, alcoholism rates are usually low on obstetric floors and in adolescent units; however, both women and young people are showing an increase in alcoholism rates.

By contrast, thermal injury treatment units have many alcoholics. Unless there is preexisting nerve or vascular disease, stroke, or some other very clearcut explanation, almost all freezing injuries will be found in alcoholics, particularly in urban populations.

Many fire deaths are alcohol related. A study of third degree burns showed over 40 percent to be alcohol related, usually women who fell asleep while smoking as well as drinking and using other sedative drugs.[7]

Trauma floors are excellent areas to seek alcoholics: victims of automobile and pedestrian accidents, falls, fights, private aircraft, snowmobile, home injuries, and drownings and near drownings, particularly late afternoon boating accidents. Assaults in the home are common in conjunction with alcohol; thus we must consider alcoholism in an assaulted patient's spouse or in the parent of a battered child.

Psychiatrists often find alcoholics admitted for attempted suicide. Because many are in conflict with family members, it is important to find out if different perceptions of the patient's drinking pattern form a part of that conflict.

We must learn to ask about drinking behavior in a variety of settings. For example, suppose we note a chest film on display in an emergency room corridor x-ray viewing box. The film depicts a male with the mild degenerative bone changes of early middle age. If there is evidence of old rib fractures in different stages of healing and in different parts of the rib cage, one accident could not possibly account for them. Suppose there are signs of old tuberculosis and metal clips from old gastrointestinal surgery visible in the epigastrium. Here is a person with evidence of multiple traumatic episodes and a history of ulcers and tuberculosis, who uses a hospital emergency room rather than a private physician. The chances that this person is an alcoholic are excellent.

OBTAINING PATIENT'S HISTORY

While it may not be difficult to relate heavy drinking to a particular argument or injury, to a single episode of aspiration pneumonitis, or to an impulsive overdose, the confusion of cause and effect in chronic alcoholism may require deft questioning to untangle. Most alcoholics are as naive about their disease as their physicians. If we realize that this is a progressive illness that changes and develops through the years, we can begin by asking questions that do not seem particularly threatening.

What we are after is a story of alcohol use through time, as perceived by the patient himself or by those close to the patient. Understanding the epidemiology of alcoholism will prove useful. More fundamental is familiarity with the way in which the disease usually develops in an individual.

While there is still debate about the role of genetics in alcoholism, there is no question that this is a familial illness. If there is alcoholism in a patient's family, that patient is more at risk than if there is not. Less well known is the fact that 30 percent of the wives of alcoholic men will have had an alcoholic parent.[8] Since heavy drinking in young people shows a strong positive correlation with both peer group pressure and use of alcohol and other drugs by parents, a quick family history is certainly in order, including current and preceding generations.

This information is usually offered quite freely by the alcoholic. For example, a male alcoholic may relate a history of problem drinking in his parents' home to his own difficult childhood because it makes his own drinking understandable. His wife's family history may explain what he perceives as her unreasonably critical attitude toward his drinking. His son's use of drugs could be a worry that makes him likely to drink. With all of these woes, small wonder that the patient drinks, and small wonder that he appears anxious and depressed!

The physician's impulse is to respond with sympathy, understanding, and the offer of yet another mood-changing drug as a substitute for alcohol. Physician, stay thy hand! What if the boss complained, the wife left, the money went—and the child as well—because of the patient's drinking? What if the problem has been for years that this person seeks chemical answers to human problems? Is the answer really a change of drug?

Attitude of Physician

How much a patient is likely to admit will depend on the attitude of the questioner. A hostile, angry, or harried interviewer whose line of inquiry shows that he understands little or nothing of the patient's situation will not get far.

If, however, the questioner is knowledgeable, interested, comfortable, and nonjudgmental, he can often at the end of a thorough history taking ask: "Do you feel you've been having a problem with your drinking?" He can then go on to: "Do you think you might be an alcoholic?" A surprising number of patients will answer "Yes," while many others will say, "Maybe a little bit," or, "I don't know. How do you tell?"

Sedative–Hypnotic Drugs

Personal history should include queries about use of other drugs to alleviate the tension or insomnia caused by alcohol. If, however, aware of self-prescribing in a way that might provoke criticism, the alcoholic may not give accurate answers.

A blunt question such as, "Do you take pills?" will often produce the same evasion as, "How much do you drink?" It is better to start by asking about the symptoms for which medication is likely to be used. Then ask if a doctor has ever been seen about these problems. Follow with a sympathetic, "And what did the doctor give you to help?" This will at least identify the drug, although generally not its quantity.

Many of us are unaware that alcohol is a member of a large family of sedative–hypnotic drugs. All of them act in much the same way. All can be substituted for one another, allowing for differences in strength and speed and duration of action.

This is an era of widespread use and abuse of sedatives and "minor" tranquilizers, potentially the cause of far more trouble than the so-called "major" tranquilizers (see Appendix A).

Many an alcoholic who would never drink in the morning or smell of alcohol at inappropriate times is drugged 24 hours a day by taking an alcohol substitute in tablet or capsule form. The subject may walk quite steadily, make reasonably good sense, and have no alcohol on the breath (although he probably takes extra care with mouth deodorants and gargles) and may appear to be fairly normal, particularly to someone who doesn't know him well or to someone who sees the alcoholic infrequently enough to be unaware of gradual change. The alcoholic may show a subtle decrease in mental alertness, personal sensitivity, and appropriateness of response; diction may seem more deliberate and careful, with extra spacing between words, and the alcoholic's eyes may lack sparkle.

Alcoholics are unaware that alcohol initially sedates while later heightening tension, irritability, mood swings, and insomnia. They assume that they drink to relieve these very things. If they decide to cut down on their drinking, or to cut it out, they may take tranquilizers or sedatives to deal with their discomfort. Tranquilizers or sedatives, however, usually produce the same symptoms that were caused by alcohol. Alcoholics will take them in gradually increasing amounts, either to supplement their drinking or, at times, in lieu of it. They are still chemically dependent alcoholics but now may use alcohol rarely if at all.

Women use minor tranquilizers and sedatives more often than men, although this probably reflects more frequent contacts with doctors, physician attitudes, and subsequent prescribing habits more than any intrinsic difference between the sexes.

(In my experience, patients who use illicit narcotics tend to exaggerate the amount they use, while patients obtaining pills from physicians or pharmacists usually minimize.)

It is my personal feeling that warning against the casual use of minor tranquilizers and sedatives is the single most important educational job to be done by those treating alcoholics today, since many alcoholics become dual addicts through well meaning but uninformed physicians.

REASONS FOR DRINKING

Whether on a psychiatric floor, in a surgical area, or in the internist's private office, a hallmark of alcoholism is the use of alcohol as a mood-changing drug instead of as a beverage.

Patients reporting that they drink to calm nerves, to sleep, to give courage or confidence to relieve anxiety or depression, or for nightcaps, are not social drinkers; they are self-medicating to alter feeling states. Patients often sense this and become uneasy, particularly if they are sneaking drinks.

Conflict with self or conflict with others around the use of alcohol is a sign of trouble. The patient can more easily acknowledge trouble than the fact of alcoholism.

Patients admitted to a psychiatric floor may actually prefer to be labeled mentally ill rather than alcoholic. There is less social stigma. Also, they hope that if they cooperate with treatment, gain insight, and engage in attempts to understand the reasons for their drinking, they may not have to abandon it.

They will therefore oblige with a history containing much that is accurate but featuring a reversal of cause and effect— stories of conflict with fellow workers, unreasonable employers, and lost jobs; divorce, separation, or conflict with spouse or lover; disappointment in children, who may be in trouble with drugs; tangled finances; a career that initially showed high promise but has inexplicably gone into a decline.

OBSESSION WITH ALCOHOL

As alcohol becomes increasingly important to alcoholics; it exerts a subtle influence on lifestyles. Alcholics begin to avoid people and places that do not permit drinking. Freed from self-consciousness about their own alcohol consumption, they can then honestly report that they don't drink any more than their current friends. Questions that explore hobbies and activities may therefore be revealing, for alcholics may be unaware that they have gradually selected their friends and activities for drinking purposes.

For example, a cellist who regularly plays chamber music with a group of European friends is far less likely to be an active alcoholic than is a jazz musician performing at resorts where drinking is an important part of the social scene and where performance is often rewarded with a bottle of whiskey.

As alcohol becomes more necessary and used more as a drug than a beverage, the drinker will start to feel uneasy about it. His discomfort will heighten when his behavior differs from that of peers. The drinker may need a drink before going to a party or may turn away from guests to take an extra drink, unobserved, in the kitchen. The alcoholic will usually down the first drink a little faster than do others present, feeling impatient at their leisurely pace.

The need for additional alcohol and the need to conceal that need provoke anxiety, discomfort, and rationalization. The drinker is no longer merely participating in a social custom with peers; he is a deviant.

Alcoholics may encourage others to drink more with them to conceal their need for increasing amounts.

CONTROLLED DRINKING

Alcoholics may decide to prove to themselves that they don't have drinking problems. They may try control by limiting themselves to wine or beer, to drinking only in certain places or at certain times, to substituting other drugs for all or part of their alcohol intake, or even to going on the wagon.

Most alcoholics are in some control of their drinking most of the time. Almost all can stop altogether for periods of time. What typical alcoholics find difficult is to drink limited amounts on a regular basis without at least periodically exceeding the amounts they planned to drink. They may find themselves getting drunk when they'd firmly decided that they wouldn't. They may stop drinking only to start again impulsively.

This means that the alcoholic is losing the ability to keep promises made privately to himself about drinking. Breaking promises made to other people is less significant, since the alcoholic may never have intended to keep them in the first place.

It is vital for the physician to realize that normal drinkers have no big problem controlling their drinking. When patients report that they regularly swear off drinking, or that they're trying a variety of maneuvers to regulate their intake, they're saying that they are already in trouble. Only alcoholics need to control alcohol intake.

RESISTING ABSTINENCE

An addiction, any addiction, should not be considered in terms of physical dependency alone, or only in the context of the patient's entire life situation being in a shambles. Instead, the strength of an addiction should be measured in terms of the amount of pressure a person is prepared to resist in lieu of relinquishing use of the drug.

A man or woman who is willing to live in constant conflict with the self or with others rather than stop drinking is in trouble. So is the person who is willing to give up physical health or a valued job rather than the bottle.

He or she has developed a new value system that no matter how it's rationalized indicates that freedom to drink is more important than health, work, and human relationships. This state of affairs is alcohol dependency—an integral part of the illness, whether or not the patient shows physical withdrawal symptoms.

It is also an uncomfortable situation for the patient, even though it may appear irresponsible, pleasurable, and hedonistic to an unsophisticated observer.

Denial

If abstinence is too painful for the patient to face, the way to avoid self-confrontation is obvious: deny the problem.

The patient reverses causal relationships by shifting the blame to someone or something else. Thus marital discord is not caused by drinking but becomes the reason for it. Dejection over the multiple problems caused by alcohol becomes the depression that one drinks to relieve. Insomnia and anxiety are not caused by withdrawal, but are the reasons why alcohol is needed to relax. An employer's prejudice explains failure to gain promotion. Alcohol provides a justified escape from a nagging spouse and mounting debts.

Since alcoholism is not usually seen by the patient or the doctor as a disease in its own right but is instead regarded as a symptom of something else, both parties may embark on a search for an explanation of the drinking.

Extreme care must be exercised that a quite valid effort to uncover the psychodynamics of the patient's illness does not result in an alliance aimed at supporting the patient's denial. The latter often results in continued although temporarily modified use of the addicting drug—to be followed at a later date by return to the full-blown expression of the disease.

The alcoholic patient has every motive to minimize or explain away his drinking and to deny it as a primary concern. It won't take long to find plausible excuses: virtually every adult human being has a set of present problems and a history of at least one or two genuine tragedies. If the physician joins the patient in explaining away the illness, the patient may be lost.

Most people, however, face painful life situations without turning to chemical solutions to the degree that the solution becomes a problem in its own right. Only with some effort can the physician establish that heavy drinking actually preceded most of the events presented as having caused it.

A history of accidents or injuries is usually not too hard to elicit. It pays to ask if there had been drinking at the time of traumatic episodes. We don't need a confession that the patient was actually drunk or how much was consumed—enough that alcohol and trouble are occurring together.

DENIAL BY FAMILY

Denial is not the exclusive property of the alcoholic. Spouses and children cover up for their alcoholics. They worry that medical reports may get back to employers or that the alcoholic may view them as disloyal or be angry if they divulge too much.

The family unit may present a deceptively normal exterior to the world, closing protectively around the alcoholism that is destroying it. I am repeatedly surprised by the ability of alcoholic families to preserve a facade that when it finally crumbles has concealed a truly agonizing situation for all concerned. The fear of change and of exposure evidently outweigh the pain of continuing to live with the familiar.

If the alcoholic has accused family members of being the cause of his drinking, repeatedly cataloguing their inadequacies, they will feel entirely culpable. Also, they may believe in stereotypes about families: the understanding wife and the virile husband supposedly have contented marriage partners, not rejection through alcoholism. The truth is an admission of failure.

Sometimes alcoholism will present not in the person of the alcoholic but as part of the illness of the spouse. If we make a habit of searching beyond the identified patient for clues to illness and puzzling behavior in the surrounding environment, a casual mention that a spouse drinks a lot may take on diagnostic significance.

For example, wives of alcoholics may be reluctant to accept a needed hospitalization for fear of what might happen at home if they aren't there to protect the children. They may request that no visitors be permitted so that the alcoholic can't arrive drunk and make an embarrassing display. They may receive constant phone calls from home.

As outpatients, spouses of alcoholics are often nervous, upset, and likely to request tranquilizers or sedatives for themselves. Symptoms may be vague, responding poorly to treatment. They cannot follow instructions to rest, or avoid stress, if the home is in a state of constant chaos, nor can they buy prescribed medicine if the pay check is spent in the bar rather than at the drug or grocery store.

SOBER ALCOHOLIC/PHYSICIAN RELATIONSHIP

Successfully sober alcoholics report that many doctors refuse to believe they are alcoholics.

Perhaps for the physician the subject doesn't look like an alcoholic. He isn't drinking. He's likely to be a member of Alcoholics Anonymous, whose members urge each other to inform their physicians about their alcoholism. He is doing just that, hoping for understanding, encouragement, and, more importantly, that the physician will never prescribe alcohol-containing medicines or inappropriate mood-changing drugs.

Too often this patient discovers that the doctor is uncomfortable with the entire subject, however. The doctor may even argue that the patient can't really be an alcoholic—that he was probably talked into this by ill-advised and possibly fanatic friends. If the patient is still fragile in his new-found sobriety and ambivalent about the need to remain abstinent, the naive white-coated authority's observations can result in disaster.

If patients say they are alcoholics, believe them.

To diagnose and to recognize alcoholism, then, requires us to suspect it not only in our patients but also as the reason behind unexplained illness in others. It can be seen by the sophisticated observer in social settings and in friends and colleagues as well as in those labeled as ill. It affects directly 1 out of every 20 adults and indirectly easily twice as many more. Although the urban dweller and those at the two extremes of the education ladder are most at risk, no population of drinkers is exempt. This chapter has mentioned some clues to making that diagnosis. There are many more. The National Council on Alcoholism has collected and set down in tabular form many of them in an interesting attempt to establish more precise criteria for diagnosis[9] (see Appendix B).

Alcoholism will remain invisible unless and until one is able to become willing to see it. As this occurs, the physician will become aware that much that was formerly puzzling becomes explainable and obvious. Simple truths are too threatening to be heard easily. Our society is too uncomfortable and too ambivalent about drinking for mere facts to be convincing. The scars left by prohibition were deep. The fanaticism of wet versus dry still stirs unpleasant feelings.

To search one's own feelings and attitudes and to examine one's own drinking and that of others is hard and not always pleasant work. When that is done, one is comfortable with one's own choice to drink or to abstain in a drinking world. One can differentiate between the disastrous drinking of the alcoholic, the moderate use of alcohol in appropriate social settings, and the often excessive and irresponsible behavior of the heavy drinker. When our inner ambivalence is resolved, we can then speak clearly and comfortably about alcohol with our patients.

REFERENCES

1. Rubin E, Lieber CS: Alcohol-induced hepatic injury in non-alcoholic volunteers. *N Engl J Med* 278: 869–876, 1968
2. Lieber CS: Liver adaptation and injury in alcoholism. *N Engl J Med* 288:356–362, 1973
3. Song P, Rubin E: Ethanol produces muscle damage in human volunteers. *Science* 175: 327–328, 1972
4. Lieber CS, DeCarli L, Rubin E: Sequential production of fatty liver, hepatitis, and cirrhosis in subhuman primates fed ethanol with adequate diets. *Proc Natl Acad Sci USA* 72:437–441, 1975
5. Lundy J, Raaf JH, Deakins S, et al: The acute and chronic effects of alcohol on the human immune system. *Surg Gynecol Obstet* 141:212–218, 1975

6. Cahalan D, Cisin IH, Crossley HM: American Drinking Practices; A National Study of Drinking Behavior and Attitudes. New Brunswick, N.J., Rutgers Center of Alcohol Studies, 1969, pp 260

7. MacArthur JD, Moore FD: Epidemiology of burns, the burn-prone patient. *JAMA* 231:259–263, 1975

8. Bullock SC, Mudd EH: Interrelatedness of alcoholism and marital conflict. *Am J Orthopsychiatry* 29:519–527, 1959

9. National Council on Alcoholism: Criteria for the diagnosis of alcoholism. *Ann Intern Med* 77:249–258, 1972.

Marvin A. Block

3

Motivating the Alcoholic Patient

Having diagnosed the patient's alcoholism, the physician must now present the problem to the patient. If the physician in charge is a specialist in the field to whom the patient had been referred by another physician, the problem is comparatively simple. When patients are aware of their illness or have been diagnosed as alcoholic by their own physicians, or when they have full knowledge that the physician to whom they have been referred specializes in the field of alcoholism, there is apparently some recognition on their parts that they have the problem. This does not necessarily mean, of course, that such patients are well motivated. What it does mean, at least, is that the subject of alcoholism has already been introduced and that the patients might be prepared to discuss it further. Some patients may be inclined to deny the existence of the problem in their cases—as a defense against a possible diagnosis to that effect—but at least the first step has been taken. For the generalist, or for the physician who first suspects alcoholism, particularly if the patient has presented for any one of a number of other reasons, the problem of motivation is often greater.

It is important to remember that it is in the course of the history taking and the reviewing of the diagnostic considerations that the motivation—particularly the early motivation—of the

47

ALCOHOLISM
ISBN 0-8089-1227-5

Copyright © 1980 by Grune & Stratton
All rights of reproduction in any form reserved.

patient is determined. As the physician takes the history, he will be observing the patient's existing motivations as to the drinking problem and also will be looking for areas that will aid in further discussions with the patient. Motivating the patient is determined to a greater degree by what is going wrong with the patient's life due to alcohol and the other sedatives. The patient may have, for example, physical difficulties or disturbances at home and in interpersonal relationships, or perhaps problems functioning at work. While taking the history and determining the diagnosis, the physician must keep in mind the following questions: What is it that the patient wants in life, in the way of thinking or doing or receiving? How is that interfered with by the alcohol? It is this leverage that the doctor will use when embarking upon the process of getting the patient to see what is wrong and what must be done about it.

Each patient is an individual, and the approach to his illness must be eclectic. What constitutes excessive drinking for one patient may not for another. Necessarily to be taken into account are the patient's age, weight, mental stability, background, social environment, and various other specifics to which his individual life is tied. It must also be at all times borne in mind that the early stages of alcoholism are extremely difficult to pinpoint and that the definitions and classifications of the disease covered by the term are spread over a wide range of drinking patterns.

It is not always the best technique to make a definitive diagnosis at the first consultation. Only if patients have already been told that they have drinking problems—or that their use of alcoholic beverages has awakened suspicion—is immediate diagnosis even advisable. More than one session may be required for the physician to reach a warranted conclusion. Also, it isn't always easy to get a patient to accept a positive diagnosis without protest.

Unfortunately, there is still attached to the term "alcoholism" a kind of stigma that makes mere mention of it repugnant to patients as a whole. The terms "alcohol dependence" or "problem drinking" appear to be far more acceptable to the average patient, at least during early interviews. It should be noted that some people might feel this to be ducking the issue, and they would urge quick confrontation with the use of the word "alcoholism." It is a matter of one's own strategy and technique, but many workers in the field have found it useful not to confront people at once in such a manner that might cause them to run away. Patients must often be prepared more slowly to face the issue.

EARLY RECOGNITION BY THE PHYSICIAN

Few persons come to the specialist in the incipient or early stages of alcoholism. Most appear at a time, later on, when a correct diagnosis can be made by almost anyone—by family members in particular. Generalists are nevertheless in a position to uncover alcoholism in its very earliest stages—provided they take time to elicit accurate histories from their patients regardless of the reason given for seeking medical help. Many incipient alcoholics are missed because physicians fail to develop full or accurate enough histories. There are no early physical signs of alcoholism, and the diagnosis in most cases depends upon careful history taking. Where such symptoms as gastric distress, headaches, gastrointestinal disorders, lack of appetite, insomnia, depression, etc., are present, alcoholism should be at least suspected as a possible cause. Again, where other signs or symptoms of toxicity are manifested or are complained of by patients, careful and extensive histories must be taken. Many early alcoholics volunteer no signs or symptoms that can be effectively diagnosed. Thus only a detailed history will provide the needed indications if these exist.

Many questions have been designed to expose the early stages of alcoholism. Some that have been in use for several years, effective as they may be in revealing later stages of the disease, do nothing to help unearth its beginning stages.

Such questions as the following have been used in the belief that affirmative answers would point to the existence of incipient alcoholism:

1. Does the subject drink to calm his nerves or to sedate himself?
2. Does he become increasingly irritable while drinking?

3. Does he frequently drink until he becomes quite drunk?
4. Does he drink a steadily increasing amount of alcohol?
5. Does he hide his source of alcohol?
6. Does he lie about his drinking?
7. Does he take a drink the first thing in the morning?
8. Does he miss work or shirk his duties because of drinking?
9. Does he neglect his family?
10. Does he experience periods of blackout or amnesia?
11. Has he been hospitalized for drinking?
12. Has he lost his job because of drinking?

Recent studies suggest, however, that the information developed through use of the above questionnaire relates to the later, rather than the earlier, stages of alcohol dependence. It is now recognized that such questions as the following are better geared to the search for signs of incipient alcoholism:

1. Is the *desire* for a drink a frequent occurrence, the key word being "desire?"
2. Is there a *need* for a drink at a certain time of the day, the emphasis on "need?"
3. Is there anticipation of drinking in the evening, as the day wears on?
4. Is alcohol used to induce sleep?
5. Does frequent drinking go *beyond* ritual socializing?
6. Is there a desire to get *high* and to maintain that feeling through drinking?
7. Does the absence of drinks at a restaurant or party produce *disappointment*?
8. Is the patient's drinking *criticized* by a friend or anyone who cares?
9. Does the subject resort to a drink to relieve discomfort or tension of any kind?
10. Does the care taken to keep a supply of alcohol *on hand* "just in case" sometimes amount to more than a modest consideration?
11. Is there a tendency to prefer the companionship of those who exhibit a drinking pattern similar to one's own and to *shun* as far as possible the society of non-drinkers?

12. Does the subject resent the remarks of others concerning his drinking habits?

Helpful as the above questionnaire might be, negative answers can nevertheless be misleading, but recognition of an early problem with alcohol cannot but follow from the display of any adverse effect whatsoever following the ingestion of alcoholic drinks. This is a more broadly recognized definition—a more reliable clue—in that it exposes not only physical and psychological symptoms of disorder but those of social involvement as well. Should the ingestion of alcoholic beverages, however, result in a sociologic problem, family disruptions, or serious arguments of any kind—particularly at home or at work—this could well point to an alcohol-related problem. If in such a situation a more temperate drinking pattern is not swiftly established, failure to cut down or stop the use of alcohol would be a strong indication of a developing drinking problem and a sign of the incipient disease.

Again, the point of reviewing this diagnostic information is that as each issue is examined to determine the diagnosis, one is also determining the motivational approach. For example, the patient who is suffering from gastritis and complains vigorously about inability to tolerate the symptoms invites one to discuss the alcoholic etiology of the disorder. Again, if the patient uses alcohol to calm nervousness or to relieve psychological symptoms, it would be in order to point out how the addiction may conceivably help temporarily or initially but that very soon the alcohol will result only in increased agitation requiring more alcohol (in the morning, for instance) to relieve that. Indeed, much of the agitation may be due to the alcohol and will be relieved merely by detoxification.

It could further be pointed out how alcohol interferes with social life, sexual functioning, or work and career, or how it encourages the development of character traits such as resentment, argumentativeness, lying, deception, neglect, or irritability toward people who are needed, worked with, or held dear. All this could be done while the physician is going through the above questions. Perhaps the subject has lost the companionship of friends he liked, or the esteem of others he has respected, or perhaps he has caused difficulties at home.

As one goes into the second set of questions particularly, one can also bring out to patients the progression of the degree of dependency on alcohol and get them to appreciate how much control over themselves and their lives they have lost or are in the process of losing.

Recognition by Family and Friends

It is a well known fact that the alcoholic is the last person to recognize his illness. Family members are sure to become aware that a person is drinking to excess long before the patient himself faces up to that fact. Patients may deny it, of course, quite as almost every person is likely to deny being drunk when a lack of sobriety is obvious to others. A longer period may be required for an employer to recognize an employee's excessive drinking, mainly because contact between the two may be limited to working hours, during which the worker may be careful not to expose a proclivity to alcohol. But immediate families seeing alcoholics at close range when their guards are down, are sure to detect their drinking patterns long before anyone else. When those who live with and care for alcoholics seek help, it is often because the alcoholics themselves will do nothing about their problems; they may not even be aware of them. This does not necessarily mean that nothing can be done. If a patient refuses to see the physician when begged or advised to do so, the next best thing is for the doctor to interview the drinker's spouse.

It is possible that one may involve other significant persons—co-workers, relatives, friends—if patients somehow conceal their alcoholism at home and reveal it elsewhere—at work, in other social situations, etc. If the spouse is ignorant or negative and obstructionistic, one may derive from such people the data needed to confront the patients with their illnesses or other inadequate coping mechanisms. Usually, however, the spouse is the most useful person to involve at this point, since there may be, despite the patient's denial, threats to job and career that one may learn only from the spouse. The alcoholic might, for example, be in danger of losing his auto license, or the marriage might be imperiled, or sexual functioning might be impaired, yet he denies or minimizes it. Thus the doctor may have to involve a parent, a sibling, a co-worker, a superior, a lover, or a friend; but the most important person in the overwhelming majority of instances is the spouse.

Not only may the spouse represent one of the most important factors both in the diagnosis and in the patient's motivation to recover from alcoholism, but the spouse may even represent an etiologic factor in the disease. Often enough an alcoholic's spouse misjudges the situation and wrongly assumes that the patient drinks excessively from sheer perversity. Overlooked is the fact that a serious progressive disease is involved and that the drinking is anything but misbehavior whose purpose is to agitate and annoy. Often the alcoholic partner is suffering from a mental problem or depression and resorts to the sedative of alcohol in order to mask an underlying psychological illness. In other instances, the alcoholic husband or wife may find in this readily available and socially acceptable drug a means of making life more tolerable when problems are too difficult with which to cope. Once the nonalcoholic spouse has had these conditions explained, an attitude of whining and nagging irritation may well give way to one of sympathetic understanding.

PHYSICAL EXAMINATION

Having taken a complete history, the physician has now come to the conclusion that the patient might have a drinking problem. A complete physical examination is now in order. Such a physical examination will rarely reveal any abnormalities related to excessive alcohol ingestion unless the problem of drinking has been of long duration. When overt physical manifestations are apparent, such as enlargement of the liver, evidence of capillary dilatation around the areas of the nose and cheeks, inflammation of the larynx, excessive palmar erythema, or other signs of long-standing alcohol ingestion, one can suspect alcoholism in its rather late stages. Laboratory procedures must be completed in order to determine if there have been any other ill effects from the ingestion of alcohol. A complete liver study and x-rays of the gastrointestinal tract may be indicated. Again, these findings supply useful information for discussion with and for motivation of the patient to give up alcohol for the sake of physical well-being. The implications of the laboratory data and the results of physical examinations must be pointed out to the patient.

It is important to note that the usefulness of the different areas where alcoholism is causing difficulties varies considerably. One person may not at all be moved—for whatever reason—by the physical harm experienced but may be moved instead by the fear of loss of the spouse. Another may not be fearful of that but may respond to threats to a career. This is why no overly simple, "cookbook" approach suffices. One must try here and there, feeling out the patient and getting to know him, and then try whatever tack proves most fruitful.

DENIAL OF ALCOHOLISM

Where such positive evidence of alcoholism does not exist, however (and this occurs in the majority of early cases), the patient may not readily accept the diagnosis of alcoholism as made by the physician. Since denial is a characteristic of patients suffering from alcoholism, they may refuse to admit that they have lost control of their drinking and insist that they "can take it or leave it," even though they may admit readily that they have been drinking too much. They are sure they can control their drinking and reduce the amount to what is known as social drinking—a drink or two per day. Under these circumstances, a physician is confronted with the problem of motivating patients to cease ingestion of alcohol altogether, as is the wise decision indicated for any case of alcoholism. How does one convince the patient, however?

One approach is to question patients for their definitions of an alcoholic. Most often patients will describe an advanced case—the skid-row bum or the public inebriate. There is general agreement that such a case is definitely alcoholism. "Do you think he was born that way?" is a good question to ask. Without exception, patients will agree that he was not. "What do you suppose he was like ten years before you described it?" The patient will describe a less severe case. "What about five years before that?" The description becomes less definite. The picture is now not quite as positive. By gradually going back into the development of the disease from its late stage, easily recognized, to its earlier stage, not so easily recognized, patients begin to see that their own patterns of drinking could be forerunners, if not actually early stages, of alcoholism—portrayed so definitely by the skid-row alcoholic. This technique has awakened many patients to the fact that the early stages of alcoholism are not as easily apparent but that they could develop into the full-blown disease that is so obvious at that late stage.

Where denial is still present, it is often wise to suggest to patients that tests be made of their ability to control their drinking. Such tests may be to take no more than two drinks per day and no less than one drink per day. A 3 week test of this procedure will often be very enlightening. The importance of being honest in this test must be explained, and if it is presented in a nonjudgmental way, it will usually produce the desired cooperation.

After 3 weeks of such a test have passed and the patient comes in to report on the experiment, it is usually found that on one or two occasions, or perhaps more, he has exceeded the quota that was agreed upon. Any number of excuses may be given for the breach. Nevertheless, the patient must recognize that the test has failed, since the agreed upon amount was not adhered to. This in itself will sometimes shake a patient's confidence about controlling drinking. Rationalization under these circumstances is extremely common, and patients may want to be tested again. By sheer willpower, such patients are often able to control their drinking as suggested. Over a period of time, however, the alcoholic, regardless of the stage in which he is found, will usually be unable to control drinking and will have to admit over a period of time to going beyond the agreed upon amount.

Even though the term alcoholism is used and patients may admit it is possible that they are alcoholics, it does not necessarily mean that they are willing to accept abstinence. They often will intellectually accept the fact that they are suffering from alcoholism, but emotionally it is very difficult for them to do so, and on occasion they may test themselves to prove that they are not alcoholic. The test consists of taking one drink and not drinking any more. Having done this on several occasions, patients will be convinced that they are not alcoholics. It is only a matter of time until they begin to drink excessively again. This can be spelled out to patients in advance if the therapist wishes to do so. On the other hand, over a period of time, in reporting to the physician patients may often discover these things for themselves.

If one has convinced the patient that he is alcoholic, and this may take some time to do so, the patient's desire to stop drinking must be tested. Often such patients will profess their desire to stop drinking after having been convinced that they are suffering from alcoholism but will quibble about the necessity for complete abstinence. Since alcohol is an addictive drug and alcoholism is a true addiction, it must be explained to such patients that as with any other addiction the drug to which an individual is addicted cannot be used with impunity. Eventually the patient will return to the excessive use of the drug. This is the story of every addict who attempts to use his drug moderately.

Each patient feels that his case is different and he, unlike the others, will succeed in drinking occasionally without drinking excessively. When asked why it is worth taking the risk, the patient will give any number of answers, not the least common of which is feeling uncomfortable in the presence of others who drink when he does not. Such patients feel that they are being isolated from the group and that failure to drink with others is a point of notice by them. Their wish is to drink the way others drink, a drink or two, which would be satisfactory.

Upon careful questioning, however, as to whether or not one or two drinks would be sufficient, the alcoholic patient will usually admit that one or two drinks will not result in the desired effect and that the objective in drinking at all is to attain a desired state regardless of the number of drinks it takes to obtain that state.

This is the alcoholic's objective in drinking. Alcoholics do not drink for social purposes, although this is what they prefer to believe. They actually drink for drug effect, and if carefully questioned they will admit this. They must therefore drink enough to get this effect. With the alcoholic, even in the early stages, this amount is usually more than the average drinker requires. The patient will generally recognize this fact once pointed out. It is apparent from past history that the desired state is not achieved by one or two drinks and that to cease after one or two drinks is something that the patient cannot do reliably. Such discussion often illustrates to the patient the fallacy of rationalizing.

Disulfiram

How do we evaluate the motivation of the patient who, at that point, professes willingness to accept abstinence? Here is one place where the use of disulfiram (Antabuse) may serve a distinct purpose. Patients are offered the pills with the warning that if they have consumed anything with alcohol in it in the previous 24 hours it would be unwise to take these pills, since they might become severely ill. Many patients who come to the physician with the express desire to stop drinking will demur when offered the pill, even though they have told the therapist that they have had nothing to drink for several days. Upon being presented with the pill, however, and admonished about not taking it if they have drunk in the previous 24 hours, they will admit to having had a drink or two very recently. This again is one way of determining the motivation of the patient as well as the patient's honesty.

Some patients who profess a desire to stop drinking and are then offered the pill will give any number of reasons why they do not want to take the pill immediately or feel that taking it is unnecessary and that they do not wish to use a "crutch," which the pill represents. Having professed a desire to stop drinking and having been offered a method of preventing drinking over a period of time, practically guaranteeing abstinence, and their refusing such an offer, they will often have proven themselves that the professed motivation is not sincere. Many patients, after having refused the disulfiram (Antabuse) and had this brought to their attention, will reconsider their original statements of the desire to stop drinking and recognize the insincerity of those statements. After thinking about it for several minutes, some of these patients who are truly well motivated will change their attitude and accept the use of disulfiram (Antabuse). Such a test has proved to be very valuable in changing the minds of many individuals when they discover that their original intentions were not honest. Confronted with the evidence of the frequency of the problem and the necessity for doing something about it, they often change their minds and accept the drug as a method of attaining abstinence. (See Appendix D.)

APPROACHES TO MOTIVATION

Some of the patients are indeed quite ambivalent. They would like to stop drinking, but other forces within them push them on to continue—physiological, psychological, social factors. Thus they may be driven to deny, to minimize, or even to defend the alcohol use so as not to have to come to terms with the decision they must ultimately make to give it up. This denial and minimizing must be confronted.

Convinced that the patient before me is alcoholic and detecting in that patient a hesitation concerning the diagnosis, I have found certain procedures very valuable. If the patient has a child ranging from 6 to 10 years old, they are more effective. If there is no such child, I usually present the patient with a hypothetical problem. "Supposing you had a 6-year-old child who is found to have juvenile diabetes, a very serious condition, as I am sure you know. How would you go about convincing your 6-year-old child that he can go to all the birthday parties with the other children but must not eat the candy, the cake, or the ice cream that all the other children can have? Your child looks at you and says, 'Why not?' and you answer that he has been found to have a serious illness requiring that he refrain from having these 'goodies' of which he is so fond. Your child looks at you and asks, 'Who says I have this illness?' You reply, 'the doctor.' 'The doctor doesn't know what he is talking about. I feel fine, there is nothing the matter with me, and I like candy and cake and ice cream,' the child replies, with what seems to him perfect justification.

"How," I ask the patient, "would you go about training that child to desist from eating those things that he must not have?"

As a rule, a kind of perturbed look comes over the face of the patient, and by far the vast majority will answer, "I don't know, I don't know what I would do." I then respond to that by saying, "You know it must be done for the child's sake and for his health and his life. How would you go about it?" Again, the patient looks at me and answers, "I don't know what I would do." I look straight at the patient and say, "This is the job I have with you. You must believe that my diagnosis is made with the utmost sincerity and for your benefit. You must take my word for it that abstinence is the only answer to your problem, and to learn to live without alcohol is your job. My job is to teach you that." It is astounding how this technique will affect the patient. For the first time the alcoholic recognizes what the problem is, how difficult it is to explain to the patient, and what must be done. I have found this approach very effective.

Another situation with which I have been confronted on many occasions is the patient in whom the diagnosis of alcoholism has been made and who feels that he cannot stop drinking completely. On so many occasions patients suffering from alcoholism do not wish to abstain but wish to be able to drink on occasion, infrequently in most instances, when they feel the overwhelming desire to have a drink or when they feel that abstinence would mark them as alcoholics among other drinkers who are not so afflicted. Since alcohol is an addictive drug, most in the field agree that attempting to accomplish this feat of an occasional drink will lead only to disaster over a period of time. It is possibly true that certain individuals might be able to take a drink now and then and by sheer willpower refuse to drink more. However, in the long run, particularly when they find that one drink has not produced any severe adverse effects and does not immediately lead to excessive drinking, the occasional drink becomes more and more frequent until the patients are back in the pattern that originally brought them to their alcoholic conditions. To many such patients, the idea of not being able to drink at all represents a horrible prospect. After some discussion of this situation, my usual statement to them is, "I could take you to any hospital in this city, and to any bed in that hospital, and there isn't a patient in that hospital who would not trade places with you if all he had to do were to give up drinking in order to achieve a recovery." Almost without exception, the patients will admit that this could very well be true. Then I add, "Here you have an illness that has an answer. All you must do is sacrifice alcohol. Is that too great a sacrifice to retain or regain your health?" I have had only one exception to the affirmative response. That 33-year-old man stated that he would rather live only to 58 and drink than to achieve the accepted three score and ten years alloted to us if he had to sacrifice his drinking. At 33, he thought he could take that risk. Unfortunately, he did not stop drinking, and his life ended at 41. I often cite this to my patients as an example of what alcohol can do to the person who refuses to recognize its dangers, particularly after a diagnosis of alcoholism has been made.

Another common problem that I have encountered stems from patients who ask, "Why me? What have I done to deserve this?" I responded by calling to the attention of the patient the fact that anyone who contracts a disease of any kind asks, "Why me?" I then add, "Do we have a choice as to what disease we may have? Illnesses occur in people without their asking for them and without their choice of illness. The mark of maturity is to accept these problems as they come and meet them in the best possible way. No matter what the illness, whatever must be done to recover from it must be followed through with conscientiousness and it will usually result in success. For those who continually repeat the question "why me," I refer them to the book by Bill Gargan with the title *Why Me?* Bill Gargan had a laryngectomy for cancer. For years, he went about the world lecturing on the subject and teaching people who had similar conditions to learn how to speak with the air swallowed into the stomach and expelled through the esophagus. *Why Me?* has been an inspiration to many people afflicted not only with cancer but with other serious diseases as well.

Speaking of cancer, I have used this as well as other diseases to induce people with alcoholism to refrain from drinking. "If you were to have a cancer in your body that I assure you would never get any worse if you ceased to drink alcohol, but if the cancer would continue to grow if you continued to use alcohol, would you give up drinking?" Without exception, under these conditions, even the most reluctant patients have stated that they would give up drinking. I then draw the similarity between the progressive disease that cancer represents and the progressive disease that alcoholism represents. This also clarifies for the alcoholic patient certain inevitabilities if the proper steps are not taken to control the illness.

I also compare the severe diabetic patient with the alcoholic patient. Each of such patients must refrain from ingesting the materials enjoyed. On occasion, a well-informed patient will challenge me with the fact that insulin may be used for diabetics, whereby they can continue to eat the various foods that they enjoy without any particular harm. My response to that is, "If it were possible for us to produce a drug that would neutralize the affect of alcohol so that it would not be harmful and would not produce the effects that alcohol does in the body, would you then be satisfied to use alcohol under those conditions? Bear in mind that you would feel no affect of the drug at all. It would just be a matter of swallowing the alcoholic beverage with no effect to be felt." After giving some thought to that statement, the patients will usually look up at me in consternation and say, "There would be no point in drinking under those circumstances." "Exactly," I reply. "This calls to your attention the fact that it is the drug effect for which you are looking, and it is the drug effect that makes you the alcoholic who requires that drug effect." I also use this procedure in discussing the problem with those who insist that they drink because they enjoy the taste—also a rationalization in most cases.

There are many such approaches toward motivating individuals to stop drinking. However, for the most part, patients will not respond properly unless they themselves can see the damage that the alcohol has produced. In severe cases—where cirrhosis of the liver has produced hemorrhage from the varicosities at the base of the esophagus, or where edema is the result of that cirrhosis—there is no doubt that patients are aware of the effects of excessive drinking. Even among such patients, however, I have found those who were not convinced that they were alcoholic. Many of these patients are self-destructive in their tendencies and—regardless of any reasoning or logic being used—are bent upon destroying themselves. Such patients—and very often these represent cases of depression—require deep psychiatric therapy to relieve their conditions. For the most part, however, if the patient has any intelligence to which to appeal, many of the discussions that I have described will bring about the proper motivation for abstinence.

Even with success in achieving abstinence for many patients, it must be borne in mind that slips will occur. This does not necessarily spell failure, since slips can be used advantageously as a lesson when applied properly. It is human for people to begin to doubt the diagnosis when after a period of abstinence they feel no particular desire to drink. Curiosity is then aroused as to what a drink might do. Many believe that it is impossible that they cannot take one drink and stop. This conflict in their own minds as time goes on—whether or not they are alcoholic, particularly when they have no desire to drink—continually haunts them. "What kind of an alcoholic can I be if I don't even feel like having a drink? That can't be alcoholism. Alcoholics are supposed to crave drink. I not only do not crave it, I don't even desire it. How can I be alcoholic?" They mull this over in their minds week after week until they feel they cannot go on without making sure that they either are or are not alcoholic. "How do I prove it? Simple—I take a drink. If I continue to drink after that, there'll be no doubt about the alcoholism and I must stop forever." Thus the conflict and argument in their minds goes on until at last they decide they must experiment. And so they do. "Take a drink, and nothing happens. Well, now I feel much better. There you are—I took a drink, I didn't continue drinking. I don't even want another drink."

The following week the same temptation returns and the experiment might be repeated. No harm, no continued drinking. The following week, the same thing. "Well, now, I'm normal just like anyone else. I can take a drink now and then and that's all." And so they take the drink now and then, but the now and then becomes more and more frequent, until they are drinking on a daily basis. Now it is Bill's birthday. "Let's have another drink." "Not me, I'm a one-drink man." "Oh, come on, don't be a spoilsport, have another drink." The thought runs through the "exalcoholic's" mind, "I've had not more than one drink every day for weeks now, I'm not going to make a habit of this, but on an occasion like this, a second drink is not going to hurt me." Thus such people yield to the temptation and take another drink. Nothing happens. The next time a special occasion arises for a second drink—why not? "I did it a few weeks ago—nothing terrible." Thus again the occasion is repeated. Two drinks, and then back to one drink the following day. The two-drink occasions arise more frequently, however. Now the patient is taking two drinks a day. It is only a matter of time before the original condition of excessive drinking returns.

I have repeated this story to numerous patients, all of whom looked at me and said, "I have been through that several times." We then go back and go over the ground again. It is these approaches, these discussions that can motivate patients not only to believe that your interest in them leads you to the diagnosis of alcoholism but to finally face up to the fact that the diagnosis is correct and that their best interests lie in complete abstinence.

THE THERAPIST'S ROLE

All too often patients feel that the therapist's attitude is toward children who have abused their toys; since they have abused their toys or broken them, they are taken away as punishment. "You have not treated them properly, so now we are going to take them away from you. You don't deserve to have toys." A tremendous number of patients have this feeling about drinking. They feel that because they have abused alcohol we are denying it to them as punishment. This must be explained very carefully in a nonjudgmental way; that punishment has nothing to do with the treatment. This is strictly a matter of health, and we are asking them to refrain from taking the very material that is injuring their health. One does not deprive diabetics of certain foods, particularly sugar, because they have taken too much sugar in the past; they are deprived of the sugar because it is injurious to them, and they must refrain from certain foods because they tend to increase the risk of illness. The same goes for abstinence regarding alcoholism.

Of course, these discussions and all the questions and answers and explanations cannot be accomplished in one session. It requires session after session of deep involvement with the patients and their lives. Very often it is a matter of teaching individuals how to live without using a drug for escape. Motivation takes time to develop in some patients and requires great persistance and patience on the part of the physician. One must not give up too easily and write a psychological funeral oration. As long as there is contact with the patients, and as long as they give the doctor a chance, one must persist, no matter how endless the rebuffs seem.

Many patients will ask me what my program is. My statement to them is that this is a reeducational program, where they can unlearn many things that they have learned in the past and can learn to live in a complex and often difficult world without resorting to a drug to escape from problems. A favorite expression of mine in discussing instances with patients is that one gives an anesthetic to do away with pain, but that this does not do away with the problem that has produced the pain. Alcohol is used as a rule as an anesthetic for many alcoholic patients to do away with the pain of living in a world that to them is often unhappy and difficult. One can allay this pain by using alcohol, but the problems that have brought about the desire for such oblivion and anesthesia have not been solved. As one would teach a child to live in a complex world and meet its problems in a mature way, one must learn to live in this complex world and learn to meet one's problems the same way. It is very often advantageous to

discuss the alcoholic patient's problems as a parent would discuss
it with a child. Parents particularly understand this, especially if
they have had difficulty with children.

Fees

Another problem that confronts physicians, particularly
those in private practice, is the matter of payment for services by
alcoholic patients who are already concerned about financial matters. All too often, by the time patients reach the physician for
help with an alcoholic problem, they have already become financially embarrassed. One of the most common dodges when the
matter is discussed is patients claiming they cannot afford the
fees that the doctor commands when they are already in financial
trouble. Where insurance policies cover the care of alcoholic patients, this problem, to some extent, is alleviated; however, for
those patients whose policies have already lapsed or who do not
have that kind of protection, the financial burden represents a
problem.

Poorly motivated patients will often use this excuse as a
method for not continuing treatment. Their rationalization tells
them that the doctor who is not to be paid will no longer be as
interested in pursuing treatment of the patient. With a conscientious doctor, of course, the financial returns are secondary, the
main interest being the welfare of the patient. When I encounter
such a patient, I use the following technique: "You are already in
financial trouble and here am I trying to help you, while at the
same time adding to your burdens and difficulties. Can you see
the position in which this puts me? Still, I feel it is worth it
because I know that if you follow my advice and take the treatment seriously and stop drinking, you will eventually recover
your health and be able to increase your earning capacity to
where you will be able to pay, not only for your treatments with
me, but to get rid of your other debts as well. But I expect to be
paid. If you are conscientious about your treatment and your response, I will bear with you and will accept partial payments
while you are under my care. If there is a balance after you
are fully recovered, I will expect you to pay that balance when you
can. I do want you to know that I appreciate the fact that your
financial burdens are being increased by coming here. There is

one important fact, however, that I would like you to know. Doctors rarely can guarantee anything in the treatment of a patient, but with you, there is one thing that I can guarantee—and that is that *it will cost you less to come here than to continue drinking.*"

SYMPATHY AND EMPATHY

All of these techniques are advantageous, and one could not possibly enumerate all the possible approaches one could use. A few that I have given may help the therapist to induce the somewhat reluctant patient to a motivation that will result in abstinence. Over a period of time, with patience and understanding, this can be done. Certainly, one must apply both sympathy and empathy for the patient and identify with the patient and with his problems.

An important part of the motivation is the overcoming of denial. Denial can be expressed as "they do not like me"—which manifests itself as isolation. Although alcohol is used by many patients initially to overcome shyness (through its disinhibiting function), inevitably shame and guilt over the alcoholic's behavior will result in even more withdrawal and isolation.

One can counter this by giving patients recovered alcoholics with whom they can identify—whose background or gender or occupation or social standing or alcoholic history is like theirs. These persons can tell their own stories, take the patients to *appropriate* Alcoholics Anonymous (A.A.) meetings, and introduce them to others. Then their defensive shyness can diminish, their relationships spread out, and their sense of isolation decrease.

The physician must have contacts in the community of A.A. or the local National Council of Alcoholism group to find such people to "Twelve Step" the patient. The same thing can be done for the family through Al-Anon and Alateen.

Do not become too critical if patients slip. Understand that they have not done this to annoy you, nor should it be considered a failure if they do slip. Encourage them to try again. Use the slips as proof of what you have discussed with them. Your sympathy, your empathy, and your understanding will encourage them to go on.

It is comparatively easy to diagnose and treat alcoholic patients who wish to get well and are perfectly willing to give up drinking without protest once the diagnosis has been made, but for the alcoholic patients who feel that they are being discriminated against, who feel that the fates have worked against them, who feel that in overcoming a sense of inadequacy they can by forcing the issue continue to drink and succeed in drinking without getting drunk, bringing about motivation is a most difficult task. It can be *done,* and it can be done successfully in the vast majority of cases. It takes patience, understanding, and a desire to help unfortunate human beings who have been caught up in a web of dependence upon this socially acceptable and readily available drug.

This demonstration of the understanding of the patient's problems, and the addition of those problems that the therapist is making, often brings about in the patient on appreciation of the physician as well as a willingness to cooperate. Based on past experience the patient also appreciates that the guarantee that the doctor describes is a reasonable one, and this often marks a turning point in patient attitude and provides for additional motivation.

Every practicing physician should study the early psychological symptoms as I have listed them earlier in the form of telltale affirmative answers to questions. If any of those questions are answered in the affirmative, the patient should be admonished regarding a developing drinking problem, and a record should be kept by the doctor. If at any future time those same questions should be put to the patient and same affirmative answers obtained, there can be no doubt that the illness has more or less firmly established itself and is to be watched, studied, and pursued. If the patient has not changed drinking habits and is continuing to drink excessively, either by his own admission or as confirmed by family, friends, or employer—with patient permission, of course—it must then be pointed out in no uncertain terms that the patient has lost control of his drinking. If, on the other hand, the patient has been able to control his drinking and the questionnaire elicits only negative answers, then and only then is it appropriate to wait upon further reports to ascertain whether or not the patient has successfully passed the test and escaped the suspected early stages of alcohol illness.

There is also a difference between understanding patients and allowing sympathy for them to lead to permissiveness. Many physicians, perhaps because of their own drinking patterns, fail to suspect alcoholism where it is definitely present and will allow patients to consume one or two drinks a day on the theory that that much alcohol can be metabolized without damage to his physiology. This is fallacious. One must always bear in mind that alcoholism is a drug addiction no different from other drug dependencies and that the use of any drug upon which a patient has to any degree become dependent will eventually lead to its excessive use.

FINAL THOUGHTS:

Prognosis

There is no guarantee that every patient who comes to the physician with the problem of alcoholism will completely recover. Too many factors are involved in the life of an individual for a single therapist to contend successfully with a particular alcoholic's every possible need. With patience, medical knowledge, and understanding of the victim's physiology and psychology, however, the therapist is in a position to be of great help, and in most cases the prognosis is bound to be favorable, if not excellent. As with any disease, the earlier alcoholism is recognized, diagnosed, and treated, the better will be the results.

Misdiagnosis

Let me put a word in here regarding the possibility of a misdiagnosis. Suppose that the patient who is being diagnosed as an early alcoholic really is not. Of what have we deprived this person? Were alcohol a necessity to life, then we should be grossly remiss, I believe, in setting such a patient down as a definite alcoholic before checking and double-checking our diagnosis for accuracy. But alcohol is not a necessity of life, and it is a drug that can lead to dependency. Should an individual have displayed some indication of having a problem as a result of that drug's use, surely to deprive that person of its further use in no way cuts him off from anything critical! Many persons who have chosen total abstinence live full and happy lives. As much can therefore be said of anyone who is deprived of alcohol, even though it can be shown that it never in any way disadvantaged or caused that person harm.

Working with the Spouse

A final word as to the value of promoting the alcoholic's motivation to seek help through interviewing—and sometimes even treating—the spouse. The most common question put by workers in the field of alcohol disease is, "What can be done if the patient who is obviously alcoholic denies the problem and refuses to seek treatment for it?" The answer I regard as most appropriate is, "If the victim will not seek help, the spouse should do so." One can motivate the patient indirectly through the spouse's own treatment—either psychotherapy, other forms of counseling, or Al-Anon.

In many instances, failure of the nonalcoholic spouse to understand the other's problem with alcohol gives rise to a relationship that threatens the very marriage itself—and thus through countersuggestibility, born of hostility, causes the victim of alcoholism to be all the more stubborn in refusing to seek treatment. If anything, the alcoholic's view of the total situation leads to denying alcoholism, refusing to modify drinking habits, and seeing no reason for treatment.

Where such a chaotic relationship exists, an interview with the alcoholic's partner—wherein the nature of alcohol involvement is carefully explained—will often result in a changed attitude on his or her part. Understanding the character and cause of the sick one's suffering, relief from which is sought in a readily available drug, may well alter the attitude of the well partner and replace hostility with sympathy. This in time may lead the alcoholic partner to become more accommodating and cooperative—often to the point of voluntarily seeking help, or at least advice, even though not personally feeling the need for such resort. This gives the therapist an opportunity to discuss the problem with the patient who otherwise might never have appeared in the office.

Although the primary goal of treating the nonalcoholic spouse may well be just to salvage her, this in turn may also influence the alcoholic indirectly through the withdrawal of the secondary rewards of drinking. For example, as the spouse acquires increasing distance from the alcoholic's illness and develops a detachment and separateness from the situation, the purpose of the alcoholic's drinking (such as revenge through humiliation and embarrassment) may well lose its effectiveness. Furthermore, the growing separateness and possible loss of the spouse—a threat now not merely words but a real possibility—can push the alcoholic into treatment. (It is crucial that these threats—loss of job, spouse, etc.—be deeply meaningful and actual, not just empty words that have no effect and might even reinforce the drinking.)

It is a common occurrence that such leapfrog interviews in the end motivate the victim of alcoholism to submit for treatment. Denial, one of the characteristics of alcohol disease, is a factor to be carefully investigated and overcome—and that denial well may be overcome through atttempting to modify the attitude of the victim's spouse.

The Physician Himself

One other point is to be mentioned: what goes on in the mind of the physician himself. As noted, doctors must be patient. They must not have the alcoholic's cure at stake for their own purposes, for self-aggrandizement or for reassurance as to ability as a doctor, for then they would not be able to tolerate the patient's resistances and denial or recidivism without getting angry and taking it personally. Physicians must be patient, tolerant, and persistant and must be convinced themselves of what they are doing and the correctness of it. Only thus can they tolerate, for example, a patient's anger should that form of defense and resistance occur. Doctors must not fear that; it is part of the illness itself. If discussion has really frightened the patient, that anger towards the physician might conceivably be instrumental in the patient's working out his own particular path to recovery, using another helping area—A.A., or another physician.

The doctor, as noted, must have solved his own problems with alcohol and alcoholism and must be convinced of the seriousness of this disorder and the temptations and dangers in a society that minimizes its harmfulness, jokes about it, and even encourages it. The physician must be willing to tolerate the anger and even oppositional and obstructionistic behavior in family members and others who regard the diagnosis as a disgrace or who have some hidden stake in the patient's being ill. Again, Al-Anon or counseling or even psychotherapy here might be necessary for the relative if that person is important in the patient's life situation. (One example is the husband or wife whose alcoholic spouse is always home, drunk, but who, now on his or her way to sobriety, is frequently out at A.A. meetings and elsewhere, exposed to others of the opposite sex; the nonalcoholic spouse's latent jealousy and fears now flare up, and the spouse might much prefer the alcoholic to be back home, drunk again, in a controllable situation once more.)

Physicians therefore must be convinced that alcoholism is a disorder, an illness, a disease, and not just a weakness, a nastiness, not just someone's fault. They must not become punitive or judgmental, certainly not toward the patients and not even toward family members, etc., whose help they may be able to use and on whom patients may be very dependent. Here too physicians must have resolved their own problems over their own feelings of dependency. They must not despise dependency as a weakness and must not be punitive toward or rejecting of the dependency feelings and behavior on the part of patients—especially in the relationship when the patient may desperately need gratification of such needs. A doctor might well permit it, might even encourage it in order to have some influence over patients to guide them and get them to stop drinking and begin on the road to recovery—even a path to recovery that at first exists for the sake of the dependent relationship with the physician.

On the other hand, as the relationship develops, the therapist must avoid luxuriating in patient dependency and must encourage patients to take their own paths away from the doctor. Between the beginning game and the end game—as it were, in the middle game—no matter what area of the patient's life is being worked on, the doctor must always keep in mind the primacy of the alcohol problem and must always keep an eye on the patient's motivation as to that. It is always the first and foremost consideration. The physician must thus wend his way carefully.

Motivating an alcoholic patient is a matter of perspicuity and judgment. The approach must be eclectic and suited to the individual involved. A few techniques have been described, but many more can be added through experience and observation as one treats more and more victims of this prevalent illness.

Richard Baum
Frank L. Iber

4
Initial Treatment of the Alcoholic Patient

Alcoholism presents a spectrum of clinical and diagnostic problems to the physician, among which the management of acute intoxication and subsequent withdrawal is often one of the most difficult and most frustrating. The difficulties occasionally inherent in the acute drunkenness situation—lack of cooperation of the patients, the unreliability of the history, and the typically inconvenient time of occurrence—may limit initial goals pragmatically to providing shelter, securing safe withdrawal, and identifying intercurrent illness of only emergent nature. On the other hand, many drinking patients are alert, cooperative, and concerned about assistance; in these persons it is desirable to arrange for ongoing treatment for alcoholism and a thorough health checkup.

INITIAL ASSESSMENT

The initial assessment of an alcoholic or potentially alcoholic patient must be appropriate to the patient's needs and accomplish three things. It should establish a doctor–patient relationship based on a clear statement that there is an alcoholism problem with which the doctor is concerned and will assist. The degree of alcohol use and the alcohol-nutritional health problems that can

73

ALCOHOLISM
ISBN 0-8089-1227-5
Copyright © 1980 by Grune & Stratton
All rights of reproduction in any form reserved.

be readily established should be inventoried. A general plan of action should be formulated to provide for the needs of patients and their alcoholism. This discussion will emphasize those circumstances that require prompt treatment; even though these are infrequent, they are of great importance.

To determine whether or not there are problems requiring immediate attention a history and physical examination are conducted, much as with any other patient. Patients who have or will develop life-threatening problems are rare but must be recognized. A rare patient will be a very poor or reluctant historian. In these, a minimum of historical information is needed to manage the patient; this information should be obtained from the family, the patient, or occasionally a drinking companion.

Life-threatening withdrawal does not develop in patients drinking less than 2 weeks; thus it is quite useful to determine the length of time the patient has been drinking during the current episode. History of recent injuries, regularly used medication, medications taken in the recent past, and allergies are also helpful. It is also useful to ascertain a history of any form of convulsions in the past, since patients with such a history are likely to have seizures in the withdrawal period that can be prevented by treatment with phenytoin (diphenylhydantoin).

In patients appearing ill, intoxicated, or uncooperative, certain physical examination features are to be emphasized. These permit the physician to construct an inventory of problems for treatment as well as an assessment of their urgency (Table 4-1). The physician must make some assessment of the likelihood of alcohol withdrawal syndrome and the estimated intensity of the withdrawal. A patient drinking uninterrupted for many years will have a more intense withdrawal than a person drinking but a few weeks; severity of withdrawal in the past predicts severity at present; signs appearing in the first six hours often indicates that the process will worsen. Table 4-2 indicates some of the common signs of withdrawal that may be recognized.

Physical examinations stress those areas requiring immediate intervention or that are potentially life threatening (see Table 4-1). Death in the acute situation is generally due to head trauma, infection, cardiac arrhythmia, pancreatitis or ruptured viscus, or inadequately treated withdrawal. Fractures and lacerations are apparent to all staff. The patient should be undressed

Table 4-1
Necessary Physical Examination

Life-threatening problems
    Vital signs
    Consciousness and neurologic status
        Arousability
        Movement, reflexes, and gross sensation in all extremities, head, and
            trunk
        Inspection and palpation of head for injury
        Cranial nerves II, III, IV, VI, VII, IX, XI, and XII
      Chest, for infection and adequacy of respiration
      Heart, for rate and arrhythmia
      Abdomen, for ileus and severe pain

Withdrawal
    Agitation
    Alarmability
    Apartness or hallucinations
    Heart rate

---

and examined thoroughly for evidence of trauma or infection. A careful neurologic examination, including visualization of both optic discs and tympanic membranes and evaluation of chest and abdomen, are essential. Skin lesions and questionable fractures are common problems that can wait for evaluation and treatment until the patient is able to fully tolerate these.

Most serious abnormalities are obvious and are reflected in distortions of the level of consciousness or of vital signs. Temperature of more than 100.5°F (38.1°C) is generally due to infection or aspiration and never should be attributed to withdrawal without further careful evaluation of the chest for pneumonitis and of the body for occult infection. Additionally, respiratory rate greater than 20 or pulse greater than 110 requires an explanation or careful serial observation. The level of consciousness or of interaction with the observer and the environment must be assessed carefully because small changes in either direction are among the most significant observations. For this reason, the same person should both make the initial assessment and continue the observation to remake the assessment an hour or two

Table 4-2
Stages in Alcohol Withdrawal

---

1. *Earliest—Patient sensations*
   Sensation of internal uneasiness
   Consciousness of visceral function, nausea, churning, tightness

2. *Minimal—discernable by observer*
   Fidgits—many unnecessary movements
   Agitation
   Chain smoke, drink many cups of coffee
   Pulse increased 20+ beats/min

3. *Moderate*
   Severe agitation
   Pulse 20–50 beats/min increased
   Difficult to keep patient in bed
   Short spells of lapse of attention
   Involuntary tremor *may* be marked

4. *Severe*
   Hallucinations—auditory, visual
   Irrational fears, sensitive to noise
   Extreme agitation
   Usually unable to cooperate
   Pulse 50 beats/min increased
   Muscular hyperactivity
   Severe diaphoresis

5. *Extreme*
   All of stage 4
   Totally irrational
   Extreme diaphoresis
   Extreme tachycardia
   Convulsions

There are 6–30 hours required to move from stages 1 to 5.

later. Hypertension is very common in the withdrawal period, with levels of 190/120 mm Hg common in persons who have no hypertension a few days later.

If the patient is coherent, is a reasonable historian, has not had severe withdrawal symptoms upon cessation of drinking in the past, and has no substantial agitation or restlessness at the time of examination, further close observation is not necessary. Such a patient may return home in the care of another person. If there is depression of the level of consciousness or agitation, however, observation over the first 6 hours is almost essential for safety. Obtundation secondary to alcohol intoxication will not persist beyond 3–4 hours after the last drink, and failure to brighten during this period is excellent evidence of head injury or of a different intoxicant concomitant with alcoholism. With-drawal symptoms develop in the first 12–24 hours after cessation of drinking, and close observation provides the basis for treat-ment during this period.

INITIAL LABORATORY EVALUATION

The assessment on the first visit may utilize a blood alcohol level. If the patient totally denies drinking, this may establish that alcohol has been ingested on a regular basis (up to 4 hours before the blood tests). If there is a disorder of consciousness or behavior, the blood alcohol level should be 200–400 mg/dl to ac-count for either of these. A level above 100 mg/dl corroborates an alcoholism history. Severe alcoholics develop many laboratory abnormalities that usually return to normal within a week of no drinking and are more important in being misleading about major organ disease than they are helpful in diagnosis (Table 4-3). If convenient, delaying routine screening tests of hematol-ogy, liver function tests, uric acid, and electrolytes for 1–2 weeks will permit the most common alcohol-induced abnormalities to disappear. Obviously indicated tests to evaluate pain, severe or-ganomegaly, or fever should be performed promptly.

Table 4-3
Common Changes in Usual Laboratory Tests in
Alcoholics

Test	Change
WBC	May not rise if folate deficient
Hematocrit	Often depressed 3–7 percent
Blood sugar*	Often wide swings accompanying poor carbohydrate intake and stores
Electrolytes	Increased anion gap due to lactate
Potassium and phosphorous	Often quite low
Uric acid	Elevated for 2–5 days
Liver tests	25 percent abnormal

All return to normal in 1 week of abstinence and normal eating.
*Requires 1 week of adequate carbohydrate intake to become normal.

Chest x-ray and electrocardiogram are not needed on all patients but are helpful adjuncts needed in about 10 percent. Tuberculosis is common among inner city alcoholics, and skin tests are often administered to aid in recognition. Arrhythmia is commonly recognized during detoxification, but its meaning is not clear. Intervention is rarely required.

MANAGEMENT OF WITHDRAWAL

Alcohol withdrawal is a state of central nervous system irritability produced upon the cessation or sharp withdrawal of ethanol intake after 2 or more weeks of drinking. The cardinal features of withdrawal are agitation and autonomic hyperactivity characterized by diaphoresis, tachycardia, and tremor. The syndrome begins 6–24 hours after stopping ethanol, reaches a peak within 72–96 hours, and then subsides. This time course is almost always seen and is of substantial value in diagnosis. Fever, severe illness, or intercurrent major infection may accelerate the course and exacerbate the severity of withdrawal. The most severe forms of withdrawal—alcoholic hallucinosis and delirium tremens—occur in the period 2–5 days after the last drink and are characterized by severe agitation and hallucinations that are often paranoid in nature. Delirium tremens has a mortality of as much as 20 percent but can always be prevented by early treatment of withdrawal. Table 4-2 indicates diagnosable stages of withdrawal. Recognition of the earlier and milder stages offers ample time for the gradual treatment of the patient.

All of the symptoms and signs of alcohol withdrawal are exacerbated by diminished sensory input. By this we mean that unfamiliar surroundings and unknown people may agitate the patient. Successful therapy of alcohol withdrawal requires creation of many environmental changes that calm the patient. Some of these are listed in Table 4-4, which emphasizes that the patients should be surrounded with familiar, nonstimulating, nonthreatening things. Restraints, intravenous infusions and bedsides should be avoided.

Alcohol withdrawal can be accomplished the majority of the time at home if there is a motivated alcoholic with an interested family member or friend. If there is substantial agitation, if a

Table 4-4
"Do's" and "Don'ts" in Treating Withdrawal (Sensory
Withdrawal Syndrome)

	Do's	Don'ts
Visual	Lights on Familiar people Civilian clothes	Lights off Shadows
Touch	Comfortable chair Low bed Regular clothes	High bed Restraints Intravenous
Sound	Light music Soft conversation with patient	Abrupt noises

convulsion has already occurred, or if there is a major intercurrent infection such as pneumonia, withdrawal should be performed in a supervised locale under the care of a physician.

Some detail is given to withdrawal under supervision of a physician or a trained person because it shows the features that are important in the more severe problems; an understanding of these will render the treatment of the less severely ill person quite easy. Often the patient is unable to give up alcohol, and withdrawal must be conducted under skilled supervision to assure that withdrawal in fact occurs. Many institutions and many third-party insurance plans now provide skilled alcoholism detoxification and this is often the most available, face saving and effective means of starting alcoholism therapy.

Nearly all patients will feel better with the use of medication. Medication should be temporary, used only during the withdrawal period, and should feature assistance to the patient during this difficult time. Nearly all patients will show disturbed sleep pattern and some features of depression during the first few days of withdrawal, but sleeping and antidepressant medications should rarely be used. Generally vitamins, antacids, antidiarrheal agents, and mild analgesics (such as acetaminophen) are used in all, and minor tranquilizers (as outlined in Table 4-5) are used in most.

General supportive care should be provided. The patient should be kept clean and comfortable. Most subjects upon stopping drinking are overhydrated and have increased total body

Table 4-5
Features of Drugs Used in Withdrawal Treatment

Drug	Unit Dose for Withdrawal	Half-Duration of Dose (hr)	Significant Side Effects
Chlordiazepoxide*	100 mg	24–40	None
Diazepam*	10 mg	12–24	None
Hydroxazine*	100 mg	10–14	None
Chlorpromazine	50 mg	12	Hypotension, spasms
Pentabarbital	100 mg	4	Respiratory depression
Phenobarbital	100 mg	16	Respiratory depression
Paraldehyde	15 ml	1–3	Respiratory depression, foul odor
Chloral hydrate	1 g	1–3	Respiratory depression

*Agents of choice.

sodium; therefore intravenous fluids are rarely needed. Food should be offered three to five times daily, and if refused the patient should be encouraged to take a sugar-containing solution such as Kool-Aid, a nondiet soda, or juice. Unlimited access to coffee should be avoided because of its stimulant effects. Thiamine (100 mg) and folic acid (5 mg) are given parenterally to all of our patients, and a multiple vitamin capsule is ingested daily.

The aim of treatment is to prevent severe withdrawal and to comfort the patient. Total withdrawal takes about 3–6 days. The ideal alcohol withdrawal drug would substitute completely for alcohol at all nervous system sites and once the patient were saturated would disappear slowly, with a biologic half-life of about two days. In this way withdrawal would be completed without requiring medicine beyond the first day. The drug should be completely safe so that overdose would not suppress respiration or have other harmful side effects. No ideal drug exists, however.

Treatment of withdrawal requires prompt and continual therapy. The hallmark of therapy is the need for the individualization of management. The amount of medication required to control withdrawal routinely varies among patients by a factor of 10 over a 24 hour period—many patients require only reassurance and comfort and little or no medication, whereas rarely patients manifesting severe withdrawal can require 2 g or more of chlordiazepoxide in the first day. Decisions regarding dosage of medication can thus be made only by careful observation of the patient over time.

Therapy is most effective when begun promptly. Patients are often medicated within 10 minutes of entering our detoxification unit, with history taking and physical examination continuing after initial medication. The need for prompt and continual therapy coupled with the rarity of severe intercurrent illness has led us to employ specially trained nurses and technicians as primary therapists functioning under a set of standing orders designed to allow therapy to be tailored to the individual with physicians providing backup help. [*Ed. note:* One of us (S.E.G.) has often observed such patients for an hour prior to giving medication in the hospital setting in order to avoid excessive sedation for that patient who has taken a large dose of a hypnotic drug just prior to entering the treatment facility.]

For the sake of simplicity we use a one-drug regimen with chlordiazepoxide as our agent of choice because it is safe and has a long half-life, which minimizes the number of treatment decisions necessary after attaining initial calming. Essentially all patients can be successfully treated with this regimen. Rarely in patients having suspected head trauma with neurologic complications it is advisable to use a short-acting drug in order to interfere with the level of consciousness as little as possible. We use chloral hydrate with these uncommon patients, who must be carefully and closely followed by physicians.

People with a history of convulsions are begun on phenytoin by mouth. We use a prompt dose of 300 mg without a loading dose and repeat this dose daily for 5 days and then stop. Patients treated with diazepam which has marked antiseizure activity, do not require phenytoin therapy.

External environment influences therapy to a large extent (Table 4-4). Calm surroundings, soft music, and someone to talk to are often vastly more effective than medication. It is essential to avoid aggravating the patient during periods of confusion. For this reason we do not use restraints or bedrails. These have been found to be counterproductive, agitating the patient and at times producing serious injury when the patient managed to get out of bed despite these precautions. Our policy is to place a mattress on the floor so that such confused patients cannot fall during this period. Confused patients must be protected from matches, glass, or other potentially sharp objects and should not be allowed to smoke.

Agitation, nausea and vomiting, and inability to sleep are hallmarks of withdrawal and do not require special strategy but respond to the regimen outlined. Sleeping medication and antiemetics are not used. Nausea and vomiting are quite common during the first 24–48 hours. This does not present a special problem, however, since alcoholics are uniformly overhydrated and intravenous fluids and electrolyte therapy are not needed unless nausea and vomiting are protracted or intercurrent illness produces dehydration. Patients will often approach the doctor with a list of complaints, expecting specific medication for each one. This situation is best handled by delaying tactics, since complaints tend to be short lived.

A variety of other medications are useful as adjuncts in alcohol withdrawal therapy. Thiamine, folic acid, and multivitamins are routinely employed, since deficits of these substances are not infrequently found in alcoholics because of either poor diet or malabsorption; treatment is the most economical approach. Antacids are employed as needed and antidiarrheal agents and laxatives are used similarly. Acetaminophen is used for analgesia instead of aspirin because of the deleterious effects of salicylates on the gastric mucosa. We allow the responsible nonphysician persons in attendance to employ liquid antacid, bismuth subsalicylate, milk of magnesia, and acetaminophen at their discretion. Our policy has been to avoid the use of soporific tranquilizing and sedative medications other than our primary treatment agent because we have found that multiple agents produce complex dosage problems without adding much to therapeutic efficacy. It is highly useful that *all* employees become familiar with a single primary treatment agent—multiple treatments and additional drugs should not be used.

The period of withdrawal can be demonstrated to last for up to 3 months by psychological testing and EEG criteria, but all life-threatening situations occur within the first week and sedative therapy is not needed beyond this point. As soon as patients appear receptive they should begin to receive counseling and planning for further stages of rehabilitation. Patients tend to be depressed in this period and need *positive programs* and *assertive statements* to become involved. Their own responsibility for their rehabilitation should be stressed and reinforced if possible by giving them responsibility for their own well-being during treatment by assigning work in the treatment facility. Occasionally a brief written contract of what the patient must do and what the alcohol therapist will do is helpful.

Accentuation of symptoms is occasionally seen during the course of withdrawal therapy. Most commonly this is the result of agitation arising from more realistic and perceptive interaction with the environment or to lessening amounts of therapeutic medication. Delayed alcohol withdrawal is not a real phenomenon; however, other drugs—both physician prescribed and illicit—are commonly used by alcoholics, and these may produce symptoms of withdrawal. The outlined plan will successfully handle these problems. Tremor is aggravated in withdrawal but is an unreliable index. Currently it seems more closely related to magnesium depletion than to alcohol.

Outpatient withdrawal (see Table 4-6) can be carried out in patients who are normal on screening examination when a re-

Table 4-6
Criteria for Outpatient Detoxification

Low volume and duration of drinking
Previous success at efforts to withdraw self
Youth and good medical health
High motivation
Home or other caretaker support mechanism
Absence of solid sedative addiction (as opposed to ethanol or paraldehyde)
No history or current evidence of seizures or severe withdrawal syndrome
No history of severe psychiatric complications such as suicidal tendencies or paranoid states

By outpatient detoxification is meant detoxification at home or in a sobering-up station without trained personnel, as contrasted with inpatient detoxification in an acute care facility, such as a hospital, or in a lay detoxification unit with trained personnel and hospital backup. The desirable hand-off to longer term rehabilitative effort (in- or outpatient) may or may not be associated with either of these and must be considered by the physician in the disposition of the patient.

sponsible nondrinking person is available to remain with the patients. Patients who are under 40 years old or who have been drinking less than a month are particularly good candidates for such management. In the outpatient setting we give the nondrinker 25 (25 mg) chlordiazepoxide capsules with instructions to give one capsule hourly as needed. In the uncontrolled setting drug therapy is not effective and we do not give medication to unsupervised alcoholics.

INTERCURRENT ILLNESS

Alcohol withdrawal syndromes are modified by and modify concurrent illness. It is essential in each patient with withdrawal to search carefully for those problems requiring immediate medical attention and to be alert to the problems of alcohol withdrawal in those patients seen primarily for medical emergencies.

The primary medical emergencies are infection, especially pneumonia, acute abdominal crisis, especially pancreatitis and perforated viscus, and decompensated liver disease. These problems can be somewhat masked by the changes in the patient's mental status brought on by alcohol and withdrawal but should, if severe, be recognized by physical examination. Liver disease with jaundice is a special problem because of the difficulty in differentiating withdrawal from hepatic encephalopathy and the danger of causing deepening hepatic coma with sedative medication. Typically withdrawal is characterized by agitation, irritability, and hallucinations, while delirium tremens shows confusion, hypersomnia with inversion of normal sleep pattern, and absence of hallucinations. EEG and serum ammonia levels can be helpful in distinguishing the difference, but the two can coexist. It is our policy to treat with short-acting medications—especially paraldehyde or chloral hydrate—in this situation even though it requires much more work and more frequent dosages.

Chronic illness usually cannot be dealt with in the withdrawal period. Cirrhosis, malnutrition, hypertension, and peripheral vascular disease, occasionally with leg ulcers, are common chronic problems requiring long-term therapy, which can best be accomplished if it is included as a feature of treatment for chronic alcoholism. For this reason our alcoholism followup clinics take care of medical problems of this nature.

Alcoholic patients who present with another medical problem and subsequently develop withdrawal symptoms are treated in much the same way as any others. It is evident, however, that therapy should be aimed at allowing treatment of the emergent medical problem to continue unimpeded. Since this frequently means maintenance of i.v. lines, catheters, and other accoutrements of modern medicine, and since the aim of withdrawal therapy is for repression of almost all agitation, dosages of medication employed tend to be higher.

FREQUENTLY ENCOUNTERED ALCOHOL-RELATED DISEASE

Peripheral neuritis, gastritis, and liver disease are frequently encountered alcohol related disease. With restoration of a good diet and continued abstinence these *all* improve with time. The times of improvement of some of the more common illnesses are indicated in Table 4-7.

Table 4-7
Times for Major Improvement in Alcohol Related
Diseases (With Abstinence, Good Diet, Vitamins)

Improve in 1 week

Gastritis	Many anemias
Pain of peripheral neuritis	WBC and platelet decreases due to alcohol
High uric acids	Lactic acidosis
Withdrawal syndrome	Wernicke encephalopathy, sixth nerve palsy

Improve in 1 month

Memory and mental function	Pancreatitis
Intestinal malabsorptions	Myopathy
Most nutritional problems	

Improve in 3 months

Alcoholic Liver Disease	Korsakoff psychosis
Peripheral neuritis	

ON-GOING THERAPY

The ultimate test of alcoholism programs is their success in producing sobriety among their clients. We have patients seen by alcoholism counselors to plan on-going treatment as soon as is feasible, routinely within the first 48 hours.

Subsequently, counselors supervise the patient's time in our unit. Except under special circumstances patients are not permitted to leave, and visitors are cautioned against bringing alcohol. Drinking on the unit by patients or employees is grounds for immediate discharge.

SUMMARY

The treatment of alcohol intoxication and possible subsequent withdrawal requires a controlled environment to prevent further drinking and provides the optimal opportunity to recognize and treat withdrawal and plan subsequent alcohol therapy. Withdrawal syndromes can be controlled and severe withdrawal aborted by the plan of therapy outlined.

Initial therapy is limited to control of the acute situation and identification and treatment of life threatening emergencies. It is possible subsequently to plan for therapy for chronic problems—alcoholism and intercurrent illnesses. This is done most effectively when combined into a single package emphasizing the relationship of alcoholism to other health problems.

REFERENCES

Ribaudo CA, Grace WJ: Pulmonary aspiration. *Am J Med* 50:510–520 1971

Sampliner R, Iber F: Diphenylhydantoin control of alcohol withdrawal seizures. *JAMA* 230:1430–1432, 1974

Sellers EM, Kalant H: Alcohol intoxification and withdrawal. *N Engl J Med* 294:757–762, 1976

Simpson RK: Data on over 5,000 admissions for detoxification. Hamson Treatment and Rehabilitation Center, Des Moines, Iowa, 1972

Soloman A: Sensory deprivation, in Freedman MT, Kaplan H (eds): *Comprehensive Textbook of Psychiatry*. Baltimore, Williams & Wilkins, 1967

Spear PW, Protass LM: Alcoholism—An endemic disease: Five years' experience in a municipal hospital. *Med Clin North America* 57:1471–1479, 1973

Thomas DW: Treatment of the alcohol withdrawal syndrome. *JAMA* 188:316, 1964

Thompson WL, Johnson AD, Maddrey: Diazepam and paraldehyde for treatment of severe delirium tremens: A controlled study. *Ann Int Med* 82:175–180, 1975

Victor M: Treatment of alcoholic intoxication and the withdrawal syndrome. *Psychosom Med* 25:636–650, 1966

Victor M: Nutrition and diseases of the nervous system. *Prog Food Nutr Sci* 43:145–172, 1975

Victor M, Hope JM: The phenomenon of auditory hallucinations in chronic alcoholism. *J Nerv Ment Dis* 126:451–481, 1958

David H. Knott
Robert D. Fink
Jack C. Morgan

5

After Detoxification—The Physician's Role in the Initial Treatment Phase of Alcoholism

Whether through lay self-help groups or professional counseling, long-term management is an essential element in the therapeutic planning for the alcoholic.

Proper management of the detoxified patient who expresses some motivation for continued treatment is extremely important to the overall rehabilitation process. The physician must recognize that initial motivation on the part of the patient may derive primarily from a recent crisis situation. As the length of time between detoxification and active psychosocial therapeutic intervention increases, motivation wanes and the patient's attitude toward further treatment other than medical management becomes more ambivalent. It is unfortunately common for the patient to escape from any therapeutic modality at this point, but a well established physician–patient relationship allows the clinician to expedite the patient's entry into active treatment. To accomplish this, attention should be directed toward the following:

1. Motivational considerations
2. Diagnostic considerations
3. Early treatment considerations: psychotherapy, chemotherapy, referral
4. Prognostic considerations

89

ALCOHOLISM
ISBN 0-8089-1227-5

Copyright © 1980 by Grune & Stratton
All rights of reproduction in any form reserved.

MOTIVATIONAL CONSIDERATIONS

The old adage, "you can't help alcoholics until they are ready to help themselves" or until "they have hit bottom" is inherently therapeutically nihilistic. Issues of motivation arise at more than one point in the course of such patients. Block (Chapter 3) referred to those techniques useful in initiating therapy; similar methods reappear at this critical treatment phase. While internal motivation on the part of the patient is important, externally motivating factors are often necessary to overcome the denial and ambivalence that are so common when the patient's physical discomfort has been relieved. A number of very effective coercive factors are useful in externally motivating the patient into initial treatment.

Legal. Alcohol-related charges such as driving while intoxicated, public drunkeness, disturbing the peace, etc., represent manifest evidence of the patient's behavioral problems with alcohol. Punishment in the form of confinement, loss of license (driving, professional, or other vocational licensure, etc.), or fines frequently coerce a begrudging individual into treatment who later may move successfully into the long-term rehabilitation process. The physician may find the judicial system extremely cooperative in this regard and should not hesitate to contact local police or courts, local and state medical societies, bar associations, or state licensure authorities within the guidelines for confidentiality.

Job jeopardy. In those instances in which the patient is referred from a business or industry that has a policy of rehabilitation rather than termination, impaired job performance secondary to alcohol abuse and the threat to job security can be strong determinants in the patient's commitment to the initial phase of treatment. A close liason with the employer without violating patient confidentiality can be established by the physician and the treatment team and is fundamental to the effectiveness of this approach. In the Armed Services, the official lines of command have developed coercive techniques for dealing with inadequately motivated alcoholics.

Family jeopardy. Alcoholism is an illness affecting all members of the family and leading to disruption and deterioration of relationships within both the nuclear and extended families. Support of the family members in terms of dealing with personal feelings of guilt, anger, and resentment and developing a willingness to set tolerance limits on the patient's alcohol-affected behavior can precipitate a "family crisis" that frequently motivates the patient toward the initial phase of treatment. Such a family crisis may consist of an imminent loss of spouse or other loved one. That person must be advised to avoid such threats with true intent, supported in his final decision, and made aware of alternate options. These options consist not only of divorce versus continued involvement in the day-to-day drama of the disease but also of withdrawal from that participation by development of a separate and meaningful life (e.g., a career).

Al-Anon may often support such intentions (see Chapter 11) and may offer pragmatic methods for avoiding "enabling" (by enabling is meant making social and job excuses, obtaining help for family or job chores left undone by patients, etc.).

Health impairment. The myriad of medical disorders associated with alcohol abuse can be emphasized by the physician's reminding the patient that further drinking behavior will result in physical destruction and ultimately death. While it is well known that patients cannot be "frightened" from drinking strictly on the basis of the tissue toxicity of alcohol, the possibility and reality of alcohol-induced physical illness does have a motivating quality, particularly in regard to encouraging the patient to enter the initial phase of treatment. Sexual function is interfered with later in the disease; this may be introduced as a factor in motivation even though the physician cannot promise return of function in many cases.

In summary, then, the following are implicit in the physician's "externally" motivating patients into treatment: (1) recognition of the patient's ambivalence toward further treatment when they are physically improved; (2) recognition that early involvement of the "significant others" (e.g., spouse, children, employer, friends, etc.) in the external motivation process is extremely important; (3) recognition that all patients have their own "bottom"—a psychosocial plateau that can often be externally precipitated; and (4) recognition that the proper use of rational authority (coercion, external motivation) by the physician is not only a valid approach but frequently is necessary to initiate early treatment and ensure long-term commitment to the aftercare philosophy.

DIAGNOSTIC CONSIDERATIONS

The current confusion surrounding specific diagnostic criteria for alcoholism as a disease entity allows the physician to focus primarily on the pattern of alcohol use and to ignore psychopathology that is frequently associated (either etiologically or consequentially) with alcohol abuse. There is preliminary evidence that bona fide psychiatric disorders, such as the primary affective diseases (manic–depressive illness) and schizophrenia, occur not infrequently in an "alcoholic" population. The associated psychopathology can range from mild personality disorders to severe psychosis. A distorted psychological picture is usually evident when psychometrics are measured during the period of detoxication, but subsequent to this a psychodiagnostic approach is helpful in assisting the physician in the proper choice of medication and also the type of psychotherapeutic milieu that would be most beneficial. In addition to a mental status examination, the following tests are useful in determining the psychological status of the patient, in detecting major personality problem areas, and in defining any "underlying" major psychiatric disorder:

Minnesota Multiphasic Personality Inventory (MMPI). A comprehensive and general survey of psychopathology, this test measures the patient on ten distinct clinical syndromes and rates the extent of psychopathology existing in each syndrome. Proper interpretation by a qualified psychologist or psychiatrist is essential in order to prevent both misdiagnosis and misinterpretation.

Bender Visual Motor Gestalt Test. A brief examination to assess perceptual–motor functions for deficits associated with cerebral damage or dysfunction; this test is sensitive to organic impairments associated with alcohol abuse, which are not necessarily evident in a mental status examination.

Projective Human Figure Drawings.   This series of projective drawings, interpreted by a psychologist, serves as a validity check on previously administered psychometric instruments (e.g., MMPI). This examination gives clues to the clinician for planning an appropriate psychotherapeutic regimen.

It is important to bear in mind that these psychological instruments, although easily administered, are of a preliminary or screening nature. The seriousness of psychological problems as detected by psychometrics increases the longer an individual abstains from alcohol. If serious psychopathology persists not only clinically but also as measured with psychological instruments, a psychiatric referral is usually in order. Other psychological tests such as the Wechsler Adult Intelligence Scale and such projective tests as the Rorschach may also be useful in determining the pressure of organic or functional psychopathology.

The entire spectrum of personality patterns, psychiatric syndromes, and illness has been observed in the "alcoholic" population. An understanding of the psychodynamics of each patient is helpful in formulating a meaningful treatment plan and deciding on the proper referral route.

EARLY TREATMENT CONSIDERATIONS

Psychotherapy

Psychotherapy is an omnibus term and essentially involves working with patients to help them handle internal and external realities more effectively. The three essential components of psychotherapy are as follows:

Emotional support.   The most important aspect of any therapy is the patient's relationship with the therapist. It is important for patients to feel understood and that with the therapist's help they can begin to manage their lives again. Understanding the patients involves gaining knowledge of the family history, of the development of attitudes and reactions in childhood and adolescence, of the problems encountered in day-to-day living, and of the situational factors and stress that may precipitate alcohol ingestion. It is important to realize that these patients' problems and discomforts are subjectively perceived and felt, regardless of how the therapist interprets the situation. Support should be offered in a nonmoralistic, nonjudgmental way.

Practical support. Intellectual insight into problems and possible solutions is not tantamount to recovery. Patients must not only learn effective problem-solving techniques but must also be encouraged to put them into action. The consequence of behavioral change may be more painful than remaining in a "familiar hell." Practical support involves defining alternative coping mechanisms from a behavioral point of view (such as abstinence from alcohol) and insisting that patients be responsible for the choice of these alternatives.

Emotional reeducation. Quite often, anxious–depressed alcohol-dependent patients have developed defenses that protect them from admitting the extent of their problems with alcohol. It is important to be aware of and to deal with any internal or external factors in a patient's life that maintain the status quo and resist change.

Patients should begin to understand, from a mutual exploration of their responses to immediate problems, something of the personal psychodynamics and maladoptive reactions involved. The physician should try to elicit the subjective meaning patients have given to the stressful events. For example:

—Who or what is producing angry feelings?
—What does loss or threat mean to the patient and his life?
—What is the cause of the patient's ambivalent feelings?
—What role have the patient's reactions played in the excessive drinking pattern and how will this affect recovery?
—What are some different ways of coping with these kinds of stress?

On the basis of patient understanding of reactions, the therapist should help the patient learn new, more effective ways of handling himself and life situations. This may necessitate a change in friends, more rarely job, and occasionally even marriage.

Although an "alcoholic personality" does not exist as a distinct entity, there are common psychological patterns that are encountered in the initial phase of psychotherapy.

DEPENDENCY

Frequently patients with alcohol abuse problems will present with pathologic dependency. This will be expressed in one of the following ways:

The passive–dependent patient who associates being assertive with rejection and commonly employs alcohol as a vehicle for coping with unconscious resentment and anger. An effective therapeutic technique involves assertiveness training.

Inappropriately aggressive patients have "turned around" a need for dependency through the association of intimacy and interpersonal warmth with rejection. It is necessary for such persons to reject you before you have the opportunity to reject them. Their aggressiveness is a defense of their feelings of low esteem and inadequacy. Alcohol is an effective tool for maintaining this form of behavior.

Admixtures of both of these types are common. Understanding patients dependency needs allows the physician to plan therapeutic strategies emphasizing individual reponsibility while recognozing underlying disturbances in the areas of intimacy, assertiveness, and fears of rejection. Recognition that alcohol represents "a people substitute" points to the physician's role in therapeutic intervention, namely, that of establishing—either for the first time or once again—a meaningful interpersonal relationship without patient recourse to isolation or withdrawal through drugs.

OMNIPOTENCE

The alcohol-dependent patient often responds to a pathologic feeling of inadequacy and powerlessness through the psychopharmacologic effect of alcohol. This drug-induced state of omnipotence is short lived and eventually augments further feelings of powerlessness, which perpetuates further excessive alcohol consumption. The spiraling downward effect does not obviate the patient's continued drinking. The physician can play a role in emphasizing the concepts of (1) the patient's participating in his own victimization, (2) short-term pleasures for long-term suffering, and (3) pursuing alternative courses of behavior to overcome feelings of being powerless.

Psychotherapy with the alcoholic requires flexibility. There are not typical alcoholics; thus there is no typical therapy. While group and individual psychotherapy can be directed by the physician, other professionally trained persons, such as psychologists, social workers, nurses, clergymen, and alcoholism counselors, can be utilized effectively on a referral basis. Alcoholics Anonymous (A.A.) can often provide invaluable assistance to the physician. It is highly recommended that the physician learn from and cooperate with the local A.A. organization in the management of the alcohol patient.

Chemotherapy

PSYCHOACTIVE DRUGS

In selected cases, the administration of a psychotropic drug is an effective adjunct. Such drugs should not usually include the highly addicting soporifics such as barbituates, chloral hydrate, paraldehyde, glutethimide, ethchlorvynol, benzodiazepines, meprobamate, methaqualone, and methyprylon. The phenothiazines, tricyclics, MAO inhibitors, hydroxyzine, butyrophenones, thioxanthines, and lithium can be used when there is an appropriate psychiatric diagnosis present. The manner in which such drugs are explained and offered to patients will in large part determine their attitudes and compliance. Patients need to understand that (1) no such drug can replace alcohol in regard to rapidity of action and initial euphoria, (2) the drug being prescribed by the physician is far less toxic than alcohol, (3) the drug being used is not a replacement for alcohol but rather its function is to ameliorate or remove the primary symptoms of anxiety and depression, or symptoms of psychosis, and (4) drug therapy alone is insufficient to produce effective recovery.

When depressive symptomatology is sufficiently serious to mandate chemotherapy, proper selection of a tricyclic antidepressant (when there are no contraindications) can be helpful in the initial phase of treatment. Imipramine appears to be more effective in retarded depressions and amitriptyline or doxepin in agitated depressions. The diagnosis of "endogenous" versus "reactive" depression in this initial phase is less helpful in making chemotherapeutic decisions than is the severity of the signs and symptoms. Patients who present with marked symptoms of anxiety and agitation can frequently be controlled with a nondependency-producing type of antihistamine drug such as hydroxyzine. Extreme caution should be exercised in the use of sedative–hypnotics (benzadizepines and barbituates), since these compounds have a high potential for abuse by persons previously addicted to alcohol. Most physicians feel their use should be limited to the detoxification period only.

ANTIDISATROPICS (AVERSIVE THERAPY)

Abstinence from alcohol is essential in the management of the patient in this initial phase. Selection of the patient for Antabuse (disulfiram) therapy should include the following criteria:

1. Does the patient thoroughly understand the rationale of Antabuse therapy?
2. Are there any contraindications to Antabuse (e.g., hypersensitivity, concomitant psychosis, severe organic brain syndrome, strong suicidal potential)?
3. What is the apparent level of the patient's motivation?
4. Does the patient understand that abstinence is a means to an end (recovery) and that its use is only adjunctive in the overall treatment process?

By emphasizing the use of Antabuse as an "insurance policy" rather than a "crutch" and stressing that a period of abstinence will allow the patient to make essential behavioral and attitudinal changes without the use of alcohol, the physician adopts a positive approach to Antabuse therapy (see Appendix D).

Referral

The multiplicity and complexity of the psychosocial and physiologic problems and needs of the detoxified patient make it nearly impossible for the physician to assume total responsibility for care. By designing an individualized treatment plan that includes other resources, the physician can appropriately direct and guide the patient into a treatment *system*.

Great care must be exercised in referring patients who have suffered repeated rejection to any other therapeutic resource. They must be reassured of your continued support, interest, and availability. Referral must not be used by the physician to justify rejection of a difficult, frequently noncompliant patient.

Selection of referral sources depends on availability and quality of other therapeutic environments and on the needs of the patient.

RESIDENTIAL AFTERCARE—QUARTERWAY HOUSE, HALFWAY HOUSE

Patients who are homeless, whose home situations are volatile and disruptive, or who suffer from significant social instability often require the type of organized therapeutic environment offered by residential aftercare. This is frequently preferable to a long-term hospital inpatient stay, since most residential programs encourage early resocialization.

COMMUNITY MENTAL HEALTH CENTERS

Most comprehensive community mental health centers offer alcoholism treatment services that include family therapy and individual and group therapy on both scheduled and nonscheduled bases. These services are designed for patients who have had previous treatment experiences and enough family and social stability not to require more protective systems.

VOCATIONAL REHABILITATION

Job instability and unemployment are very real and pressing problems to alcoholics. Vocational rehabilitation programs, especially those with specialized services for alcoholics, can offer evaluation of individual needs, personal adjustment, prevocational and vocational training, coordination and integration of rehabilitation services, job placement and case management, and followup. Frequently it is a matter of vocational habilitation rather than rehabilitation.

The issue is a complicated one. First, there is the specific problem of the inner city alcoholic who lacks totally job skills and job potentialities (this issue is considered in Chapter 10). Second, career development, in those less deprived, represents one of the major areas in which a substantive change in self-esteem can be effected. The significance of a basic change in self-image, crucial to the development of long-term sobriety, is illustrated in Chapter 1. Physicians should be familiar with the referral guidelines of vocational rehabilitation centers in their areas and work closely with the counselors involved.

ALCOHOLICS ANONYMOUS (A.A.)

The fellowship and empathetic environment of Alcoholics Anonymous can be of assistance to some patients during the intiial phase of treatment.

At no time is the patient more open and needful of the human support that can stem from a person who has recovered from circumstances similar to those currently affecting the patient. To accomplish this:

1. Choose a specific individual whom you know from your own experience will offer opportunities for patient identification in sex, age, marital status, ethnic background, socioeconomic and occupational position, personality, and alcoholic history. Such an individual would in all likelihood lead the patient to the appropriate A.A. groups. The physician out of contact with A.A. is unable to make this rational choice for a patient.
2. Discuss in depth the patient's A.A. experience, both current and past, in order to resolve those difficulties that the patient may raise to resist this therapeutic program. A specific example lies in the nonreligious patient's difficulty with the spiritual aspects of the A.A. program.
3. The physician can not only acquire necessary clinical training by attending A.A. meetings, but can influence the local A.A. membership in various medical matters. The physician may personally make the use of antipsychotic, antidepressant, and aversive therapy credible by developing a dialogue with A.A. group members.

Forming a liaison with and cooperating with A.A. can provide, in some cases, assistance to the physician in the initial and long-term management of the patient.

PROGNOSTIC CONSIDERATIONS

Once a patient is detoxified and enters the initial phase of treatment, there are certain dangers for which the physician should prepare the patient. By discovering and identifying these dangers early in treatment, the patient is more willing to deal with them on a realistic basis in the therapeutic setting. Some of the more common problems facing the patient are as follows:

The "honeymoon period." If patients achieve effective abstinence from alcohol early in treatment, they will most likely receive positive reinforcement from family, friends, employer, etc. for the behavioral change. This will continue for a few weeks, possibly 2–3 months. Then, gradually the significant others in a patient's life will begin to take this behavioral change for granted—and indeed expect it rather than hope for it. As positive reinforcement decreases, patients may interpret this as lack of support or even overt rejection. A return to the use of alcohol occurs frequently at this time. If the patients can anticipate this and if therapy can be directed toward a patient's developing an internal rather than external system of reinforcement, the sense of vulnerability can be markedly attenuated.

The problem of sexual dysfunction. The abstinent alcoholic—particularly the male—should be prepared for the possibility of some sexual dysfunction early in treatment. If this is not discussed, the patient frequently feels as if he were impotent and she were frigid, and often is extremely reluctant to broach the subject in therapy situations. The problem is usually not one of impotence or frigidity but rather a decrease in libidinal drive and depression consequent to the removal of alcohol, which had previously caused a sexually disinhibiting effect and thus an augmented libido. Reassuring the patient and talking with the patient and mate cojointly or separately concerning seeking alternative methods for libidinal stimulation will decrease anxiety and prevent the patient from feeling emasculated or frigid.

The problem of trust versus mistrust. With a dramatic change in behavior that can occur early in treatment, the patient often seeks not only positive reinforcement from significant others but also complete trust from others that the new behavior will continue indefinitely. It is important to point out to the patient that the spouse and/or employer and/or friends may view this change with some initial skepticism, and some element of mistrust should be expected. Emphasizing the destructive effect that the drinking behavior has had in the past on interpersonal relationships encourages the patient to be more realistic in what can be expected immediately from these relationships.

The problem of dysphoria associated with an increased awareness.   Many patients imagine that with abstinence from alcohol, symptoms of anxiety and depression, which are normally resultant from situational stress, will no longer occur. In fact, anxiety–depressive symptomatology may be perceived more acutely by the patient without the chemical camouflage of alcohol. Prediction of this by the physician will ameliorate the pain and frustration that characterize the initial phase of treatment.

As a physician assessing the efficacy of initial treatment, it is important to keep in mind that abstinence is a means to an end; that recidivism ("falling off the wagon") does not necessarily mean treatment failure, and that specific signs of improvement should be established, such as the following:

—Does the patient have a realistic understanding of alcohol dependency in regard to her or his personal situation?
—Is the patient actively participating in a treatment program?
—Is there improvement in family and social relationships?
—Is there improvement in job performance?
—Is the patient exhibiting longer periods of effective sobriety and, if in the case of a relapse, are the drinking episodes of shorter duration and less destructive?

Alcoholism in its many guises and with its many complications is not a homogeneous disease entity but rather a disease spectrum. The medical practitioner can assume critical diagnostic and therapeutic roles in the initial phase of treatment after emergency care and medical management have been afforded. Working with other disciplines in the formulation and implementation of an early treatment plan is an essential component of an overall rehabilitation effort and will contribute significantly to the control and recovery of the patient.

REFERENCES

Barten HH (ed): *Brief Therapies*. New York, Behavioral Publications, 1971

Criteria Committee, National Council on Alcoholism: Criteria for the diagnosis of alcoholism. *Am J Psychiatry* 129(2):127–134, 1972

Department of HEW: Confidentiality of alcohol and drug abuse patient records. Fed Register 40(127), 1975

Fink RD, Knott DH, Beard JD: Sedative–hypnotic dependence. *Am Fam Physician* 10(3):116–122, 1974

Flemenbaum A: Affective disorders and chemical dependence: Lithium for alcohol and drug addiction. *Dis Nerv Syst* 35:281–285, 1974

Goldfarb C, Hartman B: A total community approach to the treatment of alcoholism. *Dis Nerv Syst* 36:409–414, 1975

Knott DH, Thomson MJ, Beard JD: The forgotten addict. *Am Fam Physician* 3(6):92–95, 1971

Knott DH, Beard JD, Fischer AA: Alcoholism—The physician's role in diagnosis and treatment, in Conn HF, Rakel RE, Johnson TW, (eds): *Family Practice,* Philadelphia, W.B. Saunders, 1972, 265–276

Knott DH, Frink RD, Beard JD: Unmasking alcohol abuse. *Am Fam Physician* 10(4): 123–128, 1974

McClelland DC, Davis WN, Kalin R, et al: *The Drinking Man*. New York, Free Press, 1972

B.W.: The fellowship of Alcoholics Anonymous, in Catanzaro, RJ (ed): *Alcoholism—The Total Treatment Approach,* Charles C. Thomas, Springfield, Ill., 1968, 116–127

Gerald D. Shulman
Robert D. O'Connor

6
The Rehabilitation of the Alcoholic

The practicing physician is likely to encounter the alcoholic patient in one of three settings—as a patient in an office practice, as a patient discovered on rounds in a community hospital, or as a patient seen in the emergency room of a general hospital. Since the situations that bring the alcoholic patient to the attention of the physician do differ, the circumstances of the initial contact may influence the manner in which care is offered. For example, if the alcoholic is currently a patient of the physician in an office practice, there should already be established a level of trust not present when a patient meets a physician for the first time as a result of an emergency room visit. This may make a significant difference in such things as the patient's level of honesty, willingness to "hear" what the physician is saying, and willingness to act on the physician's recommendations.

After delivering whatever acute medical care might have been required, whether in the office or hospital, the physician frequently admonishes the patient, saying, "Don't drink when you go home," or "Cut down on your drinking." The patient able to follow that simple advice in all probability would not have been seen by the physician in the first place. If only the symptoms and acute episodes of a chronic illness are treated, with no attempt to deal with the basic illness itself, then the physician has

103

ALCOHOLISM
ISBN 0-8089-1227-5

Copyright © 1980 by Grune & Stratton
All rights of reproduction in any form reserved.

not fulfilled his responsibilities and can be assured that the patient will require treatment again.

The treatment of the underlying alcoholism should be considered a specialty, requiring special skills and knowledge. For the physician who is unsure of the diagnostic criteria, or the most appropriate treatment planning, a consultation is indicated. The consultant may be another physician, most frequently an internist or psychiatrist. The consultant may also be a clinical psychologist, a nurse, a social worker, or an alcoholism counselor whose credentials are not academic but result from the experience of his own recovery from alcoholism or work in alcoholism treatment. For such consultation, nonmedical people can be used very effectively.*

Such a consultant may be found on the staff of a community hospital, or in an organized alcoholism treatment center in the surrounding community, or through a local voluntary alcoholism agency such as the various local affiliates of the National Council on Alcoholism. Not to be overlooked is the recovered alcoholic member of Alcoholics Anonymous (A.A.), who may be a patient in the physician's office practice. This person may provide valuable assistance to the physician and the newly identified alcoholic in helping carry out a treatment plan. The consultation should confirm or rule out the preliminary diagnosis of alcoholism. Unless the physician has considerable experience in dealing with alcoholism, the consultant should be used to assist in the development of a treatment plan.

PRIMARY CARE (DETOXIFICATION)

Good primary care consists of detoxification that allows the patient to safely and comfortably go through the withdrawal process. The use of psychoactive drugs associated with detoxification should be discontinued, and the patient should no longer be using antianxiety drugs or minor tranquilizers. There should be a complete medical evaluation, with special attention paid to potential cardiopulmonary, gastrointestinal, and hepatic problems. Appropriate medical treatment should be instituted, and there should

---

*The majority of direct rehabilitation service for alcoholics in this country is provided by nondegreed people.

be a plan for the future management of any unresolved medical problems. During this time, a complete psychosocial evaluation should have been done. This psychosocial evaluation should include a history of early dynamics, educational, vocational, and social and marital adjustment. There should be an in-depth history of alcohol and drug use. If indicated on the basis of preliminary assessment, psychiatric evaluation by someone skilled in dealing with alcoholism should be made. The period during primary care should be further utilized to help the patient begin to identify as having a problem with chemicals and to motivate him for treatment beyond primary care. Finally, the results of all of this activity should be put together in the form of a written treatment plan, always with the involvement of the patient. (See Table 6-1.)

Certain facilities offer this type of care as part of a more comprehensive treatment program in which primary care* is one component and rehabilitation is another. The primary care component is seen as a part of an overall treatment program if followed by referral into the facility's own inpatient or outpatient components. On the other hand, there are specialized treatment centers that offer only primary care and referral. These facilities tend to use a broad spectrum of resources following initial treatment.

Table 6-1
Ancillary Uses of the Detoxification Period

Prove diagnosis to patient (e.g., both patient and physician witness withdrawal phenomena)

Establish a relationship between physician and patient (physician's concern with and efforts to relieve the patient's suffering fosters attachment)

Obtain a detailed history

Develop a short-term and possibly a definitive treatment plan

Introduce people with whom the patient can identify (e.g., Alcoholics Anonymous)

Utilize all of the above to augment motivation for treatment and recovery

---

*The term primary care as used here refers to detoxification and treatment of complications or acute concurrent illness.

Although it is possible for the physician in office practice to accomplish some of the goals for primary care for the alcoholic, it is usually not feasible. For example, a primary care facility offers the alcoholic an opportunity to identify with other alcoholics. Optimally, primary care should be viewed as a multimodality process, leading to referral for rehabilitation, which will take place in a specialized environment organized specifically to deal with the problems of alcoholism. One very valid reason for referring to a primary care facility even when there are no other major medical problems is the patient's inability to stop drinking on his own.

It cannot be stressed too strongly that at the completion of primary care the patient still suffers from a chronic, progressive, debilitating disease that requires further treatment if the disease is to be arrested successfully and the patient stabilized. After those preliminary and basic steps have taken place, the next critical decision is the match between patient and the most appropriate type of treatment available.

The matching process is very difficult for two reasons—the clinical spectrum of alcoholism varies greatly, and there is a great diversity of treatment approaches. Some are very appropriate for certain groups of patients, but none are appropriate for all.

First, a word about the diversity of the clinical pictures of alcoholism. It is quite apparent that the 55-year-old homeless male desocialized alcoholic on skid row whose body is 10–15 years older than his chronologic age, presents a very different clinical picture from the 40-year-old upper-middle-class housewife who has never drunk in a bar in her life, who has had extensive and unsuccessful psychotherapy for a variety of somewhat vague adjustment problems, and whose use of Valium and Seconal could be characterized as regular and heavy. Yet another clinical picture is presented by the 18-year-old patient who comes to the attention of the physician for treatment of hepatitis and where the history indicates the patient's involvement in a lifestyle of drug abuse and addiction; although most of the drugs used are acquired illicitly, alcohol is the drug of choice.

The diversity of treatment approaches reflects both the diversity in patient populations and differences in emphasis on the part of therapists. The remainder of this chapter will be an attempt to bring order to this diversity and confusion so that at the conclusion of primary care the physician can better answer the question, "What next?"

REHABILITATION OPTIONS

There are two major rehabilitation approaches for alcoholics—inpatient or outpatient treatment. Within these two broad categories, there are different levels of treatment as well as different settings. All of these have bearing on the patient–treatment match. Table 6-2 illustrates the different treatment approaches and the settings in which they are most commonly found. One or more settings/approaches may be used. When used in combination, the settings/approaches may be used consecutively or concurrently, as appropriate.

A more recent approach to alcoholism treatment not included in Table 6-2 is partial hospitalization (also referred to as day treatment), which attempts to combine the advantages of the intensity of inpatient treatment with lower cost and less disruption to usual lifestyle. Below we shall also discuss treatment for the family of the alcoholic, which includes residential care with or without the alcoholic, care delivered by an outpatient clinic, Al-Anon, and Alateen.

Inpatient Rehabilitation

For the purpose of discussion, a few definitions are in order. Both short- and long-term residential treatments are sometimes referred to as intermediate care, because the intensity of treatment is considerably less than what is normally found in an acute care hospital; however, there is no doubt that care is being provided. Other terms sometimes applied to this sort of care are psychosocial treatment and, simply, rehabilitation.

We define as short term that care ranging in duration from a minimum of 2 weeks to 6–12 weeks, the most common programs being approximately 4 weeks in length. Long-term programs are those that are usually no less than 3 months in duration and may extend up to 1–2 years. Some programs are time limited, with a fixed time period that can be extended, whereas others are open ended. Short-term programs usually provide more structure and a more intensive level of programming and therapy and are more likely to view themselves as limited to initiating an ongoing recovery process. Long-term programs may or may not be structured but try to achieve more of the treatment goals within the

Table 6-2
Treatment Approaches and Options

Treatment Settings	Inpatient			Outpatient				
	Short-Term Intermediate	Long-Term Intermediate	Halfway House	Outpatient Alcoholism Clinic	Alcoholics Anonymous**	A.A. clubhouse**	Al-Anon**	Alateen**
Acute care hospital	×			×	×	×	×	×
Psychiatric hospital	×	×						
Freestanding*	×	×	×	×	×	×	×	×
Self-help					×	×	×	×

Note: each facility may, but need not, possess each of the indicated (×) modalities.
*Defined as existing separately from a larger treatment facility.
**Although meetings may take place in hospital settings, they are otherwise unsupported by these environments.

duration of the treatment program itself rather than allowing these to be accomplished over a longer period of time after discharge. Longer programs tend to have a heavier emphasis on resocialization.*

Some treatment centers make a distinction in the expected duration of treatment between those patients whose primary addiction is to alcohol and those who may have a heavy involvement with other drugs in addition to the alcohol. This is particularly true if the other drugs are illicitly obtained. Current thinking is that it may take longer to effectively deal with other drug addiction problems, particularly if the drugs are acquired illicitly. In terms of duration of inpatient rehabilitation, use of alcohol alone requires at least 1 month, solid sedative addiction prolongs this period to a minimum of 2 months, and parenteral opiate use to a multiple of this. On the whole, long-term programs tend to be separated from the traditional health care system, with less medical, psychiatric, and social service expertise. They also receive poorer third-party reimbursement than the short-term programs.

The alcoholism rehabilitation center, short or long term, is a specialized unit. Such treatment is provided through different treatment settings (see Table 6-2) and accordingly may vary in the style in which treatment is delivered. For example, an alcoholism unit in a psychiatric hospital tends to be more psychiatrically oriented, sometimes because of philosophic considerations but other times because of administrative and monetary considerations (e.g., financial support of psychiatric staff who may not be involved with the alcoholism unit). The same is true in the acute care hospital setting. Alcoholism rehabilitation units found in psychiatric or acute care hospitals tend to be more expensive than freestanding facilities, but by the same token, they are usually able to generate better third-party reimbursement. One cannot assume from these facts, however, that units found within either the psychiatric or acute care hospital setting offer either better or worse care than the freestanding unit.

Often the setting can and does determine the nature of the treatment and therefore the appropriateness of the referral.

*Resocialization is used to signify the process by which maladjusted persons attain those attitudes and skills that will facilitate their again becoming accepted members of the community. This is a particularly important aspect of treatment for addicts whose addiction has removed them from the general community (public inebriates and drug addicts who are totally integrated into a drug addiction subculture).

There are three major treatment settings for intermediate care (frequently the differences among individual treatment programs in any one group of settings may be greater than the variance between treatment programs in different settings):

1. The psychiatric hospital, without a specialized alcoholism unit
2. The alcoholism rehabilitation unit located in either a psychiatric or acute care hospital
3. The freestanding alcoholism rehabilitation unit, which is not part of another facility

The psychiatric hospital without an alcoholism unit has traditionally treated alcoholism not as an addiction but as symptomatic of an underlying personality disorder. The focus is on cause and underlying problems. When this treatment is performed with full cognizance of the need to discontinue the addicting substance as a *prerequisite* to psychotherapy or any other intervention, one can appreciate that differing disciplines arrive at surprisingly similar therapeutic approaches. If the drinking continues unabated, there is little chance for successful resolution of the alcoholism.

SHORT-TERM RESIDENTIAL REHABILITATION

The freestanding alcoholism rehabilitation program is the one that was developed about 20–25 years ago to fill a void for specialized alcoholism treatment. These programs range from highly sophisticated treatment facilities with considerable medical, psychiatric, and social services to those with very little formal program. Depending on the facility, Alcoholics Anonymous can play a minor or significant role in the treatment program. In the latter case, it is often interwoven into the psychosocial and therapeutic aspects of the program. These facilities may vary from "mom and pop" outfits run by "charismatic" and therapeutically effective individuals who have themselves recovered from alcoholism through A.A. to complex and sophisticated residences offering professional individual and group psychotherapy, vocational rehabilitation, etc. Turnover of personnel in the former may result in a disastrous change in therapeutic effectiveness, whereas the latter facilities tend toward greater stability and reliability.

Although the program content in these inpatient treatment centers varies from facility to facility, there are components common to most. In many programs there will be an education component, which focuses on the program and steps of Alcoholics Anonymous, the problem of alcoholism, and cross-addiction, and which addresses living problems, etc. Most facilities use some form of group therapy, usually as their major treatment modality. The nature of this therapy varies from discussion groups in which patients are simply seated in a circle to psychodynamically oriented groups. Individual counseling is an essential part of these programs. There may also be work therapy, occupational therapy, or recreational therapy. This type of treatment setting will complete an in-depth psychosocial evaluation (in more depth than occurs in the primary care facility discussed earlier); from this overall evaluation the staff will develop a comprehensive medical and psychosocial treatment plan. Those treatment programs with heavy emphasis on A.A. may ask the patient to do a 4th Step (a written personal inventory of "character defects") and a 5th Step (sharing with another person the information that resulted from that inventory) after the patient has completed the first three steps (since they should be accomplished in order). They may provide A.A. meetings in-house or take patients to meetings away from the facility. Family counseling will be available, although the range of services provided for the family is very broad and will be discussed later in this chapter.

Short-term intermediate care programs of approximately 4 weeks duration are effective for many alcoholic patients. Such programs not only keep patients from alcohol for 28 days but also give them sufficient time away from the potentially distracting home and job problems without creating a catastrophic disruption in lifestyle. Short-term inpatient rehabilitation programs should have relatively modest goals, and such treatment should be seen as the beginning of an ongoing recovery process rather than one that is a completed process. Reasonable goals to expect from such treatment include a beginning, meaningful identification with the problem of alcoholism, some realistic motivation for recovery, some insight into the addictive process and its effects, and, most importantly, a concrete plan for continuing recovery (an after care plan). This plan should be developed jointly by the treatment staff and the patient and should be in the form of a written contract that details what the patient, possibly the patient's family, and the treatment center will do after discharge. There should be a followup system by the treatment center. The goal of the aftercare and followup part of the program is to consolidate the gains made during treatment. The treatment center staff must have a system that allows them to "reach out" to the patient who has difficulties with sobriety and/or living problems. This may be accomplished by representatives trained at the rehabilitation facility who are assigned by geographic coincidence to follow specific patients, private therapists (physicians or counselors) acquainted with the rehabilitation plan, or, when possible, local outpatient care supplied by the facility itself.

LONG-TERM RESIDENTIAL REHABILITATION

Long-term treatment, previously described as lasting from 3 months to 2 years, shares a number of program components with short-term programs. One feature that distinguishes it from short-term programs is a concentration on the resocialization of the patient. In short-term treatment there is usually an attempt to minimize disruption of lifestyle, whereas in long-term treatment such disruption is viewed as advantageous, if not necessary, to effect recovery.

Generally, the level of intensity of treatment is less than in the short-term programs, although there are exceptions. Some programs are modeled after the drug addiction therapeutic communities, which offer not only long-term treatment but also enforced separation from the outside world and the chemicals that accompany it. This separation is achieved by telephone blackouts (no phone calls—incoming or outgoing—permitted), confinement to facility grounds, and a restrictive visiting policy. At times, visitors are totally prohibited. This type of program is usually characterized by a rigid and autocratic environment. Therapy is strongly confrontive and at times assaultive. Progress is measured by the degree of responsibility the patient exhibits. An example of such a program would be Synanon (as originally conceived).

Other long-term programs are essentially similar to the short-term programs but extend treatment over a longer time period. They lack the confrontive, autocratic style of the previous type and are considerably less separated from the outside world.

HALFWAY HOUSES

A halfway house is basically a structured transitional living situation. It is commonly used following short-term rehabilitation care. It may follow primary care when the patient has previously had inpatient treatment and it is felt that a return to short-term rehabilitation would not be as effective as a structured living situation. This type of program can be used for the patient who is homeless or for the patient who has a home but should not return to it. Examples of the latter would be the female patient who has been living with a drinking alcoholic spouse who physically abuses her. Another example would be the unmarried male alcoholic who lives alone in a room above a bar around which his entire social life revolves.

In halfway house programs there are 10–20 alcoholics living together, sharing the responsibilities for maintenance of the house but gainfully employed outside of it. The halfway house then represents their home, which provides a supportive living environment, a low level of treatment, and some A.A. meetings which are held within the house. The duration of halfway house care is usually 3–6 months, although there are programs that are open-ended, particularly for those alcoholics who suffer from chronic brain syndrome. For these people, the program may become a permanent home. Levels of program intensity in halfway houses vary, so that at one end of the spectrum there is a group living situation, while at the other end the program functions almost as an inpatient rehabilitation center.

Outpatient Rehabilitation

OUTPATIENT ALCOHOLISM CLINIC

Organized outpatient treatment is usually offered in the form of an outpatient alcoholism clinic and may directly follow primary care when judged sufficiently intensive to meet the patient's needs. It may also be used following residential rehabilitation when continued structured treatment is indicated. It may also be provided to a patient who is currently a resident of a halfway house. There are some specialists in alcoholism who provide this service in their office practice, but the key here is to distinguish between outpatient treatment for the alcoholism problem and more traditional psychotherapy for the treatment of other problems. The latter usually is not effective unless begun 6–12 months after the cessation of drinking, and often the patient has had some form of alcoholism treatment during that period of time. In cases where traditional psychotherapy is required, some kind of alcoholism treatment, even if only supportive, should be taking place simultaneously.

Some outpatient alcoholism clinics are occasionally part of a larger mental health clinic or community mental health center, while others are alcoholism specific. These last may be located in general or psychiatric hospitals, may be part of a residential alcoholism treatment center, or may be freestanding. They specialize in providing treatment to both the alcoholic and the family members. They can be used by patients who need more structure than would be provided by A.A. alone, even after residential care, or those who are unable to "get away" for residential care. The latter problem should be checked out carefully because the real issue may well be one not of time but of resistance to treatment.

ALCOHOLICS ANONYMOUS

The oldest and most successful form of outpatient treatment for alcoholics is the program of Alcoholics Anonymous. Although informal, A.A. provides a worldwide recovery network for alcoholics. It is important to recognize that a significant number of alcoholics come to A.A., receive no other treatment, and recover; however, it appears that the combination of inpatient residential treatment in conjunction with A.A. increases the probability of recovery. In an employee alcoholism program, it was found that those patients who first went into short-term inpatient rehabilitation and then to A.A. maintained abstinence at twice the rate as those patients who went directly into A.A. A.A. is effective and should be part of any treatment program, inpatient or outpatient. We would strongly urge any treatment person who will be working with alcoholics to attend some open A.A. meetings to learn more about the program of Alcoholics Anonymous.

One variation of the A.A. program is the A.A. clubhouse, a place that is open for long periods of time during the day and/or evening and that represents a place where the alcoholic can go, spend time, and chat with other recovering alcoholics. This setting will often provide a variety of benefits such as the replacement of the drinking environment, a new social group for the patient, and a supportive environment for a significant segment of the day.

It has been our experience that a number of professionals are ambivalent about utilization and referral to A.A., particularly if their patient is resistant to A.A. What is not understood is that the patient's resistance to A.A. almost always represents resistance to sobriety because it poses a major threat to the alcoholic. The patient, and often the professional, may not recognize this, and therefore both may offer other reasons for not using A.A. The practice of good medicine, however, dictates that the physician employ those approaches that have the greatest probability of creating positive change in the patient, even if the patient "doesn't like it." The attitudes of the referring physician about A.A. will have a major effect on whether or not the patient will accept the referral.

AFTERCARE

Although aftercare is not a separate treatment option, it is included here because it is offered in an outpatient format. Each treatment program, inpatient and outpatient alike, must have its own aftercare program. Aftercare is provided in a variety of ways, including: (1) aftercare groups conducted at a treatment center, (2) on-going phone and letter contact between the treatment center and the patient, (3) aftercare groups set up in the patient's home area if the patient lives some distance from the treatment center, and (4) "refresher courses' and postdischarge sessions. Most aftercare/followup programs continue from 3 months to 2 years after discharge. They may also include the family of the alcoholic patient. Aftercare, in the final analysis, should be viewed not as another kind of treatment but as a component and therefore a continuation of the initial program. It is important to recognize that this differs from the usual alcoholism treatment offered in an outpatient clinic in that the goals are very limited and deal with the problems of reentry while simultaneously attempting to consolidate gains made during inpatient treatment. Aftercare does not provide ongoing alcoholism treatment or psychotherapy, as is the case in an outpatient alcoholism clinic.

When patients are involved in aftercare groups, they may come back to the facility in which they received the original treatment for a period of 4–12 weeks, although some programs may extend from 1 to 2 years. The longer aftercare programs begin to blur the distinction between aftercare programs as previously defined (the purpose of which is to consolidate gains in treatment) and outpatient alcoholism treatment or psychotherapy. These shorter programs are time limited and do not take the place of either more intensive treatment, when necessary, or Alcoholics Anonymous.

There are times when the alcoholic patient requires specialized intensive care for the treatment of other, emotional or psychological adjustment problems. As stated above, such treatment is most effective if begun 6–12 months after sobriety, and such treatment should not be considered alcoholism treatment per se.

Family Treatment

Appropriately, the family of the alcoholic is receiving growing attention. Almost all treatment programs currently have some kind of family program, which may range from a one-time evaluation and counseling session with the family to inpatient residential treatment for one or more of the family members. Residential treatment of the family member may coincide with the residential treatment of the alcoholic during all or part of the time the alcoholic is in inpatient treatment. Brief family residential treatment usually occurs in the last stages of the alcoholic's treatment and may range in time from 3 days to 1 week. Some inpatient treatment programs are beginning to mimic what outpatient alcoholism clinics have done for a long time, taking the family members of the alcoholic into treatment, even if the alcoholic himself or herself is not in treatment.

A number of treatment centers are now providing an aftercare program for the family as well as for the alcoholic patient. Two excellent outpatient resources for family members and/or "significant others" related to the alcoholic are Al-Anon and Ala-teen (for the teenage children of alcoholics). Both are very similar in philosophy to A.A. and are oriented primarily to helping the family members/"significant others" with their own living problems.

The Choice of Treatment Option

Simply listing and describing treatment options does not answer the question, "Why choose any of them?" At the risk of being repetitive, we reiterate that alcoholism is a chronic illness and that primary treatment or detoxification alone addresses only the physical and medical aspects of the disease process. Something now has to occur with reference to the psychosocial/behavioral aspects of the illness if real recovery is to begin. Said another way, the problem for alcoholics is not stopping drinking. Many have stopped hundreds and thousands of times. The problem is *staying* stopped.

The physician has two responsibilities in this area. The first is to choose the appropriate type of treatment program, and the second is to choose the best treatment facility within that type for the patient. There are a number of parameters that can be used in making a decision about referral to postprimary care. Once again, for the physician who is uncertain about referral, because of a lack of familiarity either with the treatment resources or with the specific needs of this patient, we strongly urge the use of consultation with people knowledgeable about diagnosis and treatment planning for alcoholics.

Patient Variables and Choice of Treatment

At this point, the authors of this chapter would like to identify a bias. If both inpatient and outpatient rehabilitation are available, we would choose inpatient rehabilitation, which at the beginning of treatment appears to be a more effective approach (Table 6-3). The intensity of such treatment results in an initial "push" that may carry the alcoholic over some rough spots early in recovery.

Table 6-3
Advantages of Facilities Early Use of Inpatient Rehabilitation

Guaranteed period of abstinence
More rapid learning about illness and alternate coping
  mechanisms than likely to be achieved as outpatient in A.A.
Impresses patient with gravity of problem
More rapid opportunity to achieve identification and relate to other
  patients with alcoholism
More integrated health care delivery

Given this bias, we would not like to describe some of the patient variables that can be used in selecting the most appropriate resource.

COEXISTING MEDICAL PROBLEMS

Obviously, the patient who has serious medical problems that will require ongoing medical treatment will need to be in a rehabilitative setting where such treatment is easily obtained. It is usually counterproductive to have an alcoholic patient continually interrupt alcoholism treatment in order to get medical treatment at another facility. Treatment settings providing such care include residential rehabilitation centers housed in a acute care hospitals or freestanding treatment centers with associated medical care units.

COEXISTING PSYCHIATRIC PROBLEMS

The majority of alcoholics do not have such psychiatric problems as to require specialized psychiatric attention at that time. For those who do, the alcoholism treatment center may be faced with major management problems or other distractions from treatment. The most common problem is psychosis, which if adequately diagnosed can be managed by the use of an antipsychotic drug, a supportive environment, or both. Care must be exercised to ascertain that the psychiatric diagnosis is valid. Many alcoholics, when evaluated by professionals not experienced in alcoholism, are misdiagnosed because the symptoms of their alcoholism mimic a psychotic process, and they are mistakenly placed on antipsychotic drugs. It may require up to 6 weeks off psychotropic drugs in order to establish a non-drug-related psychiatric diagnosis.

If the patient does require an antipsychotic drug, care should be taken to avoid choosing a rigidly drug-free rehabilitation program. Some rehabilitation programs have recognized the dangers of prescribing psychoactive drugs to alcoholics, who frequently become dual or cross addicted. Unfortunately, some facilities have generalized from the dangers of specific drugs such as sedatives, barbiturates, and antianxiety medications to antipsychotic drugs. They sometimes go so far as to prohibit such things as vitamins, hormones, etc. Obviously, such a program will be inappropriate for the patient requiring antipsychotic drugs. There are treatment facilities that—while recognizing the potential that antipsychotic drugs have in reinforcing the addiction—will evaluate each situation individually, often permitting the use of other than antianxiety drugs when indicated. If on-going psychiatric treatment is required and/or mangement problems are in evidence, the obvious choice would be an alcoholism unit within or attached to a psychiatric hospital.

A word of caution about psychological depression in alcoholics: Depression, particularly reactive depression, is a very common symptom of addiction and does not necessarily indicate a separate affective disorder or indicate use of antidepressant drugs. Although there are some alcoholics with affective disorders, it is very difficult to make that kind of diagnosis within a few months of the cessation of drinking. Frequently, when this diagnosis is made too early it is an error. When possible, it is better to offer the alcoholic emotional support and reassurance than to immediately prescribe antidepressant drugs. The period of depression will frequently end of its own accord after a period of recovery from the alcoholism. On the other hand, if the depression is profound and associated with significant sleep disturbances, high levels of agitation, serious suicidal ideation or threats, history of previous manic episodes, family history of serious affective disturbances, and somatic and other delusions, prompt intervention is obviously required.

The patient who manifests a character disorder along with the alcoholism will require a long-term, highly structured and high confrontative *(although not necessarily psychiatrically oriented)* program. Alcoholics who are particularly immature and/or dependent may also require a long-term program that is highly structured *but not confrontive.* On the other hand, these patients may best respond to a program wherein they are confronted gently at first and to a greater degree as the transference allows. Problems such as chronic brain syndrome may require a very supportive program with a high degree of structure and of substantial duration.

DEGREE OF STRUCTURE REQUIRED

Patients with poor impulse control, those who have suffered at least a moderate degree of organic impairment, those who are younger and require major help in socialization or resocialization, those who are very immature and dependent, and those with a previous history of unsuccessful treatment generally can benfit from a more structured environment. Although this is not always true, usually the more highly structured programs are also of longer term. Obviously, a process such as resocialization will not take place in a 4 week period. On the other hand, there are some very good short-term treatment programs that are highly structured, so that both the variables of time and structure should be considered.

CURRENT LIVING ARRANGEMENTS

The patient who is living with an intact family that can provide emotional support, who has shown a gradual decline into an addiction over a period of many years, who is employed, and who can generally function in a responsible manner can benefit from either a short-term inpatient program or an outpatient program. On the other hand, the alcoholic who lives alone, or who lives with a drinking alcoholic spouse, is best separated from that living situation and should, at least temporarily, be removed from that environment. The probability of an alcoholic maintaining abstinence in early recovery while living with a drinking alcoholic family member is not very good. The family member may have been the alcoholic's drinking partner. Abstinence by the patient will represent a threat to the family member, which may result in an unconscious attempt to sabotage the abstinence of the newly sober person. In this situation the patient may be a candidate not only for inpatient residential treatment but possibly for a halfway house after residential treatment.

The alcoholic who is also a drug addict and who has supported the addiction by dealing in drugs obviously cannot go back to his old "vocation" and expect to stay straight. A return to the "old neighborhood" usually means a return to drugs.

It is important to recognize that merely separating the alcoholic from the drinking environment will not bring about recovery. In A.A., this is known as a "geographical cure." The problem is that alcoholics bring the alcoholism with them wherever they go. Sometimes the presence of the drinking or drug-using environment is either a distraction or so destructive a force that it impedes the delivery of effective treatment, particularly on an outpatient basis.

FAMILY RELATIONSHIPS

The level of psychological health and supportiveness of the "significant others" is very important. Family members, because of their own psychodynamics, can at times be tremendously destructive forces in the alcoholic's attempts to recover. Their attitudes can mitigate the gains that occur in treatment. Even those who are not themselves drinking alcoholics may unconsciously attempt to sabotage the sobriety of the patient. The family, including the alcoholic, should be viewed as a dynamic system in which the family members adapt to the alcoholism in various pathologic ways. No matter how vigorously family members complain about "their alcoholic," they often receive some sort of gratification from the situation. Some members may adopt the role of a martyr, suffering long and loudly but unwilling to do anything that might change the situation; they may attempt to control the alcoholic, the alcoholism, and even treatment; they may become rescuers who continue to help the alcoholic avoid the consequences of the alcoholism. If the alcoholic recovers, thereby changing roles in the system, the system changes. This interferes with the ability of the family members to continue receiving gratification from their respective roles, which results in a considerable threat and creates stress on the system. It is for these reasons that the situation must be evaluated to help not only the alcoholic but the family.

Depending on the extent of the family pathology, a referral to Al-Anon or Alateen may be sufficient. If the problems are severe enough, formal family counseling in an outpatient setting is indicated. There are times when the extent of the pathology is so drastic that the only solution, if the alcoholic is to stay sober, is at least a temporary, if not permanent, separation from the family. This is especially indicated in cases where the family members refuse to accept referral for treatment for themselves.

EMPLOYMENT SITUATION

Another issue that must be examined is the employment situation. Close proximity to drinking environments may be a factor leading to a referral to treatment that removes the patient from the job—i.e., residential treatment. For example, although there are recovered alcoholics who are employed as bartenders, returning to bartending early in recovery may place additional stress on the patient. Other job-related indications for residential treatment are the shifts worked and the amount of work-related travel. The patient who works varying shifts may not be able to receive consistent or intense enough treatment in an outpatient setting. Extensive travel may produce the same problem. In general, free-lance as opposed to more structured employment tends to greater isolation and is therefore less desirable.

ATTEMPTS AT PREVIOUS REHABILITATION

The treatment history of the patient has to be examined very closely. When the history indicates that a particular type of treatment program has been used without success, the physician should think in terms of a different kind (e.g., replacing outpatient with inpatient or short-term with long-term treatment). The recurrent utilization of the same inpatient treatment center, in light of repeated relapses, is usually unwise. There are some long-term treatment centers that view themselves as offering treatment primarily to alcoholics who have been unsuccessful in previous treatment attempts. It is not unusual for such programs to require a history of numerous treatment failures as a criterion for admission.

In taking the treatment history, it is helpful to distinguish between an admission to a general hospital for the medical treatment of the sequelae of the alcoholism and one characterized by direct treatment of the alcoholism itself. Although a previous history of treatment for the medical complications of alcoholism can be used to confront the alcoholic with the extent of the problem, it should not be considered as "unsuccessful" rehabilitative experience.

TIME AVAILABILITY

Although this concern is obviously important, it cannot be considered the major factor. For example, the patient who has been unsuccessfully involved in outpatient treatment over an extended period of time may simply have to find the time for residential care. On the other hand, it is appropriate to consider outpatient treatment if the patient can accomplish the objectives effectively in this setting. This is especially true if residential treatment creates a major hardship. One example would be a divorced/separated woman with young children and no one to care for them while she is in residential treatment.

Be prepared for the fact that many alcoholics will "not have the time" (as they perceive it) to do anything about their drinking. Perhaps an agreement can be made that if the patient can remain abstinent by means of outpatient care for a significant period of time, he does not have to go to a facility. Thus the need to go away (possibly threatening a job) becomes the patient's own responsibility, not the doctor's. The patient who slips, must blame the illness, not the physician's philosophy. On the other hand, when your assessment of this situation indicates that you are dealing with resistance to treatment rather than a real problem, the role of the physician is to be supportive but firm in his recommendation.

CONSEQUENCES OF RELAPSE

Certain conditions create a greater than usual risk to patients should they relapse and resume drinking. In certain instances the consequences of relapse may be disastrous. For example, the patient who has had extensive medical problems, such as esophageal varices and a subsequent portal caval shunt, must be regarded as a "last chance." This patient will not likely have the opportunity to fail more than once in a treatment experience, and all pressures should be brought to bear on such a patient to follow the most appropriate treatment program. Another situation with potentially dire consequences is the patient who may have been placed on probation; and if the patient drinks again, the probation will be revoked and the patient jailed. The situation makes the choice of appropriate treatment most critical. The same choice is critical also in situations where another drinking episode will result in termination of employment or the breakup of the family.

PATTERN OF SUBSTANCE ABUSE

When alcoholism is complicated by a history of secondary drug use, the problem is somewhat more difficult to treat and therefore may require additional time in treatment. Dually addicted or cross-addicted patients generally respond better to inpatient treatment. The method of acquisition of the drug is another issue. The patient who has acquired drugs illegally (on the street) must be separated from that drug-using subculture. In this situation, outpatient treatment is almost always a failure, since the entire subculture consists primarily of users and suppliers of the drugs. A comparable situation would be the use of a legal drug (alcohol) in which the alcoholic is a member of "taproom society." Here all of the significant others in the life of this alcoholic are drinking companions, and home is the bar. This pattern will definitely require separation from that subculture.

AGE

Age is a very significant factor. In the past, many alcoholism treatment people believed that there were significant differences between those patients who were addicted to alcohol and those who were addicted primarily to opiate drugs. What has become apparent is that the differences are based not only on drug of choice but also on age. The majority of opiate or polydrug addicts seen by the physician are young people who have been involved in an addictive lifestyle for most of their adolescent and later years. They will require longer-term, more structured treatment with emphasis on resocialization. Many alcoholics, on the other hand, particularly those whose problem drinking began later in life, are people who have accomplished something in their life and possible lost it as a result of the drinking. For them, recovery is returning to an earlier level of successful functioning rather than learning a drug-free coping style for the first time.

Some treatment programs have a relatively narrow range of patient ages, while others are much broader. Adolescents, unless they are quite mature, usually do better in a program geared to the specific needs of their age group. Young addicts also have difficulty identifying with the "older" patients in treatment. Parental consent and continued schooling are also considerations when treatment is going to be of long duration.

Older patients may need greater structure and/or longer-term programs. Experience indicates that they require more time to recover from the physical effects of the drinking, and many times in a short-term treatment program they begin to "clear" only at about the time the other patients are being discharged. When there is disruption in effective or cognitive functioning due to early arteriosclerotic changes, a high degree of structure is helpful.

SOCIOCULTURAL AND ECONOMIC FACTORS

Socioeconomic level is another variable to be considered in choosing a program. It is inappropriate to refer someone into a program when the patient will experience cultural shock, as might be the case in which a young alcoholic/drug abuser from a rural community is sent to an inner-city drug program. Also, patients should not be referred to programs too far above that socioeconomic level; the patients will feel chronically uncomfortable and out of place and will not be able to identify with the other patients. The converse is also true. Some treatment programs provide a broad socioeconomic cross section, which prevents this kind of problem. The physician must also be alert to a potential language problem (a Hispanic who speaks very poor English cannot be sent to a treatment center where there are no Spanish-speaking members of the treatment staff).

INTELLECTUAL/EDUCATIONAL FACTORS

If intellectual ability and educational level present problems, care should be taken to assure that a good patient/program match is made. When intellectual functioning is significantly impaired because of chronic brain syndrome or when the patient is borderline mentally retarded, a long-term, highly structured, relatively simple program with heavy use of reality therapy is a good choice. Analytically oriented programs that require a good deal of introspection and insight are wasted on such patients. In cases where the patient is of average intelligence but illiterate, care should be taken that the treatment center to which the patient will be referred has the capability for handling the situation.

PHYSICAL HANDICAPS

The presence of a physical handicap, such as significant hearing loss, speech impairment, blindness, or learning disability, may severely restrict the number of treatment opportunities available. A sometimes overlooked problem is the patient who lacks ease of mobility because of a handicap. If the patient is being referred to a residential treatment program, it should be determined beforehand that the handicap will not impede treatment. When considering referral to outpatient treatment, keep in mind that the major obstacle to receiving such care may be associated with travel. The necessity of using public transportation may further compound the problem.

Choice of the Specific Treatment Facility

Whatever type of treatment is chosen for the patient, you should be familiar with the treatment center itself. Begin by determining if it is licensed and by what agency and whether or not it is accredited by the Joint Commission on Accreditation of Hospitals (this is more appropriate to inpatient rehabilitation centers than halfway houses or outpatient clinics). Try to ascertain its general reputation by checking with people who are involved in the alcoholism treatment field (A.A., N.C.A., or their affiliates). Much can be determined by a request for literature from the treatment center as well as by talking with the staff or representatives directly by phone. Do not hesitate to ask very pointed questions about costs, program duration, treatment philosophy, aftercare, or whatever else will assist you in making the most appropriate referral for your patient. The ideal arrangement, whenever possible, is a personal visit to the facility. Again, when trying to choose the specific treatment facility that best suits your patient, don't hesitate to use the consultants you may have used previously to confirm the diagnosis or help with treatment planning.

The Role of the Physician Vis-A-Vis the Treatment Center

It is important that the referring physician supply the treatment agency with as much information about the patient as possible. Valuable information includes a medical history, particularly as it relates to the alcoholism, drug history (if any), and the symptoms (vocational, familial, social, etc.) that have led the physician to a diagnosis of alcoholism. Of special importance is the physician's assessment of patient identification with the alcoholism, motivation for recovery, and level of credibility when patients discuss their use of chemicals and resultant problems. There are times when the treatment program will call the physician for additional information. Be open and available to them. In return, the physician should expect to receive a history and physical examination report and a summary letter from the facility about the patient's progress, prognosis, and aftercare plans, including the specifics of the aftercare contract to which the patient is committed. (The physician may also be asked to participate in the development of the aftercare plan.) Any existing medical management problems should also be brought to the physician's attention.

Depending on the duration of treatment and on the arrangements made between the physician and treatment centers, progress reports may be sent to the physician on a regular basis. In any case, the physician should expect a verbal progress report about a patient in response to a phone call.

EXPECTATIONS OF SUCCESSFUL OUTCOME

Since alcoholism is a chronic, progressive illness characterized by exacerbation and remission of symptoms, the goal of treatment is to achieve permanent remission. No responsible treatment person would recommend any course other than abstinence. Abstinence, however, although a necessary beginning step in recovery, is not necessarily synonymous with recovery. Patients who function as irresponsibly when abstinent as they did when drinking represent something less than recovery. We are reminded of a patient at Chit Chat Farms who was a "hit man" for organized crime. After completing our treatment program, he did not drink again. As we were congratulating ourselves on the fine job we had done with him, we recognized that what we had really accomplished was to help improve his aim!

Recovery is best defined in terms of improved psychological adjustment, satisfaction with self, job performance, and interpersonal relationships. All of these things take place with greater likelihood with abstinence.

Early indications of successful treatment are a reduction of the patient's denial or minimization of the problem of alcoholism and a general positive change in attitude including a reduction of the anger originally felt toward the physician for the diagnosis and referral into treatment. Patients should exhibit greater awareness of the relationship between their other problems and the use of chemicals and should have firm commitments to follow through with aftercare plans.

CONTINUED ROLE OF THE PHYSICIAN WITH THE PATIENT

If, in fact, the physician has been responsible for getting the patient into successful rehabilitation, then the major part of the physician's role has been completed; however, this does not and should not terminate the relationship involving the patient's alcoholism. The physician may be required to continue the treatment of the sequelae of the alcoholism. He can remain an ongoing supportive resource to the alcoholic and his family, recognizing that alcoholism is a chronic illness and that there may be a relapse. The doctor's continued involvement with the patient around other medical problems can be helpful because there is now an awareness of and sensitivity to such things as the danger of prescribing elixir of terpin hydrate with codeine for a cough. The physician has now played an extremely valuable role by recognizing and communicating to the patient that primary care alone is insufficient and by referring the patient to appropriate rehabilitation. On-going emotional support can be an invaluable aide to the now-recovering patient. Followup contact will help prevent relapse or help constructive referral if a relapse occurs.

Joseph J. Zuska
Joseph A. Pursch

7
Long-Term Management

The long-term treatment of the alcoholic requires rethinking of
the "medical model" and the usual definitions of alcoholism that
place the site and cause of the disease within the individual.[1] A
more appropriate working definition for the long-term management concept is as follows: Alcoholism is an illness that is a recip-
rocal relationship between the individual and the social environment. It is characterized in the individual by the developing
dependency on alcohol resulting in alienation, dependency, loss of
self-esteem, role dysfunction, and an apparent irreversible inability to safely ingest alcohol. The illness is characterized in the
community by responses and practices that actively create social
pressure to drink and that reinforce individual alienation and dependency. The illness is further characterized by denial of the
problem by the individual and/or the community, unless and until
visible dysfunction results in recognition.[2]

Long-term recovery has no time limit—it is a lifetime program dealing with a chronic, relapsing illness, and although less
and less professional aid will be necessary after the first year or
two, the physician interested in the long view may well maintain
contact with patients indefinitely. Indeed, many of them may
become the physician's close friends—a phenomenon that is often
discouraged in other fields of medicine.

131

ALCOHOLISM
ISBN 0-8089-1227-5

Copyright © 1980 by Grune & Stratton
All rights of reproduction in any form reserved.

The physician then must be prepared to enter into a lifetime relationship with recovering alcoholics and their families. This means accepting them as equals and being willing to attend significant happenings in the course of patients' progress, such as an Alcoholics Anonymous birthday celebrating each year of sobriety. The physician must be willing to share his feelings and, yes, even shortcomings when counseling alcoholics or participating with them in group settings. Above all, the physician must be aware of the limitation of the one-to-one relationship in a disease that has medical, social, and spiritual facets. Not only other physicians but also other agencies, recovery homes, paraprofessionals, volunteers, and especially a peer group of recovered alcoholics will be needed from time to time. A thorough working knowledge of appropriate community resources is essential. By enmeshing alcoholics and their families in a continuum of services that includes Alcoholics Anonymous and maintaining a close personal interest as a physician–friend, one can play a pivotal role in guiding alcoholics and their families into recovery.

As the physician's interest and knowledge grows, he will often participate in community education on matters of early diagnosis and prevention and stimulate the development of appropriate curricula in medical schools and schools of nursing. Such outreach accomplishment increases physician credibility and convinces patients of his genuine and abiding interest in their problems. A fringe benefit to the physician will often be a lessening of his own drinking.

The essence of this concept is that one cannot adopt a classical psychoanalytic model in the treatment of the alcoholic. Patients seeking psychological treatment implicitly request that the therapist play a role in their life patterned on figures from their pasts (the magical father, nurturant mother, etc.). In classical analysis the therapist rejects this role and instead analyzes (i.e., destroys) it. In psychotherapy, on the other hand, the therapist utilizes this role. For the alcoholic, such a relationship can lead the patient to, and help maintain, sobriety; however, it is critical that the therapist avoid excessive involvement such as to facilitate the very behavior he is attempting to treat. An example of this may be observed with the overly dependent patient who uses alcohol (i.e., slips) as a means of controlling the therapist— exactly as the patient had previously done, for example, with a spouse. Thus a balance must be established between participation in the patient's life experiences and excessive dependence.

GOALS OF LONG-TERM TREATMENT

A case of alcoholism cannot be closed in a few weeks or months of treatment; solid recovery requires at least 2 years in most instances.

The self-medication of anxiety and depression with alcohol over a span of years has resulted in exacerbation of these symptoms partly because of the drug and partly because of the failure to learn healthy means of dealing with moods that are common in normal existence. Recovery from alcoholism is a long, slow, relearning process with continued wide mood swings even after many months of sobriety[3] (see Fig. 7-1).

The question often arises as to when the alcoholic can return to work after a course of treatment. Although it is important to consider the type of work, degree of responsibility, the supervisor's cooperation, the severity and duration of the illness, and the progress made in early recovery, it is usually felt that the sober alcoholic who is participating in a sound program at least twice weekly can return to work 4–6 weeks after the onset of treatment. In some cases it may be necessary to assign recovered alcoholics to less stressful jobs temporarily or to part-time work or in unusual cases to advise them to change jobs if present employment is too productive of anxiety.

From a physical standpoint, recovery proceeds rapidly in the first few months and is fairly complete at the end of the first year. By the end of the second year, physical and emotional health are leveling off and often reach above the level of most of the drinking years.

Figure 7-2 indicates a feeling expressed by most recovered alcoholics that sometime between the first and second year of recovery they rise above their pretreatment levels in feelings of well-being and ability to work. Statistics reported by industry corroborate this impression (Fig. 7-3).

Many alcoholics in telling their stories state that they are glad they became alcoholic because their recovery carried them in growth of emotional and spiritual maturity beyond the level of

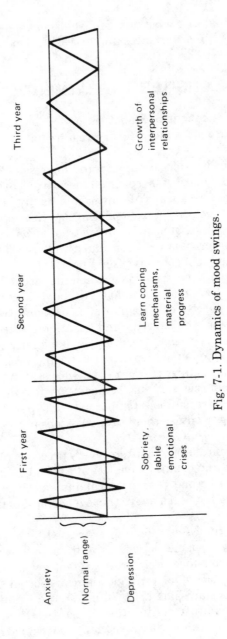

Fig. 7-1. Dynamics of mood swings.

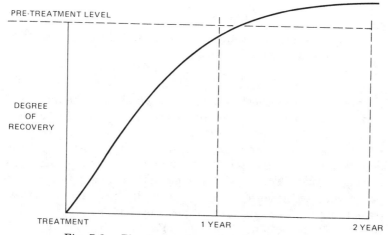

Fig. 7-2.   Physical and emotional health levels.

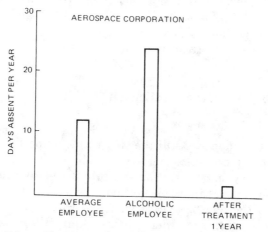

Fig. 7-3.   Alcoholism recovery statistics reported by an aerospace corporation.

their predrinking period. Certainly, many alcoholics with long sobriety are stable, dependable, and concerned over the welfare of their fellow humans to the point that their earned sobriety must be viewed as a strong plus factor.

Many crises, including relapse, will occur, especially during the first 2 years after treatment. By developing and maintaining a warm, open relationship with the alcoholic and the alcoholic's family, the physician will be more apt to be consulted when such crises occur.

In response to the emotional turmoil that these crises often produce, the physician might be tempted to refer the patient for psychiatric care. This should be avoided if at all possible until the patient has had at least 1 year of sobriety in the A.A. program. An exception to this underscores the specific need of a small number. perhaps 2−5 percent, of these patients who require early psychiatric consultation for possible use of specific therapy for schizophrenia, manic depression, or other severe psychiatric disturbance. When psychiatric opinion is finally sought, this consultant should be a psychotherapist who is thoroughly familiar with the principles of A.A. and who understands the priorities involved in abstinence.

Enhancing motivation for remaining in treatment is one of the most important building blocks in nourishing the recovery process. Clearly pointing out the alternatives, giving positive feedback to the patient of improvements noted, and, above all, allowing the patient to have a choice in selecting treatment modalities are strong motivating factors.

DISULFIRAM AS AN ADJUNCT TO TREATMENT

Total abstinence is still the single most important criterion for day-by-day progress, and resumption of drinking must be viewed as a symptom of relapsing into active alcoholism. The main reason for abstinence being so necessary to recovery is that no reliable therapy has yet been found that would enable alcoholics to recover from their illness while still drinking. As a matter of fact, society has a curious contradiction in its thinking that alcohol is an addicting drug that would probably not be approved by the Food and Drug Administration if it were a new discovery but that alcoholics must be defective in some way because they cannot control the use of alcohol as a social pleasure. We are reluctant to come forth as we do in tobacco, opiate, and other drug dependencies and point to the drug in question as being high in addiction potential and dangerous when repeated use occurs; with alcohol, we say that the normal state is to master the drug and be able to use it at will without harm. This attitude has begun to be questioned.[4]

Total permanent abstinence is the goal of therapy because the histories of thousands of alcoholic individuals who returned to drinking after a period of sobriety have revealed a progressive downward course with resumption of the active illness of alcoholism. One might summarize the reasons for abstinence thus:

—Alcohol causes alcoholism in the alcoholic individual (the drinking is the disease)
—Meaningful participation in a growth program cannot be obtained under sedation (alcohol or pills)
—The alcoholic is addicted to alcohol and needs a great deal of it to feel comfortable (more than is safe to drink)
—The required spiritual changes necessary for recovery cannot be made while drinking

Disulfiram (Antabuse) is a useful chemical barrier to impulsive drinking, especially the first year or two of sobriety. Instead of having to make many decisions not to drink during a particular day, the patient on disulfiram need make only one—the taking of a single pill.

Disulfiram is advised in the following circumstances:

—For patients who are willing to take it
—To test motivation when it is in doubt
—During periods of stress (examinations, spouse ill, etc.), particularly after the stress is over
—For the impulsive drinker
—For the repeated failure in rehabilitation
—For the drunk driver or parolee who is sentenced to enforced administration and rehabilitation

Disulfiram is a safe medication with relatively few side effects, which can generally be controlled by temporary reduction of dosage. Disulfiram, by interfering with the action of aldehyde dehydrogenase, results after ethanol ingestion in the rapid accumulation of its catabolite, acetaldehyde. Within minutes after alcohol is consumed the face turns beet red, and sweating, palpitation, dyspnea, tachycardia, hypotension, nausea, and vomiting occur. The intensity and duration of the symptoms depend on the dose of Antabuse and time interval since last dose, the amount of alcohol taken, and individual variation of response.

Disulfiram must always be prescribed with the full knowledge and consent of the patient. Although any alcoholic substance, including mouthwashes, aftershave lotion, food sauces, and cough medicine, can produce a reaction, the likelihood has been exaggerated anecdotally, and when it occurs it usually means that alcohol has deliberately been consumed; however, the patient should be given a list of common products containing alcohol and be thoroughly briefed on the symptoms of the reaction. Ayerst Laboratories issues an identification card that patients should carry at all times in order to alert medical personnel that they are taking Antabuse. Initiation of the alcohol–Antabuse reaction as a part of treatment is no longer considered necessary.

Treatment of the alcohol–Antabuse reaction is mainly supportive to restore blood pressure and administer measures to control shock when present. Most reactions are mild and last 30 minutes to several hours. Intravenous antihistamine (benadryl 50–100 mg) or ascorbic acid (1000 mg) will usually suffice.

Antabuse is slowly excreted; therefore reactions to alcohol usually occur for up to 5 days (more rarely as long as 2 weeks) after cessation of its administration. The drug is usually given as a 500 mg tablet daily for 5 days followed by 250 mg daily thereafter. No alcohol must have been consumed during the 12 hours prior to starting Antabuse.

Side effects are generally mild and consist of fatigue, somnolence, headache, dizziness, skin rash, gastrointestinal distress, and a peculiar taste and odor (garlic-like) to the breath. The last is due to the presence of carbon disulfide in the breath and can be controlled by reducing the dosage.[25] Side effects generally disappear in a week or two or may be controlled by lowering the dosage for 2 weeks and then returning to previous levels.

There are few contraindications to Antabuse. Ruth Fox, after experience with several thousands of cases, withholds it only in overt psychosis or a decompensated heart.[5] The drug may be given with practically any condition as long as the risk of treatment is weighed against the risks of continued drinking. It has been taken for many years without ill effect. Antabuse should be used with caution with isoniazid, coumadin, and dilantin administration. Rare instances of psychosis have been observed following administration of Antabuse.

Certain judges and traffic courts have sentenced drunk drivers to enforced Antabuse administration. The drug is given three times weekly for 1 year after a physical examination. Pharmacists and alcoholism treatment centers have been authorized to supervise the administration of Antabuse in these programs, which have shown some promise particularly when coupled with A.A. counseling, education, and peer group sessions.

Antabuse administration may be continued indefinitely but is usually needed only in the early months or years of sobriety. The patient's willingness to take it is a sign of commitment to sobriety and that denial is lessening. Decision to terminate the drug is best made jointly by the physician, spouse (or "significant other"), and Alcoholics Anonymous sponsor acting in consultation with the alcoholic on the strength of sobriety as evidenced by the alcoholic's progress. Important guidelines in this decision are as follows:

—Active participation in A.A. (no longer *needs* to drink)
—Coping with crises without recourse to drinking
—Improved family relationships
—Dissolution of denial
—Social ease (diminution in social anxiety)
—Growth in self-esteem
—In excess of 12–24 months of sobriety

The use of disulfiram while patients attend Alcoholics Anonymous meetings causes them at times to be criticized by some members who reject all drugs as "crutches." They need to be counseled that crutches are necessary to tide one over a period of disability and that willingness to "go to any length" to achieve sobriety can be a source of quiet pride. Fortunately, Antabuse is more acceptable today by most A.A. groups, and such criticism is on the wane (see Appendix D).

As a part of the goal of abstinence one must teach alcoholics how to become social deviants in a culture that not only encourages drinking but tolerates heavy drinking and intoxication. A key point in this endeavor is to advise them to be open with their friends and relatives about recovery programs (most of them know only too well about the drinking problem) and refuse alcoholic beverages when offered by saying frankly, "No thanks, I am an alcoholic." This action will usually stop all pushing and offering of drinks except by those who are involved in the alcoholic's illness and in need of treatment themselves or who are practicing alcoholics and feel uncomfortable when a drinking friend is abstinent. As a general rule it is well to counsel alcoholics who have just been discharged from inpatient treatment programs to avoid cocktail parties and bars until they have developed a solid base of sobriety—this usually requires at least a year.

Gentle coercion is often necessary to accelerate the motivation process.[6] The physician is in a favored position to point out worsening health problems in a nonjudgmental, supportive manner—not as a scare tactic. On the other hand, health improvement is a strong positive motivating factor and should be shared adequately with the patient. Other coercive levers are the possible loss of a spouse and children, loss of a driver's license, job loss, revocation or suspension of a professional license, and loss of any skill or talent that the patient values.

ALCOHOLICS ANONYMOUS

There is no longer any doubt that Alcoholics Anonymous is responsible for the sobriety of more alcoholics than any other single treatment modality.[7, 8] It is available in 92 countries and offers long-term continuity to a program with "contented sobriety" as its goal. Alcoholics Anonymous emphasizes action and places the responsibility for recovery squarely on the shoulders of the alcoholic. Participation in Alcoholics Anonymous does not damage the therapeutic alliance with a counselor or physician. Physicians desiring to become better acquainted with alcoholism as an illness and its continued management should attend various Alcoholics Anonymous meetings in their communities. Much can be learned and observed, and striking changes can be noted in individuals who are "surrendering" to the process and who are genuinely participating. Not the least of what is learned will be that alcoholism is generally misdiagnosed and mismanaged by physicians.

Attendance at Alcoholics Anonymous meetings should be prescribed with the same degree of seriousness as a cardiac consultation, and patients should feel that the doctor respects Alcoholics Anonymous as a potent and valuable step in recovery.[9] Having their physician attend an occasional meeting is refreshing to alcoholics, convinces them of a genuine human interest, and allows for sharing the recovery process. Physicians who cannot enter into the ways suggested above are advised to refer their alcoholic patients to someone who can for long-term care and followup.

Much can be said about the advantages of Alcoholics Anonymous,[7] but suffice it to say for our purpose that alcoholics can find warmth, friendship, firm guidance, appropriate and supportive confrontation, resocialization, no need to drink, and growing confidence in their own recoveries by a regular working attendance. As a matter of fact, one of us[10] first became interested in alcoholism through feelings of envy when he noted the striking changes that were occuring in naval patients who were coerced into Alcoholics Anonymous attendance for 10–20 meetings and could not at first understand what was causing those changes. He was at a loss to explain a healing phenomenon that he, a physician, could not bring about.

Early in his Alcoholics Anonymous affiliation the alcoholic should select a sponsor from the community network of alcoholics recovered through Alcoholics Anonymous. The sponsor will guide the alcoholic's progress and advise in crises. The problems of recovery are so many and varied that a sponsor is a welcome member of the interdisciplinary team, and conflict with the physician or any other therapist need not arise. As a matter of fact, conferences can be held when a crisis such as relapse occurs and a course of management decided upon as the result of discussion between physician, sponsor, "significant other," marriage counselor, Al-Anon member, etc. Care should be taken to shift dependency of the patient to the program rather than to any particular individual, however.

A.A. is a worldwide fellowship of men and women who are
banded together to solve their common problems of alcoholism
and to help fellow sufferers to recover.[11] The only requirement for
membership is a desire to stop drinking. By sharing their experience, strength, and hope as recovered alcoholics and guided by a
philosophy embodied in the "Twelve Suggested Steps" the members are able to maintain sobriety.

The Twelve Suggested Steps*

1. *We admitted we were powerless over alcohol—that our lives
    had become unmanageable.* (Taking this step implies giving
    up and surrendering to the program and admitting one is
    whipped as far as control over drinking is concerned.)
2. *We came to believe that a power greater than ourselves could
    restore us to sanity.* (Giving up one's ego control and throwing
    oneself on the power of the group, God, or whatever we believe
    to be our higher power.)
3. *We made a decision to turn our will and our lives over to the
    care of God **as we understood Him**.* (Surrender to a spiritual
    program—*not a religion.)*
4. *We made a searching and fearless moral inventory of ourselves.*
    (Must be written in order to thoroughly examine all the mate-
    rial that one has been rationalizing, minimizing, denying, or
    distorting in various ways.)
5. *We admitted to God, to ourselves, and to another human being
    the exact nature of our wrongs.* (Reading and discussing step
    four inventory with another person of our choice.)
        The vast majority of people who fail in A.A. have not
    taken the fourth and fifth steps.
6. *We were entirely ready to have God remove all these defects of
    character.*
7. *We humbly asked Him to remove our shortcomings.*
8. *We made a list of all persons we had harmed, and became
    willing to make amends to them all.*
9. *We made direct amends to such people wherever possible, ex-
    cept when to do so would injure them or others.*
10. *We continued to take personal inventory and when we were
    wrong promptly admitted it.*

---

*Reprinted with permission of A.A. World Services, Inc.

11. *We sought through prayer and meditation to improve our con-*
    *scious contact with God **as we understood him**, praying only for*
    knowledge of His will and the power to carry that out.
12. *Having had a spiritual awakening as the result of these steps,*
    we tried to carry this message to alcoholics, and to practice these
    principles in all our affairs.

It is important in using A.A. as a referral source to realize
that A.A. gives no concern to the reason for drinking and considers all such reasons merely as excuses. A.A. feels that alcoholics
drink because of a compulsion to do so and that they have lost the
power of choice as to whether or not to drink even when they are
not aware of such loss. It is believed that alcoholics are unable to
help themselves in this situation in spite of any amount of
willpower, intelligence, or moral integrity. Relief comes from accepting powerlessness and then accepting help from an outside
source. *Alcoholics cannot keep themselves sober but end up sober*
by trying to help other alcoholics stay sober even when the latter do
not find sobriety.

The A.A. program is a spiritual way of life; this fact must be
understood by physicians who are managing an alcoholic in A.A.
The physician's tendency to prescribe for patients mind- and
mood-altering medications is the greatest cause of conflict with
A.A., and such patients would be better served by being informed
that their symptoms were of emotional origin, and turning to
their 12 step program would be preferable to medication in the
average case. The physician should not accept the responsibility
for relief of distress in these individuals unless it is disabling.
Very often the anxiety symptoms have an unconscious desire to
drink or a resentment as their origin, and it is safer for such
patients to work the A.A. program without sedation.

"A.A. doesn't work for me" is a commonly heard statement
that need not force the physician to quickly assume the responsibility for producing an alternative for such a patient. The A.A.
program will work for anyone who "thoroughly follows our
path";[16] however, not all patients are willing to make the necessary surrender immediately, and it may be necessary to try other
methods of treatment until patients become ready for A.A. In
their attempts to avoid A.A., patients may complain about the

"religious" approach, the cigarette smoke, the coarse language of the repetitive "drunkalogues." We feel that these are all excuses and can be avoided if the patient is sincere by merely shopping around in the community for a satisfactory meeting.

In general, it is surprising how many meetings of all types and sizes one can find not only in one's own locale but throughout the world. There are speaker meetings, discussions, participation or question and answer meetings, and special meetings for beginners, men only, women only, or people under 30 or 40 years old. Some meetings concentrate on a study of the "Big Book," others on the Twelve Steps and Twelve Traditions or on just certain steps such as the 4th or 11th. Some meetings are "open" to the public; others are "closed" and admit alcoholics only or those who are trying to decide whether or not they are alcoholic. In addition to the more than 12,000 meetings listed with the A.A. General Service Office in New York City, there are a great many unlisted meetings of A.A. members who get together just for the pleasure of holding a meeting. Such groups may be composed only of priests, physicians, attorneys, movie stars, politicians, military personnel, homosexuals, nonsmokers, agnostics, or others who wish to share common problems. Members of "special interest" groups are far more likely to stay sober if they also attend regular membership meetings where all are considered to be equal and suffering from the same disease.

Beginners' meetings are smaller, more intimate, and have question and answer sessions to aid newcomers. New members usually are not asked to speak about their own experience with drinking until they feel ready to do so and may pass if called upon. They are asked to read a chapter from the Big Book from time to time as a means of developing comfort in appearing at the podium in front of a group. When newcomers feel ready to do so they may volunteer or respond when called upon to tell their stories in front of the group. This type of ventilation helps to develop honesty and remove guilt. Within a few weeks a spiritual transformation begins to take place as the result of not drinking "one day at a time." The emphasis is on "today," and the desire to drink is put off for 24 hours by following the successful experience of those who have achieved significant sobriety.

It is important that the physician realize that neither alcoholism nor A.A. is restricted to skid row derelicts or "hopeless" drunks. Just as the majority of alcoholics in the U.S. are not bums and not on skid row, so also are the members of A.A. successful business and professional men and women of social stature and financial means. The physician, then, should be willing to recommend A.A. knowing that *it can work and is working for all classes of society.*

Anonymity is at the very heart of the program and is best expressed in the Twelve Traditions.[11]

Tradition Eleven states, "Our public relations policy is based on attraction rather than promotion; we need always maintain personal anonymity at the level of press, radio, and films."

Tradition Twelve: "Anonymity is the spiritual foundation of our traditions, ever reminding us to place principles before personalities."*

For newcomers, anonymity serves to allay their fears of being labeled as alcoholics by everyone they know. The larger significance of anonymity, however, is the key to understanding the strength of A.A. It is a symbol of personal sacrifice without the dangerous rewards of fame and fortune that might be reached for by an individual seeking publicity as an A.A. member doing great work for alcoholics. The latter behavior would most probably reinflate vanity and might very likely result in a relapse that would tend to destroy the unity and credibility of the A.A. fellowship and imperil its very survival. Breaking anonymity at the private level is desirable whenever the alcoholic is ready for extending a hand to another.

A.A. World Services publishes five books. The first is *Alcoholics Anonymous* (also known as "The Big Book"), which comprises the personal stories of recovered alcoholics. The initial 164 pages outline the A.A. Recovery program as written by the original members, who stated in the preface to the first edition:

We of A.A. are more than 100 men and women who have recovered from a seemingly hopeless state of mind and body. To show other alcoholics *precisely how we have recovered* is the main purpose of the book.

---

*The Eleventh and Twelfth Traditions are reprinted with permission of A.A. World Services, Inc.

For them, we hope these pages will prove so convincing that no further authentication will be necessary. We trust this account of our experiences will help everyone to better understand the alcoholic. Many do not comprehend that the alcoholic is a very sick person. And besides, we are sure that our way of living has its advantages for all.*

This book deserves serious study as a part of any rehabilitation program and is an excellent vehicle for discussion and readings. It should be read by the physician just as any other book dealing with clinical medicine.

The only authority of the A.A. program is the book *Alcoholics Anonymous* and perhaps the *Twelve Steps and Twelve Traditions,* which is an elaboration of the meaning of the steps and traditions, and *A.A. Comes of Age,* a history of A.A. and *As Bill Sees It,* which features brief excerpts of the writings of the cofounders of A.A. selected for daily reading. A new paperback entitled *Living Sober* has an excellent selection of A.A. approaches to the problem of what to do when the desire or compulsion to drink returns. In general, an A.A. member who is actively engaged in the A.A. program is not troubled by the desire that previously had been an obsession or irresistable compulsion. Members are often so impressed with this change that they consider it miraculous.

The ease with which members stay sober is often a trap in that they may feel they no longer need the meetings or other A.A. activities. Drinking almost invariably follows, which sooner or later results in a progressive downhill course that is as bad as or worse than that which had originally brought them into treatment. In this sense the alcoholic is not considered as "recovered" but only as "recovering" even after many years of sobriety.

As progress is made in Alcoholics Anonymous alcoholics are encouraged to begin "twelfth-step work"—the helping of other sick alcoholics. This reinforces their own progress, makes them feel needed, and is one of the strong factors behind the success of Alcoholics Anonymous. Twelfth-step work should be encouraged by the physician, who, for example, can offer to assist recovering alcoholics by medical evaluation of the "baby" and help arrange

*Reprinted with permission of A.A. World Services, Inc.

for treatment when requested. There is hazard when the "baby" fails, and one must caution novice twelfth-steppers not to get too emotionally involved. Helping another alcoholic in efforts to remain sober can be of the greatest importance to the progress of patients in their own recoveries.

As patients grow in confidence and ability to cope with stress, they can often assist the physician as volunteers by indoctrinating new patients into Alcoholics Anonymous and participating in community educational work with the physician. An advantage is that the physician can hand-pick a particular recovering alcoholic to indoctrinate a new patient. Many recovering alcoholic patients, and their spouses, will seek further training in alcoholic rehabilitation as a step toward becoming qualified counselors. This should be encouraged only after 1 year or more of sobriety has been attained.

INDIVIDUAL AND GROUP COUNSELING

As an adjunct to patients in Alcoholics Anonymous or for those who initially refuse to attend, it is valuable to arrange for or refer them to an ongoing series of group or individual counseling sessions conducted by a professional or paraprofessional familiar with the complex disease of alcoholism. The group should be open-ended and consist mostly or entirely of other alcoholics who are in various stages of recovery. The peer group identity is a necessary ingredient of long-term management and is valuable in dealing with anxiety, isolation, loneliness, anger, and especially with the inconsistent messages that alcoholics receive from the community.

The individual counseling sessions should involve support, confrontation, ventilation, and clarification of current living problems. The primary focus should be on total abstinence and a "here and now" approach, coupled with a firmly stated *avoidance* of a search for "why the patient drinks." A constant theme of all sessions should be that patients are being prepared for group counseling and A.A. because they have a disease that is best healed by group counseling and peer group support.

PSYCHOTHERAPY

Psychoanalytically oriented psychotherapy of the recovering alcoholic, be it individual or group therapy, is doomed to failure if the patient is using alcohol or any other sedative drug. Even supportive psychotherapy of the alcoholic is ineffective if the patient is still drinking. Because of the alcoholic patient's manipulativeness and because of the therapist's tendency to search for the "underlying cause" of the drinking, the patient will gradually get sicker.

Only a relatively small number of recovering alcoholics will actively seek out or need intensive psychotherapy. This kind of therapy should not be undertaken until the patient has 1 or preferably 2 years of uninterrupted sobriety and a thorough grounding in Alcoholics Anonymous or another support system. If drinking or use of some other medication is resumed, the psychotherapy should be temporarily or permanently stopped because it indicates that the patient still needs to use sedatives to control anxiety or depression. Peer group support should continue.

PASTORAL COUNSELING

Spiritual counseling by a minister trained in alcoholism is an important addition to the interdisciplinary team for patients that express a need for this type of support. Renewed faith in a higher power represents a recovery from the effects of excessive narcissism and offers hope and meaning in the growth out of alienation and isolation from family, friends, and the church of one's belief.

EDUCATION OF THE ALCOHOLIC PATIENT

During the initial few weeks of treatment the alcoholic is usually exposed to lectures by physicians, recovered alcoholics and others along with films and discussions on the nature of the disease of alcoholism. This should be continued and should include the changes that must be made in the patient's life if recovery is to be achieved and maintained. Such education is an important part of the growth process. Physicians willing to undertake the long-term management could well arrange for a monthly evening discussion group on subjects pertinent to their patients' needs. Spouses or significant others should be included.

THE FAMILY OF THE ALCOHOLIC

It is assumed that the family and significant others become involved in treatment during the initial phase. Al-Anon for the spouse, Alateen for the children over 10 years old, and even Alatot for the younger children are helpful group meetings for family members as continuations of the learning process in dealing with their anxieties not only over the past but especially over the changes now occurring in the alcoholic as the result of treatment. Should a relapse occur, these self-help groups can be very supporting to the family.

When indicated, family counseling couples groups and conjoint therapy can be very useful providing the therapists understand alcoholism and its recovery process.

THE PROBLEM OF THE "ENABLER"

An "enabler" is anyone who has enabled or perhaps even encouraged the alcoholic to continue destructive drinking. Although the enabler can be a spouse, friend, child, roommate, homosexual partner, physician, the corporation, the military, or society itself, the enabler is usually the spouse or an adult son or daughter. The enabler will initially be quite concerned and forceful about the need for the alcoholic to stop drinking, but the enabler's enthusiasm for cooperating with the therapy tends to diminish when it becomes evident that the enabler will need to undergo some psychological changes if he plans to have a satisfying relationship with the abstinent alcoholic. The physician should get enablers to attend Al-Anon meetings as soon as possible. In these meetings enablers will learn to manage their own lives and to live comfortably with the idea that alcoholics will gradually have to accept responsibility for themselves and for the consequences of their drinking. The enabler may need the physician's support when it comes to "letting go" of some of the controls that alcoholics are trying to accept back as they gain sobriety (these are the same controls—e.g., family finances and child rearing—that the enabler had taken over, sometimes eagerly, as the alcoholic was getting sicker).

All the problems of "normal" families, such as sexual difficulties and role struggles, will present themselves in the recovering alcoholic's family and will require skillful management by use of A.A., Al-Anon, the alcoholic's sponsor, and (rarely) appropriate consultation by medical specialists.

A special problem is the marriage that was never meant to be or that began when one spouse was already drinking alcoholically. The enabler may prefer divorcing and marrying another drinking alcoholic to undergoing the necessary emotional growth. Another problem is that of the enabler who is also drinking alcoholically. Immediate introduction into Al-Anon will often lead to the enabler switching over to attending A.A. meetings in a few weeks or months. Another frequent problem is that of the female enabler presenting herself to the physician to seek help for her allegedly alcoholically drinking mate. After getting a fair idea from the enabler that the mate is in fact drinking alcoholically, the physician will have to assess the emotional maturity and economic self-sufficiency (actual or potential) of the enabler. If she cannot even imagine herself emotionally living without her mate, or if she lacks the ability to support herself financially (or the willingness to undergo preparation for it), her quest is probably doomed because she will not be able to precipitate the crisis necessary to bring her mate into rehabilitation. Dynamically, the underlying problem often is that the enabler fears that she will lose the alcoholic if she confronts him or actually leaves him. Her fear is that she may then have to get along without him. A skillful therapist who has established rapport with the enabler can often convince the enabler of the necessity for confrontation by showing her that alcoholism is a progressive, relapsing disease, that she is losing her alcoholic husband or lover gradually but steadily, and that the only way to prevent this loss is to confront and bring about rehabilitation, that otherwise the loss of the alcoholic is only a question of time—and will occur later, when the enabler has become more cynical, older, and therefore less flexible for undergoing such changes as proper mourning, getting a job, and establishing new relationships, all of which are necessary for accepting a loss and gaining personal autonomy. Not infrequently the emotionally crippled, widowed, middle-aged enabler will, in the face of the above life problems, begin to drink alcoholically herself and eventually find help in A.A.

After a brief explanation of alcoholism as a disease, she needs to be persuaded to (1) immediately begin attending Al-Anon meetings, (2) tell her husband that she has discussed their problems with the doctor, and (3) suggest that the husband see the physician. She will learn at Al-Anon how her husband's illness trapped her into anger, defensiveness, protection, and controlling, blaming, and finally enabling him to avoid the consequences of his drinking because she unconsciously has assumed responsibility for his actions. She is now the co-alcoholic and must bow out of the vicious circle if her alcoholic husband is to be helped. Actually, proper management of the spouse has often resulted in a previously uncooperative alcoholic seeking treatment.

Obviously, the sex roles in these examples may be reversed; the woman can be the alcoholic and the man the enabler. This may also occur in homosexual pairs or in families.

Society as a whole or a large subculture can also be viewed as an enabler because, like an individual, it will encourage or discourage the alcoholic's tendency to drink excessively. Normal American drinking customs suggest that we use alcohol when we feel good, when we feel bad, as a "pick-me-up," to calm down, as an "eye-opener," and as a "nightcap." At cocktail parties we use it to say hello, to "get in step," to "unwind," as an ice-breaker, courage-maker, socializer, or friendship-maker, and, finally, as "one for the road." At a dinner party we use it as an appetizer, as a main beverage (beer or wine), as an after-dinner drink, and as "more of the same" during later evening socializing until we drive home with "one for the road" toward the nightcap before bedtime.

Executives discuss business while having cocktails, and salesmen buy another round when they land contracts. If a sales pitch falls through and the customers leave, the salesman is apt to buy a double to control frustration.

In sports, we drink at the clubhouse, at the golf shack, on the beach, during the hunt, at the races. We drink cold beer at baseball games because it is hot in those bleachers, and Irish coffee at football games because it is cold in those bleachers. The winners of the World Series shower in champagne before cameras and the press, and the losers drink heavily, silently, resentfully, and alone at the hotel.

We drink when we hear good news, when we get bad news, to go off to war, to celebrate peace, to commemorate a birth or mourn a death. We drink at birthdays, reunions, Christmas, Halloween, and the New Year. Drinking goes with courting ("Candy is dandy but liquor is quicker," said Ogden Nash), with engagements, marriages, anniversaries, and, nowadays, even with divorces.[27]

An example of a subculture as an enabler is the world from which the alcoholic Navy pilot comes.

In naval aviation we drink at happy hours, after a good flight, and after a near midair collision to calm our nerves. To celebrate our first solo flight, we traditionally present our instructor with a bottle of his favorite liquor. We drink when we get our wings, when we get promoted (wetting-down party), when we get passed over (to alleviate our depression), at formal dining-in, at change of command ceremonies, chief's initiation, and free wine at "beef and burgundy night." At birthday balls we drink our door prize if we had the lucky ticket.

When a diver inspects the hull of the ship we give him "medicinal" brandy and we "prescribe" the same "treatment" (for equally questionable medical indications) for the man who fell overboard and was fished out of the Caribbean Sea on a hot day in July.

Night carrier landings from sunset to sunrise rate medicinal brandy dispensed by the well-meaning flight surgeon. We "hail and farewell" frequently, and the first liquid that wets the bow of a newborn ship at its christening is champagne. We drink from enlistment to retirement and from teenhood to old age. For those who have a predisposition to alcoholism there seems almost no escape. And those who want to abstain because they are trying to recover from alcoholism find it difficult to live with such national myths as the hard-drinking, two-fisted pioneering frontiersman, the hard-charging tiger of an aviator who can drink with the best of them, the ruggedness of the guy who can hold his liquor like a man, and the notion that "you can't trust a man who doesn't drink."*

The extent to which it is embedded in our culture may be reflected in our use of alcohol in those very religious rituals in

*Reprinted by permission from Pursch JA: Alcoholism in aviation: A problem of attitudes. *Aerospace Med* 45:318–321, 1974.

which the higher power, i.e., God, is praised or communed with.

The alcohol orientation of the enabler plays an important role in the life of the recovering alcoholic. An individual enabler can change and grow—through Al-Anon or other support systems—as recovering alcoholics can grow away from the enabler who refuses to change a relationship toward them. In the case of a subculture as an enabler, recovering alcoholics need to be enlightened about the "enabling" nature of the drinking practices of their society because the desired change in that society is going to take place very slowly and will continue to present stresses and pitfalls for alcoholics who continue to try and find peer acceptance and approval by living up to peer drinking expectation. A clear, forthright explanation of these conditions from the therapist will increase the alcoholic's chances for continued growth.

THE PHYSICIAN'S OFFICE

Recovering alcoholics should be seen at least weekly to monthly during the first year, especially when they are well—that is when they tend to drop the program. The family is requested to accompany the patient at every other visit. (Occasionally it is wise, however, to maintain separation of treatment personnel in dealing with the patient and the spouse.) Evidences of emotional growth and physical improvement are shared with patients and their continuance in the program reinforced.

The physician should try to involve at least one other person in the patient's life in the treatment of his alcoholism. This is usually the spouse, but it could also be a parent, adult son or daughter, brother or sister, friend, employer, etc. Care is needed here to reassure the alcoholic that the significant other requires education about the disease of alcoholism as much as the alcoholic does and that the other's presence does not necessarily imply a plot to defeat the alcoholic (although at times it could literally be true). The main purpose is to educate, introduce to A.A. and Al-Anon, and encourage relatives or friends to work alongside the alcoholic for their own welfare as well as to understand the disease process and its effect on relationships. The alcoholic may become angry and object to any other person being brought into the treatment. This resistance must be viewed as a part of the denial process and needs working through before progress can be made.

Attendance at Al-Anon for spouses or significant others is preferable to "advice" or "therapy" by the physician, since it puts them in touch rapidly with people who have been healed after similar experiences and offers them hope as well as a uniquely sustaining fellowship.

Secretarial and nursing staff need to develop positive attitudes toward the alcoholic and learn to accept the fact that alcohol on the breath is no more a cause for rejection than acetone on the breath of a diabetic. Comment on the breath should be made in the same manner that one comments on the presence of a rash.

IATROGENIC SABOTAGE VERSUS THE PROPER USE OF PSYCHOACTIVE MEDICATION

The prescription blank is one of the major stumbling blocks for the alcoholic on the way to recovery.[12] Many a "dry" alcoholic was returned to active sedativism by the sincere but unaware physician who did not know about the relationship between alcohol and other drugs and who therefore responded to the dry alcoholic's problem of pain, depression, anxiety, or apathy with a prescription for drugs instead of prescribing ongoing rehabilitation, A.A., and counseling. All sedatives, analgesics, minor tranquilizers, opiates, psychedelics, and stimulants should be avoided by the recovering alcoholic because their "high" or "downer" effect can easily become a substitute for the effects previously obtained from alcohol. If the alcoholic patient's anxiety is such that a minor tranquilizer would control it, then it is best that the patient learn to live with that anxiety and cope by participating in A.A. and other support programs rather than risk developing dependence or addiction to a new substance.

Since alcoholics already have cross tolerance for sedatives (e.g., barbiturates) and minor tranquilizers (Librium, Valium, Meprobamate, Serax), they will, usually in a relatively short time, begin to take these substances in increasingly larger doses, at first for stressful situations, then for daytime sedation, and finally for sleep. Eventually in combination with a return to drinking they will probably be hospitalized because of overdosage. This will complicate detoxification procedures because of the cumulative effect and longer half-lives of these drugs (about 20 hours), which may lead to patients having grand mal seizures about 10–12 days after detoxification for alcohol withdrawal was begun.

Also, the recovering alocholic must be made aware of the need for being honest with the physician and the anesthesiologist prior to surgery so that the doctors will be aware of the patient's high tolerance for sedative–hypnotics.

Drugs in the amphetamine family present chemical traps for recovering alcoholics, who are primarily troubled by depression and apathy. These patients will tend to increase their use of stim-ulants, try to titrate them with alcohol or other sedatives, and frequently end up being hospitalized with symptomatology that is initially indistinguishable from paranoid schizophrenia and that then requires a prolonged period of detoxification. A similar problem often stems from the use of amphetaminelike drugs by the (usually female) alcoholic desirous of dieting.

The recovering alcoholic who presents with pain (psychosomatic or posttraumatic) often becomes addicted to Darvon, Talwin, or opiates if these drugs are prescribed and if counseling and A.A. are allowed to diminish in importance.

Phenothiazines, because they do not produce euphoria, may be carefully prescribed for recovering alcoholics if in the opinion of a physician who understands alcoholism the patient's mental functioning will be improved by phenothiazine maintenance therapy. The same can be said for the use of tricyclic antidepressants in the case of retarded depressions and lithium for recovering alcoholics with manic–depressive disorders.

Recovering alcoholics who are being maintained for necessary brief intervals on some of the above medications may find that in some Alcoholics Anonymous groups[13] the feeling against drugs of any kind (including disulfiram) is strong and expressed frequently enough so that it could jeopardize their sobriety. The psychiatrist or other physician who treats alcoholics should be familiar with the Alcoholics Anonymous resources in his community so that he can help the patient understand the basis of the position taken by the antidrug A.A. groups. The physician should be willing and able to describe a rationale for short-term use of such drugs so that the patient is reassured by the awareness that the physician is as concerned with misuse of drugs as are these antidrug groups.

A major concern of the long-term manager must be the prevention of the unnecessary, harmful, mood changing, and mind changing brought about by physicians who are unaware of the alcoholic's suceptibility to the abuse of these drugs and of the fact that the prescription pad can sabotage the recovery process by renewing the dependence on sedative medication. Until all physicians have learned about the addiction susceptibility of the alcoholic, it will be necessary to educate recovering alcoholics about their disease so that they have the confidence to speak up when medication is being "pushed" on them by unaware physicians.

CONTROLLED DRINKING

The recent literature on alcoholism treatment reveals a growing number of papers on attempts at teaching "controlled" or "social" drinking and claims that abstinence may have been over-emphasized as the sole criterion of recovery from the disease.[14] The very word "controlled' implies that rigid and structured limits must be placed upon the drinking or trouble will ensue. A curious fact is that in no other drug addiction do we attempt to teach controlled use of the drug (with the exception of methadone treatment for heroin addiction, where the rationale is not really controlled social use but rather substitution of a prescribed drug in order to block the desired effect of an illegal one that fosters criminal behavior. Even in this instance, gradual tapering off and withdrawal of the methadone is a prelude to abstinence whenever possible, and control of the drug remains in the physician's hands). In alcoholism those who recommend controlled drinking are attempting to train the alcohol addict to self-prescribe.

Society by its "pious pushing" is constantly reminding alcoholics that they are not "normal" unless they can drink "socially" without harm. Most alcoholics try innumerable times with great suffering and loss to live up to this image but eventually learn that they cannot drink in moderation. Warnings have been issued by the American Medical Association, the American Medical Society on Alcoholism, and the National Council on Alcoholism that continued drinking is dangerous to the alcoholic (see below).

We do not deny that an occasional alcoholic may recover the ability to drink in moderation—what we question is the frequency of this phenomenon and our present ability to make it happen.[15] The very attitude on our part that drinking may be "necessary" for some alcoholics is an invitation for too many of them to try it. The experience of the authors indicates that this goal is unwise, fraught with failure, and an admission of defeat. Let careful research continue, when proof is available that a significant number of alcoholics can achieve controlled drinking *after reentry into society* and that we can select and predict which ones will make it, then we shall reconsider our opinion. In the meantime, the combined statement of the National Council on Alcoholism and the American Medical Society on Alcoholism is a safe guide:[28]

1. Abstinence from alcohol is necessary for recovery from the disease of alcoholism.
2. Although abstinence is a means of achieving recovery, other factors by which a person's life is enriched are important: improved physical and emotional health, better work performance, more rewarding relationships with the family and society, and increased economic efficiency.
3. As in many other diseases, relapses may take place but must never be thought to indicate that recovery is beyond reach. Any improvement is positive and should be recognized and encouraged as a prelude to recovery.
4. There is a need for responsible research into alternate approaches, carried out with proper controls as well as the judicious publication of results when pertinent. However, in the present state of our knowledge, we firmly believe and emphasize that there can be no relaxation from the stated position that no alcoholic may return with safety to any use of alcohol.*

The "Big Book" of Alcoholics Anonymous recommends in Chapter 3 a technique of self-diagnosis—to try a period of controlled drinking as a test to determine whether or not one is alcoholic.[16] Failure to maintain control *over an extended period* is considered indicative of an alcohol problem. Perhaps this is one of

*Position statement on abstinence reprinted by permission of The National Council on Alcoholism and the American Medical Society on Alcoholism.

the fringe benefits of a controlled drinking program—convincing alcoholics that they are unable to drink even in a controlled program and helping them decide that sobriety is the best course. Indeed, controlled drinking experiments have yielded reports that some subjects were found to be abstinent on followup studies.[17]

MANAGEMENT OF THE RELAPSE

In accordance with the medical concept of the disease of alcoholism, "The only generally accepted and time-tested technique for the treatment of this highly recidivistic illness entails the achievement of abstinence."[18] Relapse is common and seems to occur especially during the early weeks or months of sobriety and again between the 11th and 13th months. Resumption of drinking will not always necessarily proceed immediately to serious alcoholic drinking, although it certainly may and often will do so eventually. In some individuals, however, there will be a period of weeks, months, or even a year or more of "controlled" drinking without the onset of the signs and symptoms of alcoholism. Sooner or later drinking will proceed to the alcoholic variety, with a reoccurence of serious medical and social problems. Alcoholism does not improve without treatment but gets progressively worse.

On obtaining a history from the patient in relapse one often finds that a characteristic chain of events occurred after the ground was laid by one or more of the following:

—Disappointment in sobriety
—Emotional conflicts
—Peer pressure of social drinking by persons significant to the alcoholic
—Excessive mood swings
—Various life crises
—Psychoactive drug prescription after an illness or injury
—Excessive zeal as a "twelfth-stepper"— too soon
—Investing too much of oneself in the rescue of a new member of the program (i.e., a "baby" or "pigeon")

A phenomenon referred to as "building up to a drink"[19] begins with a change in mood, anxiety, and psychosomatic complaints and culminates in a state of emotional irritability and confusion referred to by sober alcoholics as a "dry drunk." This state may precede the onset of drinking by several days or weeks and can often be recognized by family, friends, or A.A. members. Treatment consists in the acceptance of the vulnerable state by the alcoholic, verbalizing feelings with a sponsor in A.A. meetings, and taking action along the lines of the recovery program. Medication is almost never advisable, although counseling by the physician can be supportive. Hospitalization or attendance at a daycare facility for a few days may occasionally be necessary.

If drinking has occurred and trouble becomes evident, the patient should be confronted, making use of the present crises to motivate, pointing out the alternatives, and employing whatever coercive levers are appropriate to reinstitute the previous program of sobriety. Hospitalization may be necessary to interrupt or prevent the drinking cycle. The physician, spouse, friend, industrial alcoholism counselor, A.A. sponsor, Department of Motor Vehicles, county and state professional societies, state professional licensing bureaus, police, and others can exert pressures that may be useful to help convince the relapsing alcoholic that serious loss can occur if drinking continues.[6] Although confidentiality is a sacred cow in the physician–patient contract, it must not be rigidly adhered to in the face of recurring disability and deterioration, particularly when a little pressure on an area valued by the patient can effect a resumption of the recovery process. Here, the physician as a kindly "SOB"* can play a major role in not only saving the alcoholic's life but protecting the general public as well. Permission in writing, authorizing the physician to contact any person or agency having a possible bearing on the patient's course, can be crucial.

THE CHAIN REACTION OF HEALTH

As alcoholics progress in their own sobriety and growth they often reach out more and more to help other alcoholics in their circles of friends and neighbors. This phenomenon has been called the chain reaction of health[10] and represents real hope of a break-

*"Specialist on booze"—a personal communication from Max A. Schneider, M.D.

through in enhancing a greater rate of recovery from the serious epidemic disease of alcoholism. When the number of recovered alcoholics begins to approach a critical mass sufficient to create a herd immunity, an "epidemic of health"[20] could be initiated in our communities—a distinctly possible outcome from the partnership of Alcoholics Anonymous and the health sciences. A good example is that of the Navy rehabilitation experience, which has resulted in 85 "Dry Dock" A.A. groups located worldwide that were started by recovering men and women who had completed the treatment program.[26] This type of seeding of our communities with a growing referral network of recovered alcoholics unashamed of their illness and willing to assist health professionals and paraprofessionals, such as counselors, social workers, A.A. sponsors, etc., is an exciting prospect.

EVALUATION OF LONG-TERM MANAGEMENT

Criteria for the evaluation of the effectiveness of long-term care would emphasize the number of patients and their families that remain in treatment versus those that drop out. Sobriety, employment, and ability to relate would be basic. An additional factor of great significance is the number of "alumni" or recovered alcoholics managed by the physician or program who remain in touch and volunteer their services when called upon to help guide a "baby" into recovery. How many of them are willing educators of the community? Case finders? How many have sought additional training and have entered the field of alcoholism?

An additional indicator is the comparison of the frequency of use of medical facilities before and after alcoholic rehabilitation. In a study of 161 alcoholic patients, the Naval Health Research Center reported that for subjects in the 2 years before treatment 4251 days were spent on the sick list as contrasted with 1985 days in the 2 years following treatment.[21]

OTHER MODES OF THERAPY

Aversion therapy, systemic desensitization, behavior modification, hypnotherapy, acupuncture, transcendental meditation, megavitamin therapy, and therapy with lysergic acid diethylamide (LSD) all have their advocates.

The very fact that so many modes of therapy are available for alcoholism, and have their apparent successes, indicates that there is no specific technique of treatment. In fact, technique may not be as important as the therapists' warmth, understanding, and acceptance of the alcoholic as an equal with optimism about the recovery process.[22]

At the present time it is generally agreed that the only recovery method that has proven widely successful is Alcoholics Anonymous. Research on effective therapists suggests that an important characteristic is the commitment to the client.[23] "The inmost growth of self grows only in relation to another" (Martin Buber). Certainly this characteristic and principle is what A.A. is all about.

THE PHYSICIAN'S ROLE

The physician, in the long-term management of alcoholics and their families, should be an intelligent shoehorn for the introduction into A.A., Al-Anon, Alateen, and other community helping agencies. The physician is also a friend, educator, counselor, and crisis interventionist in addition to being an important initial contact for the necessaary development of growth in interpersonal relationships. To do this, the physician must have his own house in order as far as attitudes and personal use of alcoholic beverages are concerned.

A few simple rules:[12]

1. Don't assume responsibility for keeping the patient sober—that is the *patient's* problem.
2. Be careful with your prescription pad—it is one of the greatest hazards to sobriety.
3. Don't try to treat the patient alone.

SUMMARY

Long-term recovery involves abstinence and restructuring and reshaping the alcoholic's life not in terms of "cure" but aimed at helping him find new friends that value sobriety instead of a social group that just tolerates it.[24] The physician as an important member of the interdisciplinary team will be more successful in matching patient needs with the community services if he understands and respects those services as at least equal in value to his own effort.

Long-term recovery of the alcoholic therefore is an ongoing growth process without an endpoint, implying that the case can never be closed.

REFERENCES

1. Beauchamp DE: Alcoholism as blaming the alcoholic. *Int Addict* 11(1):41–52, 1976.
2. Dodd MH: Alcoholic recovery homes; A community model at work in the home and community. Presented to the Alcohol and Drug Problems Association Conference, Recovery Home Section, San Francisco, December 1974
3. Fox V: Dynamics of substance abuse management. Eleventh Annual Distinguished Lecture Series in Special Education and Rehabilitation, University of Southern California, 1973
4. Hayman M: The Myth of social drinking. *Am J Psychiatry* 124:585–594, 1967
5. Fox, R (ed): *Alcoholism: Behavioral Research, Therapeutic Approaches,* New York, Springer, 1967
6. Knott, DH, Beard JD, Fink RD: Alcoholism: The physician's role in diagnosis and treatment. Presented as a scientific exhibit at the American Academy of Family Practice, 23rd Annual Scientific Assembly, Miami Beach, October 1971
7. Hayman M: Current attitudes to alcoholism of psychiatrists in Southern California. *Am J Psychiatry* 127:7, 1971
8. Trice, HM, Roman PM: *Spirits and Demons at Work: Alcohol and Other Drugs on the Job,* Ithaca, N.Y. State School of Industrial and Labor Relations at Cornell University, 1972
9. Rogawski AS, Edmundson, B: Factors affecting the outcome of psychiatric interagency referral. *Am J Psychiatry* 27:7, 1971
10. Zuska JJ: Beginnings of the navy program Alcoholism. *Clin Exper Res* 2(4):352–357, 1978
11. Twelve Steps and Twelve Traditions, New York, A.A. World Services 1965
12. Ohliger P: No pills to alcoholics. Orange County, Calif. *Med Assoc Bull,* February 1974
13. Bissell L: The treatment of alcoholism: What do we do about long-term sedatives? *Ann NY Acad Sci* 252, 1973, pp. 396–399

14. Ewing, JA, Rouse BA: Outpatient group treatment to initiate controlled drinking behavior in alcoholics. *Alcoholism* (Zagreb) 9:64–75, 1973

15. Hirsch J (ed): *Opportunities and Limitations in the Treatment of Alcoholics*, Charles C. Thomas, Springfield, Ill, 1967

16. Alcoholics Anonymous: The Story of How Many Thousands of Men and Women Have Recovered from Alcoholism. New York, Alcoholics Anonymous Publishing, 1955

17. Chalmers DK: Controlled drinking as an alcoholism treatment goal: A methodological critique. Paper presented at Proceedings of the North American Congress on Alcohol and Drug Problems, San Francisco, December 1974

18. Gitlow SE: Alcoholism: A disease, in Bourne, PG, Fox R (eds): *Alcoholism: Progress in Research and Treatment.* New York, Academic Press, 1973, p 5

19. Valles J: From Social Drinking to Alcoholism. Dallas, Tane Press, 1972, pp 89–115

20. Seixas FA: A possible effect of major efforts to treatment of established alcoholism: Initiating an epidemic of health. *Prevent Med* 3:83–96, 1974

21. Bucky SF, Edwards D, Berry NH: A note on hospitalization and discharge rates of men treated at the Navy's alcohol centers. Report No. 75–41, Naval Health Research Center, San Diego, May 1975

22. Emrick CD: A review of psychologically oriented treatment of alcoholism. II. The relative effectiveness of different treatment approaches and the effectiveness of treatment versus no treatment. *J Stud Alcohol* 36:1, 1975

23. Swensen CH: Commitment and the personality of the successful therapist. *Psychol Bull* 77:400–404, 1972

24. O'Briant RG, Lennard HL, Allen SD, et al: *Recovery from Alcoholism: A Social Treatment Model.* Springfield, Ill, Charles C. Thomas, 1973

25. Paulson S, Kraus S, Iber F: Development and evaluation of a compliance test for patients taking disulfiram. *Johns Hopkins Med J* 141(3):119–125, 1977

26. Pursch JP: What do you do with a drunken sailor? Address at the 40th International Convention of A.A., Denver, July 1975

27. Pursch JA: Alcoholism in aviation: A problem of attitudes. *Aerospace Med* 45:318–321, 1974

28. Position Statement Regarding Abstinence, National Council on Alcoholism/American Medical Society on Alcholism, Sept. 16, 1974

Frank A. Seixas

8
The Medical
Complications of
Alcoholism

In recent years, an accumulating body of research has led to the
identification of a large group of diseases specifically engendered
by alcohol addiction. Some of these pathologies arise directly from
the toxic effect of ethanol upon the tissues and others from the
malnutrition which at times accompanies alcoholism.

Alcohol generates a large caloric yield (7 cal/g) without supplying any essential nutrients. Alcoholics may therefore suffer
from severe malnutrition without feeling hungry or suffering
weight loss. While this dietary deficiency is extremely important
in itself, it has become increasingly clear that direct toxic effects
of alcohol on tissues responsible for absorption, modification, and
storage of essential nutrients augments such malnutrition. For
instance, high-dose ethanol produces histologic abnormalities of
the intestinal mucosa, decreased absorptive capacity, and altera-
tions in intestinal motility. In addition, it interferes with the
cellular metabolism of vitamin B_6, folate, and iron, and impairs
absorption of vitamin B_{12}. The acute or chronic gastritis commonly observed in alcoholics further accentuates these deficiencies. Nutritional deficits in the B vitamins, certain bivalent ca-
tions (Mg^{2+} and Fe^{2+}), vitamin C, and essential amino acids have
all been observed in association with alcoholism.

The huge energy load associated with the oxidation of large
quantities of ethanol (via alcohol dehydrogenase and aldehyde

165

ALCOHOLISM
ISBN 0-8089-1227-5

Copyright © 1980 by Grune & Stratton
All rights of reproduction in any form reserved.

dehydrogenase to form acetaldehyde and acetyl-CoA, respectively) result in a marked decrease in the ratio of NAD to $NADH_2$ and interference with the citric acid (Krebs) cycle. This metabolic derangement results in changes in the manner in which the body handles innumerable vital substances: acetate, lactate, pyruvate, urate, indolalkylamines, catecholamines, sex hormones, and other steroids, lipids, lipoproteins, cholesterol, fatty acids, carbohydrates, etc. These may lead to acute disorders: uric acid elevation precipitating attacks in those with gout, an acute rise in blood pressure (resulting from elevated catecholamine synthesis, especially in a patient with labile essential hypertension), acute hypoglycemia (usually in either a malnourished or diabetic alcoholic subject). In each instance, treatment may be required only acutely (be it colchicine, alpha- and possibly beta-adrenergic blockade, or parenteral glucose, respectively), and the underlying chemical aberration clears spontaneously within a few days if abstinence is guaranteed.

The roles that these metabolic defects play, if any, in eliciting specific tissue pathology (primary cardiomyopathy, hepatic cirrhosis, etc.) is not yet completely elucidated. At this moment a classification of consequences of alcoholism possesses the potential for multiple etiology (direct toxic, malnutrition, or both) and for multiple prognosis as well (e.g., the highly reversible picture of fatty liver versus the much more serious prognostic import of hepatic cirrhosis). The metabolic derangement, when severe and persistent seems at this time to be sufficient to lead ultimately to pathologic changes, although some still favor the view that such metabolic abnormalities require a futher noxious influence (hereditary, viral, or as yet undetermined), in order to achieve pathologic permanence. What is reinforced strongly by investigative studies is the immense quantity of alcohol ingested by people with alcoholism. It is this quantitative aspect, made possible by the development of tolerance which allows the ingestion of such large quantities over long periods of time, that makes possible the conception that permanent structural damage can ensue from such a seemingly innocuous chemical as ethanol. From a practical therapeutic viewpoint, abstinence is currently the one major preventive or treatment modality, but clinical investigations continue to explore intermediate mechanisms in detail. Nowhere have such studies been more encouraging than those concerning the liver.

THE LIVER

The most conspicuous physical effect of taking high quantities of alcohol is fatty infiltration of the liver. This results largely from increased hepatic lipogenesis. The fatty liver appears clinically as hepatomegaly accompanied by minimally disturbed liver functions and, rarely, mild jaundice. Only recently it was determined that as much as half the increased weight of the fatty liver derives from protein—in particular, degenerated tubulin from cell membranes. This discovery may vastly alter our concepts of the benignity of fatty liver. Discontinuance of alcohol is however associated with remobilization of the fat. The changes in intracellular structure seen on electron microscopy are less easily changed and may provide links to the development of more serious pathology. There have been a number of unexplained sudden deaths among alcoholics in which the only postmortem finding was a fatty liver (hepatic steatosis, lacy liver). These have been attributed to many factors including sudden and severe hypoglycemia; cerebral fat amboli have also been postulated but not demonstrated. Paroxysmal arrhythmias independently related to drinking have also been suggested as the cause of these sudden deaths.

Alcoholic hepatitis is considerably less common than fatty liver. The condition is characterized by jaundice, fever, leukocytosis, and, sometimes, liver tenderness. Hepatic functions are disturbed, and a rather typical histologic picture with the presence of inclusions called Mallory bodies has been described. Unfortunately the prognosis with this illness must be very guarded. There is not only a 30 percent mortality rate early in its course but the notable propensity for later conversion to hepatic cirrhosis.

There is very strong evidence that alcoholic hepatitis is the common pathway from fatty liver to hepatic cirrhosis. This evidence comes from animal studies in baboons fed liquid diets with 50 percent of the calories derived from alcohol. Animals went through each stage, ending with typical cirrhosis. It is now accepted that the pathology of alcoholic cirrhosis varies in the amount and distribution of fibrous tissue, and can include both the small nodular "classically Laennec" type and the large nodules once associated with the "post necrotic" variety. Studies in France and Germany have shown that prolonged high levels of ethanol ingestion were more conclusively related to the incidence and occurrence of cirrhosis than were dietary deficiencies.

Hepatic cirrhosis should be considered when one finds a patient with a firm, possibly enlarged liver and/or spleen in conjunction with a series of symptoms and signs that depend on the altered structure and diminished function of the liver. This includes a wide variety of abnormal liver chemistry tests including hyperbilirubinemia with jaundice, hyperglobulinemia and hypoalbuminemia with ascites, and hypoprothrominemia with bleeding. The splenomegaly stems from portal hypertension, in consequence of which one also finds esophageal varices, hemorrhoids, and a "caput medusae" in individual cases. In fully developed cases, one may observe weight loss, spider nevi, palmar erythema, Dupuytren contracture, gynecomastia, testicular atrophy, and parotid enlargement. Hepatic failure, gastrointestinal hemorrhage, clotting abnormalities, and an elevated incidence of hepatoma all serve as paths to the often fatal outlook of this illness.

Management of cirrhosis consists of abstinence, prolonged bed rest, and carefully balanced nutritional therapy. The reader is referred to more detailed texts for methods to control portal hypertension, gastroinestinal bleeding, ascites, hepatic insufficiency, and coma. Although there are some cases (approximately 15 percent) of cirrhosis unassociated with alcoholism, i.e., those secondary to schistosomiasis, chronic infectious hepatitis, or kwashiorkor, and separate cirrhotic disease such as Wilson's disease and biliary cirrhosis, the failure to make and formally list the diagnosis of alcoholism when applicable along with cirrhosis on the hospital record may account in part for the frequent failure to advise appropriate treatment of the alcoholism. Advice to cut down on ethanol ingestion is a useless shibboleth under such circumstances. Active and aggressive treatment for alcoholism is required in order to attain effective therapeutic results for the cirrhosis.

THE PANCREAS

About 50 percent of cases of pancreatitis stem from alcohol ingestion. The precise etiology is still under investigation, but more and more emphasis is being placed on the direct effect of large doses of ethanol over long periods of time.

Ethanol in low doses results in an increase of pancreatic secretions of low viscosity. In high doses over long periods of time, the secretions are decreased in volume and become highly viscid. The pancreatic ducts become obstructed by protein plugs. This induces subsequent inflammation with acute attacks of pancreatitis. Other pathogenetic ideas have been advanced. In an attack of the acute disease, one may note abdominal pain, vomiting, fever, and shock. For acute episodes, Kowlessar has outlined initial treatment comprised of bed rest, cessation of oral nutrition, and continuous nasogastric suction to suppress pancreatic secretion. Intravenous hyperalimentation may be indicated in the more serious cases. Fluid and electrolyte balance must be attained. Pain is severe and requires relief by the parenteral administration of analgesics such as meperidine and, for some patients, continuous epidural block. The possibility of respiratory failure calls for vigilant monitoring. Postattack management consists of a bland low-fat diet, continued abstinence from alcohol, and anticholinergics such as methantheline. One can survive many acute attacks but progressively pancreatic tissue becomes destroyed. Calcification occurs as well as the formation of pseudocysts. In some patients not responding to treatment, surgical interventions such as cholecystostomy, enterostomy, drainage of the peritoneal sacs, and total or partial pancreatectomy have been employed with some success. Repeated attacks compound the damage with increasing frequency, until multiple acute episodes give way to a condition of chronic pancreatic insufficiency. The patient complains of abdominal pain and weight loss with steatorrhea. Mild diabetes may complicate the picture and require insulin.

GASTROINESTINAL TRACT

Alcohol is a stomach irritant and may produce acute gastritis characterized by nausea, vomiting, pain, and other signs of indigestion. Acute duodenitis has also been observed. Chronic atrophic gastritis is characterized by loss of the glandular portions of the mucosa with some irregularity of the epithelial cells

and inflammatory infiltration of the stroma. Whether it is especially frequent in alcoholism is controversial. At times, persistent
vomiting may lead to a tear or rupture of the esophagus at the
esophagogastric junction, the Mallory–Weiss syndrome, which
requires prompt recognition and surgical management. Otherwise discontinuation of ethanol in association with a bland diet
will likely result in prompt recovery from the usual peptic problems incumbent upon excessive ethanol ingestion.

Ethanol not only irritates the upper gastrointestinal tract,
producing gastritis and aggravating peptic disorders, but it induces an enterocolitis as well. In explaining this symptom, a
transient steatorrhea, defective sodium and water uptake, and
lactose malabsorption have been described. Shortened villi in the
small intestine are induced, as well as ultrastructural abnormalities in small intestinal mucosal cells. The diarrhea and colic
commonly disappear with abstinence.

THE HEART

For many years, heart disease in alcoholics was thought to
be rooted solely in malnutrition. Researchers working during the
last 15 years have determined that chronic alcohol intake has a
direct toxic effect on the myocardium. G.D. Talbott divides alcoholic heart disease into three clinical entities: toxic, conductive,
and nutritional.

Toxic alcoholic heart disease is also known as alcohol cardiomyopathy. It is the outcome of at least 5 years of chronic
ethanol abuse. Cardiac architecture is permanently altered by
the sequence of fat deposit, inflammation, and interstitial fi-
brosis. The initial development of the disease is often asymp-
tomatic, and irreversible structural damage with extensive
hemodynamic implications may have occurred by the time it is
diagnosed. The most important change in the heart muscle is
decreased elasticity.

The first observable clinical manifestation is dyspnea, usually exertional but sometimes presenting as a nocturnal
paroxysm; in either case, the difficulty in breathing is often accompanied by moist basilar rales as well as elevations in blood
pressure and pulse rate. Arrhythmias are prominent in the clini-

cal course. As the disease progresses, the heart becomes massively enlarged. Intracardiac thrombosis and recurrent embolization may occur. Progressive congestive failure with edema, ascites, and pulsations of an enlarged liver become noticeable. Atrial and/or ventricular gallop sounds are commonly noted. Cases have been described in which cardiomyopathy occurs in combination with acute skeletal myopathy.

There is a fairly poor prognosis for toxic alcoholic heart disease because it tends to be detected in advanced stages. Management consists of abstinence, months of complete bed rest, digitalis, and a diuretic. A high-protein diet may prove beneficial. When this regimen has been faithfully adhered to, dramatic reductions in heart size have been reported.

Conductive alcoholic heart disease can result from the serious electrolyte imbalance that ethanol has long been known to produce, but also may relate to direct effects of alcohol on the bundle of His or cardiac muscle. Various arrhythmias include auricular fibrillation, ventricular and superventricular tachycardia, auricular and ventricular premature contractions, and mild to severe intra- and sinoventricular blocks have been seen.

It is highly likely that the same mechanisms are involved in conductive alcoholic heart disease and the arrhythmias of the withdrawal syndrome. In both, alcohol-induced electrolyte imbalances or other mechanisms may lead to such effects as cardiogenic shock, ventricular flutter or fibrillation, cardiac standstill, and sudden, usually left-sided congestive failure, any of which may be lethal.

Talbott has noted that these arrhythmias can be controlled with an oral solution containing high doses of magnesium and potassium in a fructose base with varying concentrations of other electrolytes. Some advise β-blocking drugs for this purpose. Abstinence, of course, is indicated.

The alcoholic's common combination of poor diet and faulty metabolism may result in severe thiamine deficiency and malutilization. The result may be a potentially fatal nutritional heart disease: beri-beri. Fortunately this has become fairly uncommon in this country since the introduction of nutritional supplements in many staple foods. The clinical manifestations are those of congestive heart failure, of the high-output type, in conjunction with the peripheral neuropathy so characteristic of beri-beri. The conventional therapeutic regimen of digitalis and diuretics is often ineffective. Patients may respond immediately to thiamine, administered orally or intramuscularly, but prolonged cardiac injury has been known to result from beri-beri. Vitamin supplementation, particularly B complex and C, is a useful dietary adjunct, and avoidance of alcohol is imperative.

THE NERVOUS SYSTEM

The thiamine depletion that causes nutritional alcoholic heart disease is also responsible for a number of debilitating neurologic conditions frequently encountered in the alcoholic.

Peripheral neuropathy is one of the most striking and widespread of these syndromes. It appears clinically as progressive numbness, pain, and paresthesias in the legs and/or arms, as well as motor weakness, usually bilateral and symmetric, of the peripheral parts of the limbs (feet more involved than hands). As a rule, the lower extremities are affected first; walking becomes difficult or impossible.

The disease is reversible with thiamine, but recovery may take many months. Treatment consists of immediate bed rest, a diet rich in calories and vitamins, polyvitamin supplements, and unfailing abstinence. To prevent contractures, the affected limbs should be splinted, and physical therapy should be instituted as soon as possible. There have been recent reports that thiamine dipropyl sulfide may have a faster therapeutic effect.

Toxic or "tobacco–alcohol" amblyopia is a neuritis of the optic nerve leading to progressive failure of central vision and difficulty in distinguishing red from green. Clinical testing reveals impaired visual acuity and bilateral central scotomata. The condition is reversible with thiamine.

Wernicke encephalopathy, sometimes accompanied by peripheral neuropathy, is a brain disorder in which severe thiamine depletion results in acute hemorrhagic lesions primarily in the brain stem and the hypothalamus. It results from prolonged alcoholism. Patients suffering from Wernicke encephalopathy are unable to move their eyes conjugately either horizontally or vertically (ophthalmoplegia). They exhibit nystagmus, ataxia, disorientation and confusion. In the syndrome's earliest stages, thiamine rapidly reverses the ophthalmoplegia and should be combined with intensive oral and parenteral polyvitamin therapy as well as abstinence.

Wernicke encephalopathy is nearly always found in conjunction with Korsakoff psychosis, the clinical totality being referred to as the Wernicke–Korsakoff syndrome. While Korsakoff psychosis had a similar etiology, the neuronal lesions are less localized than in Wernicke syndrome, and brain damage is usually permanent. The loss of neuronal substance is evidenced clinically by defective memory, and confabulation, as well as peripheral neuropathy in some cases. Treatment parallels that for Wernicke encephalopathy, but mental recovery takes months and in many patients does not take place at all, resulting in permanent mental injury. Even with the more satisfactory outcomes there is usually some residual memory impairment.

Alcoholic cerebellar degeneration is a syndrome in which atrophic cerebellar changes produce progressive unsteadiness of gait and stance and, in some cases, mild to moderate nystagmus, hypertonia, and deep tendon hyporeflexia. The disease has a rapid course, reaching maximum severity and then stabilizing within days or weeks of onset. Abstinence and nutritional therapy may produce some limited abatement of symptoms.

Central pontine myelinolysis and Marchiafava–Bignami disease are rare neurologic conditions found almost exclusively in malnourished chronic alcoholics. Both diseases are difficult to diagnose clinically; they are normally discovered on autopsy.

In central pontine myelinolysis, a dense concentration of demyelinized lesions in the pons produces rapidly progressing weakness of the bulbar innovated musculature, which first manifests as dysphagia and dyathria. Within days, there is aphonia and total inability to swallow as well as complete ophthalmoplegia, fixed or dilated pupils, and lack of corneal response. Initial quadriparesis is usually succeeded by hyporeflexic or areflexic quadriplegia, which may be rigid or flaccid. In the terminal stage, death is preceded by a sequence of drowsiness, stupor, lethargy, and coma.

Marchiafava–Bignami disease involves severe atrophy of the corpus callosum, the lesions resembling those of central pontine myelinolysis and multiple sclerosis. Progressive psychological deterioration occurs within days or months of onset. Patients exhibit agitation, confusion, hallucinations, negativism, impaired judgment, and disorientation. The neurologic damage is evidenced physiologically by dysphagia, echolalia, disturbance of gait and motor skills, incontinence, grasping, sucking, perseveration, and delayed initiation of action.

Although generating considerable disagreement, the notion that ethanol alone could produce a chronic brain syndrome distinct from those central nervous system disorders resulting from nutritional deficiencies has achieved broad acceptance. In its most extreme form, cerebral degeneration (alcoholic dementia) is an irreversible progressive dementia characterized by confusion and memory loss, spacticity of the lower extremities, an "astasia–abasia" type of gait disturbance, retropulsion, fine picking movements, digital and labial tremulousness, and dysarthria.

In its earlier phases, this syndrome may be ubiquitous among those patients ingesting large quantities of ethanol for protracted periods. Subtle interference with mentation and memory such as to lead to difficulties with job or school performance and failure to appreciate the logical consequences of specific behavior are common. One may judge change in mental status of a patient not previously known by reference to a standard such as previously accomplished schooling or job performance.

Severe hepatic insufficiency also induces cerebral dysfunction known as encephalopathy and usually accompanied by high blood ammonia levels. Hepatic coma is preceded by neurologic dysfunction, producing varyingly severe neuromotor, mental, and behavioral aberrations. Onset of coma may be signaled by a "flapping tremor" (asterexis), an abnormal flexion–extension movement of the unsupported hand. Early detection and prompt institution of therapy for cirrhosis may avert the terminal stages. Hepatic encephalopathy may also complicate the course of cirrhosis after shunt operations for portal hypertension.

THE MUSCULOSKELETAL SYSTEM

Over the last two decades, clinicians and researchers have defined an alcohol-induced muscle disease affecting the muscles of the thoracic cage and the proximal muscles of the extremities, characterized by acute muscle tenderness, pain, muscle weakness, frank rhabdomyolysis, and, sometimes, myoglobinuria. This syndrome, which may cause death by acute tubular necrosis with renal failure, is fortunately quite rare.

More commonly one sees muscle pain, tenderness, and weakness involving the proximal limb girdles especially and occurring in conjunction with and for up to a week following the acute alcohol debauch. Careful study has revealed a leakage of muscle enzymes with transient elevations of SGOT and CPK. Return to full function within 5–7 days is the rule, but a chronic myopathy may intervene should ethanol ingestion persist. Occasionally the chronic myopathy appears in the absence of a preceding acute episode. Wasting and weakness of the proximal limb girdles is the rule, and diminished response of blood lactic acid elevation to ischemic exercise may be observed. Distal limb findings of a similar nature should always make one suspect dysfunction of the peripheral nerves rather than a myopathy.

Myopathy improves with abstinence and adequate nourishment. J.P. Knochel cautions that the administration of glucose, fructose, or carbohydrates to malnourished alcoholics undergoing withdrawal may precipitate acute hypophosphatemia leading to further muscle injury and other complications in patients who previously had only the subclinical form.

Inebriation is connected with a high incidence of traumatic fractures due to falls, brawls, and automobile accidents. In some alcoholics, the risk of fracture is increased by osteoporosis. The normal homeostatic cycle of bone formation and bone resorption is disturbed by a combination of calcium depletion, poor diet, and decreased activity. The resulting "metabolic" fractures (i.e., those superimposed upon osteoporosis) most commonly observed are in the hip, wrists, humerus, and spine, whereas the usual locations of the "traumatic" fractures of the alcoholic are ribs, legs, and skull.

Osteonecrosis of the hip is a rare syndrome seen mainly in patients with alcoholism. Limping and severe hip pain, usually bilateral, progress to femoral dislocation as the head of the femur necroses. It has been suggested that the bone tissue dies as a result of hyperlipemia, fat emboli obstructing the blood supply of the femoral head. Previous treatment with cortisone may also play an etiologic role in this condition.

When osteonecrosis is suspected, usually from hip pain seen in alcoholics with no other signs of arthritis, the patient should be taken off weight bearing immediately. Needless to say, drinking should cease at once. Hip reconstructive surgery is often needed.

BLOOD

Ethanol interferes with hematopoiesis at all levels, producing a number of anemias and clotting disorders.

At the nutritional level, the restricted diet may be deficient in B-complex vitamins, especially B_6, B_{12}, and folate. Although an iron deficiency anemia is not uncommon among alcoholics, this does not usually result from a nutritional deficiency but rather from excessive iron loss (via gastritis, hemorrhoids, or varices). In fact, consumption of alcoholic beverages high in iron (occasionally due to manufacture) may result in hemosiderosis. Alcohol also speeds the development and manifestations of hemochromatosis where the genetic predisposition is present.

Whereas the gastrointestinal mechanisms responsible for iron absorption usually seem to be intact despite alcohol ingestion, the same is not true for folates. The restricted quantities of folate ingested by the heavily imbibing alcoholic undergo "double jeopardy," so to speak, since the alcohol induces a mucosal block to their absorption in the small bowel.

Further, those B-complex vitamins that are unaffected by the hazards noted above may fail to find adequate storage mechanisms in a liver previously injured by ethanol.

Finally, the limited quantities of folate capable of reaching the hematopoietic cells often are blocked from exercising their usual biochemical effects by ethanol. Direct interference by ethanol results in a maturation block of all the marrow cellular elements (red cell, white cell, and platelet). It is an effect complicated by the relative deficiency in pyridoxal phosphate, the conversion to this active congener of B_6 having been interfered with by ethanol. Thus both megaloblastic and sideroblastic marrows may be seen during ethanol ingestion.

Discontinuation of ethanol ingestion in conjunction with an adequate diet is followed by a rapid return of hemotopoiesis—often with the appearance of reticulocytes, which should not delude the observer into the mistaken impression of a hemolytic syndrome (although hemolysis may also occur).

Abnormalities of the WBC series include not only a synthesis block resulting in leukopenia but also defects in function. Both diminished leukocyte mobilization and chemotactic properties have been noted.

The maturation arrest of thrombocytes is complicated by a decreased platelet lifespan, abnormal platelet function, and the possibility of diminished clotting factors resulting from a damaged liver.

INFECTIOUS DISEASES

Ethanol is known to have an as yet unclear role in impairing the mobilization of polymorphonuclear leukocytes as well as in decreasing serum bactericidal activity against *Escherichia coli* and *Haemophilus influenzae*. Conjoint introduction of alcohol and bacteria into rodents results in elevated mortality when compared to that due to sepsis alone.

Pulmonary tuberculosis is an infectious disease frequently associated with alcoholism; the population of tuberculosis hospitals shows a disproportionately elevated percentage of alcoholics. The tuberculosis is often complicated by peripheral neuropathy and liver disease. Although ethanol is not a primary cause of tuberculosis, its effect on leukocytes may lower resistance to the infection and undoubtedly compromises any long-term therapeutic plan. V. Hudolin has found a definite correlation between improved cure rates and abstinence.

The heavy smoking that almost universally accompanies alcoholism (even heavier during withdrawal) is a complicating factor in bronchopulmonary disease. Poor bronchial toilet associated with excessive sedation may account in part for the high incidence of suppurative bronchopulmonary disease in patients with alcoholism. A Danish study of brewery workers, however, failed to demonstrate elevation of mortality rates due to infection among those with high ethanol ingestion.

CANCER

There is little doubt but that ethanol ingestion can be dose correlated with elevated incidence of cancer of the larynx, esophagus, and liver. There is a strong likelihood that this may be true of cancer of the oropharynx and possibly of the pancreas as well. Cigarette smoking can be shown to represent a further, separate, untoward factor. The type of alcoholic beverage apparently influences carcinogenesis, since certain specific regions of wine-producing countries reveal disproportionate elevations of esophageal cancer.

Although the incidence of alcoholism varies widely among the European wine-drinking nations, Spain and Italy as well as France share the same onerous burden of elevated levels of these malignancies. The Danish study of brewery workers demonstrated elevated overall mortality rates as well as higher incidence of the above-noted neoplasms among those supplied with "free" daily "six-packs" of beer. Other malignancies, such as colonic, occurred in normal number. Other studies, however, show increased incidence of cancer both of the cardia of the stomach and the colon. The increased incidence of cancer seen among alcoholics may be due at least in part to the enhanced capacity of these individuals to activate procarcinogens in the intestine, according to C.S. Lieber.

SURGERY

Because of alcohol's cross tolerance with other members of the hypnotic–sedative group of drugs, one may expect an abnormal response to preoperative and general anesthetic medications. In addition, the sudden cessation of sedative ingestion coincident with surgery and/or injury–illness frequently results in an acute withdrawal syndrome, often delirium tremens, in the immediate postoperative period (within 3 days for ethanol and 7–10 days for solid sedative withdrawal). Obviously, the elevated incidence of pulmonary and hepatic dysfunction, poor wound healing, and metabolic abnormalities must be considered in preoperative decision making as well as during and after surgical care.

PERINATAL AND PEDIATRIC

Ethanol ingestion during pregnancy has been incriminated in the production of fetal abnormalities (the fetal alcohol syndrome, FAS). FAS encompasses diminution of birthweight, size, and intelligence, as well as an association with various physical–developmental–behavioral abnormalities. Although FAS appears to be correlated with a level of ethanol ingestion in excess of 2–3 oz of hard spirits per day, there is no reassuring evidence at the present time regarding the absolute safety of lesser quantities of ethanol during pregnancy. Rarely, one may observe a withdrawal syndrome in a new born of a mother suffering from a high level of ethanol addiction immediately prior to parturition.

PSYCHIATRIC

Psychiatric complications of alcoholism are protean, but suffice it to mention some of the more relevant. Depression and psychotic states may occur secondary to the use of alcohol and may clear within some weeks of abstinence. Therefore it is difficult to establish objectively a clinical psychiatric diagnosis (of primary depression, paranoid, or other psychotic states) during or immediately following alcohol ingestion. The patient must be abstinent from alcohol and other hypnotics for at least a period of weeks (1–6) before a diagnosis of a primary psychiatric disorder can be clearly established.

In addition, the self-medication with alcohol by a patient in a primary depression may convert a retarded depression into what appears to be an agitated depression—the agitation being more a pharmacologic result of the drug. One would do well to consider alcoholism when confronted by any agitated state, since alcohol-induced agitation may be confused easily with psychogenic anxiety.

The chronic mental patient (with chronic schizophrenia, chronic organic brain syndrome, or a character or personality disorder) may function adequately at some level until adaptation is compromised by use of ethanol or other hypnotics; at this point the patient may decompensate. Use of alcohol will interfere with attempts at therapeutic intervention and should govern the initial therapeutic approach before treatment of the underlying disorder.

The term pathologic intoxication has been applied to circumstances in which an unreasonably small quantity of ethanol induces a bizarre, violent, and destructive behavior pattern. Its very existence has been questioned.

It is apparent from this brief survey that alcohol can generate multisystem problems of extreme gravity, any number of
which may be present in an individual patient. It must be emphasized that the drug produces this damage primarily when consumed in large quantities over extended periods of time.

The thousands of alcoholics who die from suicide, starvation,
accidents, withdrawal complications, and the myriad pathologic
processes are all victims of a single disease; regardless of specific
manifestations, these disease entities would not be possible without the patient's ability to more or less comfortably take in un-
physiologic volumes of alcohol (i.e., tolerance). While the count-
less symptoms may range all the way from indigestion, anxiety,
and broken bones to cirrhosis, dementia, and unbearable family
tragedies, they all arise from one underlying pathology for which,
ultimately, there is only one remedy: total abstinence from alcohol. Only in this manner may the medical complications of alcoholism achieve maximal rates of regression.

From the point of view of one interested in avoidance of
physical complications, total abstinence remains the basis of any
successful therapy for the alcoholic.

REFERENCES

Bayliss RIS: Medical disorders associated with alcoholism, Third Sym-
    posium on Advanced Medicine, in Dawson AM (ed): Baltimore, Wil-
    liams & Wilkins, 1968, pp 328–339
Jones KL, Smith DW: The fetal alcohol syndrome. *Teratology* 12:1–10,
    1975
Kissin B, Begleiter H (eds): *The Biology of Alcoholism: Clinical Pathol-
    ogy.* New York, Plenum, 1974, vol 3, pp 291–586
Lieber CS: Alcohol and the alimentary tract. *Adv in Alcohol* 1 (10), 1979
Noble EP (ed): Third Special Report on the U.S. Congress on Alcohol and
    Health. Washington, D.C., U.S. Dept. of Health, Education and Wel-
    fare, NIAAA, 1978, pp 35–78
Seixas FA, Eggleston S (eds): Work in progress on alcoholism. *Ann NY
    Acad Sci* 273:146–302, 1976
Seixas FA, Williams K, Eggleston S (eds): Medical consequences of al-
    coholism. *Ann NY Acad Sci* 252:10–377, 1975
Tuyns AJ: Alcohol and cancer. *Alcohol Health Res World,* 20–31, Sum-
    mer 1978

Lynne Hennecke
Vernell Fox

9

The Woman with Alcoholism

It is difficult to find in the vast literature on alcoholism any studies done on the alcoholic woman before the 1960s. Even today, many publications fail to make clear until the last paragraph that conclusions are based on all male samples.[1] The implicit notion, then, is that there is little if anything that differentiates the alcoholic woman from the alcoholic man and that research findings can simply be extrapolated to include her. Too often this assumption has led to an insensitivity to the special treatment needs of the alcoholic woman. When these needs are appropriately addressed in treatment, the usual assumption of a poor prognosis diminishes considerably.

Although the ratio of women alcoholics to men alcoholics is not known with any precision, estimates vary from 1:4 to 1:2.[2] A recent study has attempted to relate this ratio to a genetic paradigm for transmission of alcoholism.[3] We do know that drinking for women has increased as society has become more permissive of her drinking behavior, e.g., drinking in public. This permissiveness, however, has not extended to a relaxation of social attitudes toward women's drunkeness. Studies[4,5,6] indicate that not only do both sexes report more intolerance towards female drunkeness but even among alcoholic women the attitude expressed is one of disgust. The negative evaluation concerns the

181

ALCOHOLISM
ISBN 0-8089-1227-5
Copyright © 1980 by Grune & Stratton
All rights of reproduction in any form reserved.

area of social roles, that is, the drunken woman unable to provide nurturant behavior and unable to employ the customary sexual restraints. The notion of moral weakness, therefore, is more explicit for women than it is for men. These attitudes have both helped to reinforce the alcoholic woman's denial of her disease and diminish her chances of seeking or being offered treatment. Even the physician shares this negative attitude. A report[7] on physician attitudes towards the alcoholic woman notes that the physician "believes the alcoholic woman to be sicker than the alcoholic male." Most of the physicians reported their awareness of their patients' alcohol problems, although less than 15 percent came to him for that specific complaint. Unfortunately, many of the physicians were loath to deal with the alcoholism in any open and direct way.

The double stigma of alcoholism and alcoholism in a specific person (woman, Jew, cleric, physician, etc.) presents a major obstacle to recovery unless the dignity of the disease concept is projected to the patient by the physician.

PHYSIOLOGICAL CONSIDERATIONS

Although compelling evidence of a relationship between sex hormone levels (particularly estrogen deficiency) and alcoholism is not available at this time, some alcoholic women relate drinking episodes to their menstrual cycle, particularly the premenstrual period. An alert therapist should consider this phenomenon particularly if the patient is prone to "slips." Strategies such as ibuprofen therapy for the prevention/relief of dysmenorrhea,[8] extra A.A. meetings, telephone contact, etc., should be planned with the patient to help her negotiate this difficult period.

Alcoholism may lead to such menstrual irregularities as missed, scanty, or overly heavy periods. These irregularities, as well as forgetting to employ contraceptive measures during drinking bouts, can further complicate her susceptibility to and awareness of pregnancy. These difficulties can be exacerbated if she is unmarried or has a troubled marriage.

Spontaneous abortion and early miscarriage are more common in alcoholic women. They tend to have more premature and breech births as well as other complications in delivery.[9] The majority of alcoholic women, perhaps because of the high value that they place on motherhood and nurturance, either significantly reduce their alcohol intake or stop drinking altogether during pregnancy. For those women who do not stop their drinking, the risk of birth defects in the child becomes considerable.

The incidence of congenital abnormalities in heavily drinking women is estimated to be about 32 percent.[10] About a 12 percent risk factor has been estimated for all pregnant women (alcoholic or not) if they drink during the first trimester. The critical amount of alcohol which would elicit the full spectrum of congenital abnormalities known as the fetal alcohol syndrome (FAS) has not as yet been determined. It is likely, however, that a relatively modest alcohol ingestion during the first seven weeks of pregnancy (the very period during which women fail to recognize that they have conceived) might result in the FAS. FAS is thought to be the third most common congenital defect (Downs Syndrome = 1:600, Spina Bifida = 1:1000 and FAS = 1:2000) and the leading preventable one.

Difficulties and risks persist after pregnancy. There is a higher incidence both of postpartum death in drinking mothers, and in deaths of the newborn than in the general population. Raising a physically handicapped child presents problems—particularly to a mother who cannot cope with her own problems. The irritability of the child and the disease of the mother makes early bonding difficult.

The guilt associated with these defects can only grow worse as the syndrome is more widely publicized. Education should of course be part of the prevention strategy. For the pregnant alcoholic woman who has not stopped drinking, however, abortion might be indicated or at least seriously considered.

TREATMENT CONSIDERATIONS

Generally speaking, a certain telescoping of the disease of alcoholism, i.e., later onset and more rapid progression, differentiates female from male alcoholics. Later onset can be explained in part by the differential socialization process for males and females. The literature suggests that sex-role conflict per se may be the important stress factor contributing to women's alcoholism regardless of the direction (masculine or feminine) of the desired sex role identification.[11,12]

Parents and society as a whole tolerate nonstereotypic sex role behavior during childhood and adolescence in females but not in males. This latitude of behavior is allowed until the female is of marriageable age when her role becomes more stereotypically defined. Alcoholic drinking for women often begins with specific situational factors, some acute threat to her feminine adequacy such as marital or interpersonal relationship problems, a miscarriage, or children leaving home. This is not to imply that she had not been drinking, perhaps heavily, prior to this. Most likely she had, alcohol being an important part of her life and probably a major coping mechanism. The situational factor adds considerable weight in breaking her tenuous hold on controlled drinking or converting a latent or covert illness to an overt phase.

What is perceived as more rapid progression of the disease in females may be due in part to the earlier mentioned harsher judgment of women's drunkness. Alcoholism in men may seem to progress more slowly simply because society views much of his drunken behavior more benignly than that of the woman alcoholic. More rapid progression, however, will perhaps be linked in part to the differential rate that women metabolize alcohol.[13] Peak blood alcohol levels obtained with a given alcohol dose calculated on body weight are significantly higher for women than for men. Estrogen has been shown to modify this metabolic rate.

Both men and women alcoholics are isolated, but the isolation of women alcoholics differs somewhat from that of men. Except for the early stages of her disease, the alcoholic woman is rarely a "bar drinker." She prefers to do her drinking alone, whether she is a housewife or a career woman. She is aware of society's (and her own) view on drunkenness in women and she feels "safer" drinking alone. Moreover, a difficult and problematic identification with the mother (indicated by role conflict as seen in the higher scores on "femininity" scales and "masculine" oriented sex role preferences[11,12]) contributes to this extreme isolation by interfering in close relationships with other women. She becomes further isolated by either an overprotective family, friends, and community, or sometimes by a spouse who uses her alcoholism as an excuse for his extramarital affairs. If she happens to be working, her problem is dealt with by dismissal rather than confrontation. Even if her physician is willing to suggest that she may have a problem, he will often offer her valium or other psychotropic drugs as a substitute to help her with her "nerves."

TREATMENT

It has been the clinical experience of Vernell Fox, one of the authors of this chapter, that there has been, since the late 1960s, a steadily increasing number of women patients dependent upon various other sedative and anti-anxiety drugs. Currently, about two thirds of the female admissions report that they have or have recently had prescriptions for sedative or stimulant drugs. Over half have misused them to the extent of having withdrawal symptoms. The others have prolonged their "drunks" by substituting pills. About ten percent of the women seeking treatment for alcoholism are on, or have recently been taking assorted street drugs, rarely heroin, but all others currently in vogue. These are usually the younger women, and they are particularly frightened and difficult to detoxify.

In the late 1950s, Dr. Fox was Medical Director of the Georgian Clinic in Atlanta, Georgia. This treatment program for alcoholics had a fifty bed inpatient unit, ambulatory detoxification services, and a day hospital/outpatient component. It was available to all patients who would voluntarily come for services. When it became apparent that there were fewer applications for treatment by women than should be expected, even after the usual outreach efforts, it was decided to start a group for women only. Group therapy was the major treatment modality of the program. The commitment to the modality came from observations of the tremendous impact of peer pressure seen with A.A. groups, the staff's own experience with the impact of the group process on other patient populations, and the beginning appearance of reports in the literature of positive results from working with alcoholic patients in groups.

A technique of running this group gradually revolved that was somewhat different from the techniques generally used and described in the literature of that time and in subsequent years. The leader willingly assumed the dual role of teacher (sometimes of such basic issues as simple body functions) and reflector/clarifier/supporter. The leader's problems centered around being sensitive enough to discern easily which questions were based on an honest need for information and which were mechanisms for asking permission to express feelings or opinions.

The job grew easier as this open-ended group continued. Older patients, like the family's older daughters, picked up the teacher role and imparted, with added freshness and sibling authority, the required information. This made the leadership role easier. After a few years, one needed only to remain sensitive to gross or frightening psychopathology and to take over and relieve the group, as well as to provide the supportive link for new members to hold onto while entering the group, to referee occasional power struggles, and generally to serve as the attitude-setting "grandmother" for the group.

The interactions and ultimate success of this original "women's group" clearly demonstrated the essential need for meaningful peer group identity when treating any specific group, including women. Historically, treatment facilities have addressed the problems of the male alcoholic, and peer group identification was readily available for him but not for the woman.

While the majority of the group was heterosexual, some homosexual women also attended. Issues of age, socioeconomic status, race, and sexual preference came up regularly. The feelings surrounding these issues were usually curiosity and awkwardness about surfacing subjects. Occasionally, hostility and one-upmanship would abound, but it was almost always based on individual personality conflict. The group never polarized or subgrouped. There remained a basic central identity of "we are all women who are struggling for a real identity and sense of worth and a means of staying sober."

To facilitate the expression of her feelings of empathy, without confusion and resentment, the alcoholic woman must establish her autonomy, understanding both her right and her responsibility to accomplish this task. The group can lend support to this newly emerging sense of autonomy. In an all women's group, she will feel more comfortable to explore honestly and openly sensitive areas of life—sexuality, extramaritial affairs, child abuse, abortions, prostitution.

A two year followup study[14] showed that the initiation of a
women's group in the treatment process was a key factor in turning a virtual no success rate into a success rate that exceeded the
rate for men. For over ten years, Gitlow has used a leaderless
women's group as a mechanism through which to achieve an improved incidence of long-term recovery.[15]

The severe ego devaluation suffered by the alcoholic woman
can be helped by the joint efforts of the women in the group to
attempt to remove sex role stereotyping, sex bias, and double
standards. Women's groups are particularly sensitive to such
symptoms of subclinical depression as needing to please others,
not ever getting angry, and the underlying feeling of hopelessness
and helplessness—"I can't help myself; you must take care of me
and then I'll resent you for it." They learn that they are not alone
in their wants and needs.

Although it is critical that the patient's consort become involved in the recovery and growth process, experience with
women patients is that the accomplishment of this component of
treatment is especially difficult. It is often impossible to involve
the husband in the recovery process. Since they do not come in,
call or otherwise complain (as do their female counterparts attached to male patients), there are fewer opportunities to relate
spontaneously to their needs and involve them. To act through
the patient or to contact them directly presents problems. The
women often feel anxious, insecure, and concerned that he "would
not be interested" or "has already been bothered too much." The
male consorts almost universally respond with great defensiveness. In contrast to the stability of marriages between an alcoholic male and his female spouse, a vast majority of husbands
leave their alcoholic wives. After some months of treatment some
women gradually begin to disclose the relationships of their husbands' psychosexual pathology and their resistance to the patient's change, especially to the concept of their total abstinence.
In these instances, it is well to direct and support the alcoholic
woman in the necessary divorce proceedings or termination of the
destructive relationship. Again, the group can provide shared experience. Divorce, after the initiation of treatment and abstinence, tends to correlate with long-term recovery.[16,17]

Although active participation in A.A. will be an important
component in the recovery and maintenance process, some
women are especially vulnerable to seeking dependent relation-

ships with males in this group. What appears to be a familiar avenue (men) and thus a solution to her problems can often prove disastrous or at least threatening to her sobriety when there is trouble in the relationship. Dependency must be dealt with by developing and strengthening her autonomy.

Two practical problems that must be addressed by a treatment program for women are child-care and career guidance. Children can be an effective leverage to motivate the alcoholic woman into treatment, but they can also be an obstacle when there is no child-care resource available to her, particularly if she needs hospitalization for detoxification or long-term residential rehabilitation. Programs should optimally offer child-care facilities or minimally be able to suggest adequate and available community services and resources.

Since her role preferences are usually in the "masculine" direction, she must be encouraged to develop those that are pertinent to her self concept rather than made to feel that these preferences are deviant. In our society the primary way of implementing role preference is through occupation. The alcoholic woman, therefore, must be given career guidance.

Although her immediate practical needs might dictate the necessity of getting a job—any job—it would be wise to urge the patient to plan for a career. Work may be an anxiety binder, particularly since it structures time. This structuring is important for all alcoholics. If this is denied to the alcoholic woman, that is, if she goes back to the unstructured world of housework and child-care she runs a greater risk of recidivism. Back to homemaking (usually not her role preference) may then mean boredom, feelings of inadequacy, and dangerous isolation.

Recent studies[18] have shown that a career is the primary way in our culture to manifest one's self-concept. "I am a physician," really claims "I am an intelligent and caring person." Assessing abilities and strengths for career possibilities for the alcoholic woman, will counter feelings of inadequacy, confusion and low self-esteem, thereby strengthening her identity. Obviously the therapist should avoid entering "test situations" in which the effort to develop a meaningful career becomes the means by which the patient demonstrates her ultimate inadequacy.

Educational goals should be explored, whether a high school equivalency diploma, a college or a post-graduate degree. Community services and facilities (universities, community colleges, trade schools, tutoring classes, etc.) should be suggested. To avoid a dependent relationship, and to promote feelings of mastery, the patient should be given the task of calling these institutions for information.

Local public employment agencies routinely give an aptitude test (usually the Differential Aptitude Test) which can help the patient in several ways. Most colleges and universities require an entrance exam. The DAT has norms for several populations—college, adults, etc. By comparing her scores with these norms, she can get a fairly accurate idea about her chances of gaining admittance to an academic program. The DAT has subscores (verbal, math, spelling, language usage, clerical speed, analytical, mechanical, and spatial) which can indicate not only areas in need of some brush-up but also her strengths. Goals, then, can be discussed within this framework of reality. Another advantage of taking the DAT before attempting an entrance exam is that it serves as a practice exam and will thus help to lower anxiety for the entrance exam itself.

Trade schools should also be explored and used as resources. Many women today are interested in careers in the skilled trades. Unfortunately, union apprenticeship programs can have a high degree of sexism and racism. This represents one of a number of ways in which the alcoholic woman resembles the alcoholic man who is socioeconomically deprived. However, in New York City, a group of women (recovered alcoholics and narcotic addicts) learned cabinet-making, plumbing, carpentry, and electrical work through a CETA-funded program at the "All-Craft" Center and went on to open their own company, "The Mothers and Daughters Construction Company." Such opportunities should be explored in all communities.

There are two testing instruments that could be helpful for the patient who very possibly does not know what she wants to do. Both tests are take-home tasks. The Self Directed Search[19] assesses areas of personal preferences. The SDS came from empirical research on people in some 500 occupations (from actuary to zoologist). Thus, scores are keyed to careers to indicate how similar a person is to those in certain occupations, they do not, however, assess how well a person will do. This test is useful in suggesting previously unconsidered occupations. It can be helpful not only to the woman who is just starting a career but also to the alcoholic woman who had chosen her work mainly for adequate drinking time/opportunities or for equally destructive reasons.

A similar take-home assessment, the Quick Job-Hunting

Map (QJHM)[20] is broader. It evaluates skills one has and enjoys, where one wants to use those skills, as well as identifying places where one would like to work and how to get hired in one of those places. It provides a positive assessment of her skills and needs—again, within a framework of reality.

Needless to say, these testing instruments are not necessary in counseling alcoholic women in a career, but they are useful tools and help to facilitate wise decisions, decisions within which the woman has fully participated. She begins to take responsibility for herself, her life and thus build her autonomy. It should be emphasized that a skilled therapist might support the patient in undertaking a job long before she is ready for formal career choice or training. This may be accomplished while reminding her that the specific choice of a job is less important than the fact she is working and that jobs can be readily changed. An early entrance into the job market permits consideration of her personal potential in a rewarding manner and serves as a useful mechanism for exploration of her dependency needs and willingness to undertake responsibility. An early and fairly rapid improvement in her self image often results.

Unfortunately, the literature frequently quotes a few limited studies that have found that women do not do as well in treatment as men. It is gratifying to note that in a recent analysis of data collected by the NIAAA Alcoholism Treatment Monitoring System[21] the results with women patients were generally good. Experience has been that when programs address the specific needs of women with alcoholism, the women themselves reach out to other women within and without the program (the majority of women enter treatment referred by other women patients), and the prognosis for recovery of women becomes as good, or perhaps better than, their male counterparts.

REFERENCES

1. Blume SB: Diagnosis, casefinding, and treatment of alcohol problems in women. *Alcohol, Health Research World,* Fall 1978, pp. 10–20
2. NIAAA: *Alcohol and Health,* first special report to the US Congress on, from the Secretary of DHEW, GPO, 1971
3. Spalt L: Alcoholism—evidence of an X-linked regressive genetic characteristic. *JAMA* 241:23, 1979

4. Lawerence JJ, Maxwell MA: *Society, Culture and Drinking Patterns.* New York, Wiley, 1962
5. Knupfer C: Female drinking patterns. *Soc Prob* 12:224, 1964
6. Curlee J: Alcoholic women. *Bull Menniger Clinic* 31:154, 1967
7. Johnson MW: Physicians views on alcoholism with special reference to alcoholism in women. *Neb State Med J* 50:378, 1965
8. Pulkkuner MO, Csapo AI: The effect of Ibuprofen on the intrauterine pressure and menstrual pain of dysmenorrheric patients. *Prostaglandins* 15:1055−1062, 1978
9. Fox VL: Alcohol and pregnancy. Presented at Univ Utah School on Alcoholism and Other Drug Dependencies, Salt Lake City, Utah, June 1978
10. Ouellette EM, Rossett HL, Rosman NP, Weiner AB: Adverse effects on offspring of maternal alcohol abuse during pregnancy. *N Eng J Med* 297:528−530, 1977
11. Wilsnak SC: The impact of sex role on women's use and abuse, in Greenblatt M, Schukitt MS (eds): *Alcoholism Problems in Women and Children.* New York, Grune and Stratton Inc., 1976, pp 37−63
12. Scida J, Vannicelli M: Sex role conflict and drinking. *J Stud Alcohol* 40:1, 1979
13. Jones BM, Jones MK: Women and alcohol: Intoxification, metabolism and the menstrual cycle, in Greenblatt M, Schukitt MA (eds): *Alcoholism Problems in Women and Children.* New York, Grune and Stratton Inc., 1976, pp 103−136
14. Fox VL, Smith M: Evaluation of a chemotherapeutic program for the rehabilitation of alcoholics. *J Stud Alcohol* 20:4, 1959
15. Gitlow SE: Personal correspondence
16. Knott D: Personal correspondence
17. Gitlow SE: Personal correspondence
18. Super DE: *The Psychology of Careers.* New York, Harper and Row, 1957
19. Holland JL: *Self directed search.* Palo Alto, California, Consulting Psychologists Press, 1974
20. Bolles RN: QJHM, National Career Develop. Project, Berkeley, California, 1975
21. Women in treatment for alcoholism: A profile, Abstract of Accession, # NCA 1028327, Feb. 1977

Marvin D. Feit

10
Problems Peculiar to Patients of Low Socioeconomic Status

This chapter is designed to orient the physician to the management of low-socioeconomic-status patients who present a clinical picture of alcoholism. Upper- and middle-class patients usually present a resource-positive environment often compatible with the physician's personal background. Therefore it is quite easy for physicians to relate to these patients, to perhaps understand the presenting problems, and to develop traditional plans utilizing such patient resources as money, employment or marketable skills, and the support of family members.

The low-socioeconomic-status patients are a class of economically poor patients composed largely of minorities—blacks, hispanics, Native Americans, poor whites, and others. These patients are typically quite different in lifestyle from the physician, come from and have different cultures, have virtually no money and practically no hope for long-term employment, are perhaps limited in formal schooling, and may have obscure family relationships.

These patients present special problems to the physician. Prescriptions and treatment plans often don't work. The patients are people with whom the physician is not only unfamiliar but who possess characteristics so different as to potentially arouse fear and distrust within the physician. June Christmas notes that

ALCOHOLISM
ISBN 0-8089-1227-5

Copyright © 1980 by Grune & Stratton
All rights of reproduction in any form reserved.

Table 10-1
Problems in Management of the
Low-Socioeconomic-Status Patient

Estrangement and distrust in the therapeutic relationships (experiential
     differences → inability to identify with one another → fear)
   Within patient
   Within physician

Low resources
   Lack of funds for treatment precludes certain services (private medical
     care, many inpatient rehabilitation facilities, etc.)
   Lack of basic literacy, schooling, and job skills with which to find a
     place in the dominant culture, should such be desired.
   Lack of opportunities for establishing ego strength, identity, and
     self-respect within the culture (work, housing, acceptance of culture
     variations, etc.)
   Debilitating results stemming from the required assistance programs
     (welfare, etc.)
   Lack of support by family members possessing the above resources

---

in such an atmosphere, professional despair, combined with a
cultural connotation of chronicity, often defines the situation as
inevitably hopeless.[1] In addition, patients bring to the therapeutic situation their own anxiety and distrust, compounding the
alienation. See Table 10-1.

MANAGEMENT

There are ways physicians can manage low-socioeconomic-
status patients. First, they have to recognize that the patient has
a drinking problem; second, that the patient is different from the
physician; and third, that the patient might require a different
approach. Each of these—defining the diagnosis, therapeutic arrangement, and treatment approach—will present problems
specific for this group of patients. The physician's approach not
only must take these circumstances into consideration but must
do so in a unified and integrated manner for greatest success.
Every patient is unique, and treatment requires that the
therapist identify this uniqueness. The problem in this group is
the therapeutic distance from the patients, physician difference

from them, and physician inability to see the unique qualities of patients that are so different from his own. The physician cannot use his own background and frame of reference for understanding and empathy here.

Problem Detection and Recognition

The methods noted in Chapters 1 and 2 pertain to these patients as well.

Physicians need to develop their listening skills when working with alcoholics; this is particularly necessary with low-socioeconomic-status patients. Quite often these patients are suspicious of formal institutions in a white, upper- and middle-class-dominated society, having experienced rejection or embarrassment one or more times. They often won't admit problems in formal institutions to physicians or other helpers who do not deal with them as individuals in their own right. Often these patients are outwardly compliant, say all the right things, and appear motivated when just the opposite is actually happening. Detecting double messages and hidden agendas and assessing the extent to which a patient "owns a problem" (i.e., accepts that he is indeed an alcoholic) requires the development of listening skills. Basically one has to listen to patients rather than tell them what to do.

The art of modifying learned cultural distrust by a correcting experience with the therapist is limited by several factors, one of which is the usefulness of such distrust—its defensive and protective aspects. The "niceness" on the part of the therapist may merely convince patients that the doctor is trying to manipulate them; they then feel threatened rather than convinced and will flee at the first advance. The physician *must not try to get so very close to the patient too quickly,* but must feel the way slowly, with patience and with respect for the differences between them.

Shift in Approach

Although all patients pass through stages of ambivalence regarding their desires to stop drinking and thereby change the very fabric of their lives (e.g., fearing loss of friends, activities, sometimes families and careers), it is usually possible to convince them of the disproportionate benefits likely to accrue from abstinence. Socioeconomically deprived patients, however, present a quantitatively different problem in that giving up alcohol and its related activities may involve social and human loss with relatively modest concomitant gain. For example, for many patients the world consists only of friends who drink, and they move within a system that includes hospitals, jails, flophouses, or single-room-occupancy (SRO) hotels. In this system, patients receive security, warmth, food, personal recognition, and attention to basic needs at critical moments. Not only does life without alcohol seem no better or even worse for these patients than life with alcohol, but the physician may also be unable to appreciate a clearcut advantage to abstaining. No physician who lacks such a conviction is likely to convince a patient of the need for sobriety. Such belief, easy with better-endowed patients, is especially difficult with the economically deprived. The doctor must therefore formulate for such patients realistic and achievable aims that represent clear and self-evident improvements.

Physicians, then, must be able to view the individual operating in a social context that is usually quite different from that which they know and with which they are familiar. In order to achieve this view, physicians must begin to ask more appropriate questions. For example, in the case of a "career" drinker it might be possible to identify people to whom the patient responds, such as certain policemen or room clerks. In any event, this individual's situation may not appear as hopeless as it first seems.

The Cultural Context

There are other areas of concern that might be useful for physicians to explore. One should minimally inquire about the individual's past experience in dealing with formal institutions, what he sees as problematic in relation to drinking and in life itself, what is acceptable and unacceptable drinking behavior in his culture and environment, how he feels about seeking help, and how he has arrived at the present situation or the "pathways" to treatment. This should not be interpreted as implying that the physician should utilize any psychodynamics so discovered in an early attempt to encourage intellectualization. Such an effort commonly diverts attention from the primary task of dealing with the drinking to the more "acceptable" one of an intellectual discussion requiring little, if any, change. Understanding the patient's illness is of value only insofar as (1) it increases the strength of the relationship between the patient and physician (therapeutic alliance), (2) it helps the doctor discover what actions may be needed for intervention, and (3) it may help the physician determine the most effective means for increasing motivation (i.e., exerting therapeutic leverage).

Identification of the "pathways" to treatment can often serve to clarify the resources available to individuals and, in turn, suggest points of intervention in a treatment process. Usually these resources require physicians to look beyond their understanding of the formal or classical network of services. One cannot separate medical management from the milieu in which low-socioeconomic-status patients live or survive. For these patients, physician contact in formal institutions may be used only after their familiar network resources are exhausted. Native Americans, for instance, generally arrive in the mainstream health care system only after thinking through themselves, going next to their immediate families, then to the extended family (cousins, aunts, uncles) and social network, to the religious leader, and to the tribal council.[2] Effective management with Native Americans might necessitate continued communication as well as involving other Native Americans from the patients' own health care orientation, such as tribal leaders or healers ("medicine men"). A similar approach would need to be followed for other individuals with similarly specific characteristics.

In a cultural context, concepts vary and have different meanings and connotations to those involved. Consider the concept of family. The type of family studied most in America is the nuclear family, consisting of two partners and their children. This definition is inappropriate when applied to many of the ethnic and cultural groups comprising most of the low-socioeconomic-status patient category. For example, the one-parent family is today a rather significant part of American society, while Native Americans have a very broad definition of family, often with as many as 200 members, since they consider the extended family (aunts, uncles, cousins, grandparents, and so forth) and accept all born into such a family as full members. "Illegitimacy" and "orphan" are terms that in general mean nothing to Native Americans. Many blacks and hispanics also tend to see the family as different from the nuclear concept of family most typically taught to professionals. Socioeconomically-deprived patients do indeed have families, but they are usually different from what physicians and other professionals are often taught. Once such families are identified, physicians will be quick to recognize that the familiar functions provided by all families will be present.

Locating individuals in their cultural context is therefore an essential component of managing low-socioeconomic-status patients. It is imperative that the helper know the culture and history of the patients, since they represent their resource-positive environments from which emerge the strengths physicians can build upon in the treatment process. Although this circumstance is universally true, the physician's own experience allows ready access to the cultural information about patients whose backgrounds are similar to his own (by identification); such is often untrue in regard to the socioeconomically deprived patient. The helper must not assume such awareness but must rather question the validity of initial interpretations. These patients must be viewed in relation to their own distinctive problems and not in a stereotypic and predictable manner. For example, "Latin machismo, the coping strengths of black women, and Native American adolescent strivings for consciousness of [tribal] heritage may not apply to each individual within his or her respective minority group, or may be manifest in ways that differ so widely that to be content with a label or slogan is to deprive the person of individuality."[1]

Treatment Planning

Development of a treatment plan is another area that can be used advantageously in patient management. Physicians might enlist the aid of patients in this process by asking them to identify their problems and how they think these problems may be resolved or alleviated. Here is a moment when physicians can test the reality awareness of their patients by assessing and discussing the extent to which patients can achieve their own goals. Moreover, physicians can use this time to ask patients how they and other helpers may be useful to them. This technique would be valuable in helping patients make better use of physician services.

It is important for physicians to explore the nature of the problem(s) presented by patients. Frequently professionals accept patient statements only to learn later that such statements may be inaccurate and not helpful. One should not easily accept a patient's view as not being able to obtain a job as the reason for drinking if past data and a few questions suggest that the patient has no real history of employment and has no apparent marketable skills. Yet a job to such a patient may in fact be possible to obtain—bearing in mind that a physician may see a job as consisting of a high degree of stability, full time and with regular hours, and with a regular income, but to the patient a "job" may mean securing odd jobs, much part-time work, hustling, and a host of other things, legal and illegal. Asking such questions as how one manages one's time and how one "makes it" financially allows patients to provide clear pictures of themselves in their own environment.

Treatment plans should perhaps be viewed not as prescriptions to be followed routinely but as growth documents against which patients can measure their achievements from time to time. It should be recognized that a treatment plan developed at one time probably will need to be modified or changed several times in the course of treatment. Physicians must accept that alcoholism, as a chronic relapsing illness, may run a recovery course replete with recidivistic complications that must be anticipated. The patient should be aware of the cost and potential dangers of such "slips," but a constructive plan for dealing with them might avoid excessive loss or demoralization with treatment. In other words, discuss with the patient the difficulties that emerge in the treatment process and what alternatives might be available to him.

A major consideration in developing a treatment plan is the recognition that gross cerebral changes may occur with chronic alcohol abuse (whether through trauma, avitaminosis, or toxicity of ethanol). Frequently these changes are not demonstrated by the mental status examination or traditional psychometric techniques. The cortical deficits produced by chronic alcohol abuse are similar to the effects of aging or presenile dementia, which means that complex integrative functions would be impaired initially whereas simple sensory and motor functions and familiar learned patterns used over a lifetime would be retained until more severe stages of degeneration are reached. If alcohol use results in significant cortical damage as indicated by some research findings, it is possible that it may represent the source of loss of impulse control, inability to abstain from alcohol consumption, and difficulty in adjusting to a new psychosocial ambience. The reversibility of the alcohol-related cerebral dysfunction is ill defined, but evaluation suggests that at least 1 year of abstinence is essential for this process. It is necessary to appreciate the overt and subtle organicity that exists in this population: unrealistic expectations may only lead to a behavioral decompensation and readdiction, and abstinence from alcohol and adequate nutrition are the bases for treatment.

By their very label, low-socioeconomic-status patients present themselves as obviously in need of financial support. Such patients are usually referred to the state Department of Human Services, formerly called the Welfare Department, and if they meet the eligibility requirements for one of the various financial assistance programs they can receive monthly allotments.

The physician is generally not involved in establishing patient eligibility for Federal or state financial assistance programs; however, it is extremely important for physicians to understand some inherent strains on effective treatment plans and take appropriate steps with their patients. In effect, the social, psychological, and financial support systems of low-socioeconomic-status patients generally do not enhance the goals of the treatment plan. The usual treatment plan emphasizes support of a program aimed toward development of self-reliance and thereby self-esteem. This is not limited to retraining and other direct measures. Even that paramount therapeutic principle dealing with formulation of critical interpersonal relationships (see Chapter 7) serves ideally to promote such growth. The unresolved and problematic question is whether or not the development of a close therapeutic community and specific (narrow) societal relationships can result in self-esteem in the presence of continued dependence upon a "welfare system."

Treatment programs that address themselves also to improving the self-image of alcoholic individuals have a better chance of communicating effectively with their clientele. Such efforts need to be expanded, since these programs typically encourage patient participation in some form of social action. Physicians working in this atmosphere are often called upon to participate or to lead social political activities. The issue of whether or not such activity is appropraite for physicians depends on the setting, the administrators, the physicians themselves, and the patients. There is probably nothing worse than well-intentioned people acting inappropriately and missing the target.

Further, much research is needed to determine in which treatment programs low-socioeconomic-status patients recover best. For example, politically and socially active treatment programs may communicate effectively with their clientele, but to what extent does this improved communication result in greater patient sobriety? This and other questions suggest how much more knowledge needs to be obtained about a favorable response to rehabilitative efforts by alcoholic patients in general and low-socioeconomic-status patients specifically.

There are self-help treatment programs where professional help is not involved. Alcoholics Anonymous (A.A.) and the Nation of Islam are two such groups that involve peer assistance and improving one's self-image. Physicians have traditionally had a referral alliance with A.A. but not with other groups such as the religiously oriented Nation of Islam. Whereas A.A. often lacks appeal in poor and black communities, this latter group reports much therapeutic success and attributes it to the individual's conversion or change to a completely different way of life. Individual motivation and commitment to alter an existing lifestyle should never be minimized, and self-help treatment programs provide the atmosphere where such change can take place. Physicians can explore with their patients use of self-help treatment groups but must themselves be capable of understanding the life situation of patients and be able to recommend the more nontraditional helping group.

Organizational Support

Managing the low-socioeconomic-status patient must also include the development of supports external to the patient–physician relationship for the physician to be most effective. Physicians may rarely provide treatment by themselves for this group of patients. As part of a multidisciplinary team, and certainly as the key member, the physician ought to be quite vocal in ensuring the employment of highly trained and skilled counselors. Poor counseling can quickly undermine the developing patient relationship. One must keep in mind the past experiences of these patients to note their acute susceptibility to rejection and embarrassment. Just one negative situation may be all that is necessary for patient withdrawal to occur.

First contacts of any kind for low-socioeconomic-status patients are crucial in the treatment process. Intake may be one small part of the total program from the physician's perspective, but for the patients it is a time filled with extreme anxiety. How they are treated at intake often establishes how they perceive the staff and the program. It is often helpful for patients to see people with similar backgrounds during this phase of treatment.

Patient management is a responsibility of any physician. Clinical intervention by other professionals should proceed with the physician's being aware of what is happening to the patient. This is to suggest that simple referral to other professionals does not achieve effective patient management with this population. Low-socioeconomic-status patients can respond to physicians provided that they demonstrate an understanding of them, can determine their course of treatment, and ensure proper care. Indeed, these patients tend to regard a physician's words as extremely powerful and continually need to know that the physician is in control of the treatment process.

Physicians ought to be vocal in stating their need to be supported with a diverse staff. It is often comforting to patients to see people with similar ethnic and racial identities employed at all levels. Native Americans in Minnesota indicated a preference for securing health services from Native American workers.[3] They demonstrated this preference in the Minneapolis–St. Paul "Twin Cities" metropolitan area in relying upon Native American service agencies, while nontribal health agencies located in the same community were continuously involved in strategies to recruit Native American clients.[4]

Staff development or training programs must become integral parts of treatment programs. Regular meetings of the staff, physicians, nurses, and counselors with varying social, ethnic, health, and economic backgrounds must permit candid discussions of not only the patients' but the staff personnel's relationships and feelings toward one another. Such staff activities need to be conducted on a regular basis with content being derived from the population served. For example, "pathways" to treatment and the community services that do exist for low-socioeconomic-status patients can be covered and would probably need to be updated periodically. Also, the resources within local communities, such as unions, houses of worship, and social clubs, ought to be involved in the training of staff and in developing more creative treatment situations.

CONCLUSION

Management of low-socioeconomic-status patients usually presents physicians with special problems. On one hand, the medical procedures, techniques, and diagnosis are the same as with all patients; on the other hand, low-socioeconomic-status patients are unique in that their lifestyles, values, culture, coping patterns, and norms are often quite different from those of the physician. Hence traditional treatment planning is not effective, and physicians have to do things differently in order to effect better management of these patients. Several suggestions were offered both in the context of the patient–physician relationship and in the organizational support system around the physician as a key member of the multidisciplinary team. Physicians must be aware that clinical interventions have powerful social and political consequences for their patients and should adopt a treatment protocol that accounts for this awareness. Effective management would allow low-socioeconomic-status patients far greater involvement in and exposure to the mainstream health care system, from which one could anticipate opportunities to yield more significant results with a population too often seen as hopeless.

REFERENCES

1. Christmas J. Alcoholism services for minorities: Training issues and concerns. *Alcohol Health Res World* 2 (3): 22–27, 1978

2. Red Horse J, Lewis R, Feit M, et al: Family behavior of urban American Indians. *Social Casework* 25 (2): 67–72, 1978
3. DeGeyndt W. Health behavior and health needs in urban Indians in Minneapolis. *Health Serv Rep* 88:360–366, 1973
4. Red Horse J, Feit D: Urban Native American preventive health care. Paper presented at the American Public Health Association Meeting, Miami Beach, October 1976

James A. Knight

11
The Family in the Crisis of Alcoholism

The story of alcoholism is the story of miscarried repair—a backfiring of the effort at maintaining equilibrium in one's life. While drinking to solve some problem, attain some goal, or accomplish some purpose however major or minor, the person creates through the agent that he uses a problem greater than the original one.

Although knowledge of the causes and treatment of alcoholism remain limited, this knowledge is sufficient to encourage programs in prevention and treatment. It is often forgotten how frequently in the past major diseases were controlled with only fragments of knowledge. A good example is the control of cholera. This disease was prevalent in London in 1854. A careful epidemiologic study of the cholera patients by Dr. John Snow identified one common denominator among them: their use of drinking water from the Broad Street Pump. A rapid decline of the cases occurred after the pump had been removed. Although some living microorganism in the water was suspected as the causative agent by Snow in 1854, this was before the days of bacteriology. The causative agent, *Vibrio cholerae,* was not identified until 1883 by Robert Koch—29 years after Snow closed the pump and well on Broad Street and ended the 1854 epidemic of cholera. This example is cited only to show how absurd are the

205

ALCOHOLISM
ISBN 0-8089-1227-5

Copyright © 1980 by Grune & Stratton
All rights of reproduction in any form reserved.

critics of many health programs who proclaim that little can be done until the total truth is known about an illness.

There is an old axiom about the family that describes it as an autocracy ruled by its sickest member. One may ask how the sick member attained such a role in the family. In studying illness, among the questions one must ask is what does this illness tell about the family from whick this sick person comes? Life is filled with examples of families who have chosen one member to be sick or a scapegoat or a clown. At times, an individual family member chooses voluntarily to be sick in order to save the family. Usually the situation is less dramatic, with problems being brought by one or both partners in a marriage or with problems growing out of the marital interaction. When children come along, the family matrix may be such that it becomes productive of either health or disease. When confronted with an alcoholic patient, the therapist who asks what this illness tells about the family from which the alcoholic comes and who looks vigorously for answers will have begun the therapy of both the alcoholic and the family.

In discussing alcoholism in the family, there has been a tendency to think only of spouse or parent as the alcoholic, with little thought given to teenage sons and daughters as problem drinkers. In the United States there is an increasing incidence of new young drinkers. With an increasing prevalence of teenage drinking, there will be an increasing incidence and prevalence of teenage alcoholism.

While impulsivitiy characterizes much adolescent behavior, teenagers do attempt to learn self-control. In their efforts to attain maturity and independence and to work out their own philosophies of life, they rebel against most external controls, structure, or authority. Thus teenagers are a very susceptible population for alcohol use or abuse and the subsequent loss of impulse control. Therefore they may bring to the family the crisis of alcoholism with the same frightening fervor as that of an alcholic parent or spouse. With the increasing availability of alcoholic beverages to youngsters, the problem of teenage alcoholism promises to grow substantially. Prevention and early intervention hold greater promise than treatment. It is not easy to entice teenagers into treatment with professionals whom they view as authority figures.

PSYCHODYNAMIC CAUSATION IN ALCOHOLISM

In an effort to understand the family in the crisis of alcoholism, the therapist must have some understanding of psychodynamic causation in alcoholism. The theories of causation can be broken down into a number of categories.

1. The Freudian view contends that alcoholism results from one or more of three unconscious tendencies: self-destruction, oral dependency, or latent homosexuality.
2. Close to the Freudian view is the concept that alcoholism develops as a response to inner conflict between dependency drives and aggressive impulses.
3. Sharing much in common with the above theoretical views is the Adlerian view that alcoholism represents a striving for power that compensates for a pervasive feeling of inferiority. Alcoholic persons turn to alcohol to enhance their feelings of self-esteem and prowess.

David McClelland, the motivational psychologist, and his associates have extended the Adlerian theory in their research and have declared that the abuse of alcohol by many is motivated by unfulfilled power needs.[1] McClelland and his associates suggest that frustrated ambitions may play a role in the development of an alcohol problem. It is suggested that alcoholics may have enhanced needs for power but find themselves inadequate to achieve their goals. They resort to alcohol because it provides a sense of release and power and feelings of achievement. Since overindulgence in alcohol precludes an effective coping with the problems needing solution and leads to additional problems, this vicious cycle results in confirmed alcoholism.

Thus when persons provide themselves with drugs such as alcohol that change their pain to pleasure, depression to elation or an increase in self-esteem, impotence to omnipotence, the first step in addiction has occurred. This sudden change from frustration to gratification can be reminiscent of the experience of childhood when the mother attempts to keep the baby's frustration to a minimum by anticipating and gratifying all wishes. A little cry from the baby immediately brings everybody in the environment to identifying and responding to the baby's wishes. It is this regression, a return to the state of security and freedom from fear, that revives the old childhood wishes that never die. This is the latent and universal wish in the individual—to be taken care of and mothered.[2,3] The fact that alcohol can bring such a wish fulfillment is illustrated in such statements as, "Now I am not afraid of anything or anyone." "I can do anything I wish." "Nothing can happen to me."

With theories and psychodynamics in mind, one factor stands at the forefront: alcoholism is self-destructive behavior or at least represents a self-destructive tendency. Alcoholics appear to be willing actively, consciously, unconsciously, and repeatedly to damage themselves. The self-destructive drinking is a deliberate, strategic maneuver to accomplish certain ends. Exploration to find out what these are is a major part of the therapeutic endeavor.

According to Aristotle, the plot of a good tragedy contains three parts: prologue, climax, and catastrophe. These three stages correspond to the onset, course, and outcome of the disease of alcoholism. The prologue in the alcoholic's life may be childhood and the development of certain personality traits or a self-destructive lifestyle. The climax is the period in adulthood when the alcoholic struggles against the control of the developing illness and the loss of autonomy. The battle is between two forces— the self-destructive tendency and the wish to avoid the catastrophe. The climax yields, often suddenly, to the catastrophe, when the person relaxes the battle against the self-destructive tendency and surrenders to the bondage of alcoholism.

FAMILY DYNAMICS

Role Assignment or the Projection Process

All kinds of role assignments are made in families in order to make a family member appear to be someone different from who he is or to serve some particular purpose in the family.[4] This is a

fascinating aspect of family dynamics and enhances our understanding of both illness and health in a family. As has already
been mentioned, families choose a member to be sick, to hold the
marriage together, to be the black sheep, clown, or scapegoat. We
do not understand the many complicated factors that determine
whether a given family member accepts the designated role,
fights it, internalizes it, pretends to accept it, flees from it, or is in
conflict with it. Some symptoms are developed as a function of
efforts to escape the role assignment and others as reflections of
the designations. Some symptoms are manifested only within the
family culture, while others come into play only outside the family. A family member is often heard to say, "When I am not with
my family, I am an entirely different person."

Also, the family projection process can diagnose, classify,
and assign characteristics to certain family members. A wife may
label her husband (a moderate drinker) as alcoholic. The wife's
label is accepted by the children and transmitted to the grand-
children. The concept described here should be kept in mind when
working with the alcoholic and family. The illness may contribute
profoundly to both the family's equilibrium and disequilibrium.

Role Reversals in the Family

Karpman writes that only three roles are necessary in
drama analysis to depict the emotional reversals that are
drama—Persecutor, Rescuer, and Victim.[5] Drama begins when
these roles are established or anticipated. The real drama relates
to the switch in the roles. Fairy tales are simple but excellent
examples of the switching in action roles. Think of Cinderella,
Little Red Riding Hood, or the Pied Piper. The Pied Piper begins
as Rescuer of the city and Persecutor of the rats. He then becomes
Victim of the Persecutor mayor's doublecross (fee withheld) and
in revenge switches to the Persecutor of the city's children. The
mayor switches from Victim (of rats) to Rescuer (hiring the Pied
Piper) to Persecutor (doublecross) to Victim (his children dead).
The children switch from Persecuted Victims (by rats) to rescued
Victims to Victims Persecuted by their Rescuer.

Think now of the family in which the illness of alcoholism
resides in one or more of its members. Picture the numerous cir-

cumstances or changes that precipitate a role reversal. Most likely the alcoholic will switch periodically from victim to rescuer to persecutor—and likewise there will be reversals in the roles of the other members of the family, especially the spouse. Also, there will be reversals in the role of the therapist.

Do Alcoholics' Self-destructive Lifestyles Originate in their Early Years in their Families?

The alcoholic in his drinking behavior is following a self-destructive path. How one tries to determine why the alcoholic is self-destructive will depend on one's conceptual framework and therapeutic persuasion. It is tempting to believe that the alcoholic's lifestyle is the living out of a parental injunction or message from in childhood, such as, "Don't be," or, "Don't be important," or, "Don't belong." Of course, there are many ways of being self-destructive; thus a number of other factors contribute to the use of alcohol when it is chosen as the agent of self-destruction.

The parental message brings to mind a patient who sought help because he was hearing voices. There were two voices—a male and a female. The male voice usually spoke harshly to him and commanded him to do something detrimental to himself, such as, "Step in front of that moving car." The male and female voices often spoke to one another. If the male voice said, "Let's kill the son-of-a-bitch," the female voice would advise caution, "We better not; we could get into big trouble." While the male voice was openly hostile and destructive, the female voice generally cautioned restraint, not for the patient's sake but for their own protection. The patient found relief from these voices by reading the Bible. He would read until he came to an especially powerful verse. At that point the voices would scream, "Let's get the hell out of here before we get into trouble." This patient was an alcoholic, which he was slow in revealing. He had a bout of "intestinal flu" and could take essentially nothing by mouth for several days, including alcohol. By the time he recovered from the "flu," he was hallucinating. A review of his family history revealed that his mother was pregnant with him at the time of marriage. His parents did not want him and communicated this message to him throughout his years of dependency on them. Further exploration identified many other traits, and the family sources of these, seen frequently in alcoholics.

This patient's case history is mentioned only to raise the issue of when and where the alcoholic's self-destructive lifestyle originated and to encourage the therapist to look at the family as the possible source. Of course, why alcohol is chosen as an instrument to feed the self-destructive tendency deserves continued study. No single factor will emerge in answer to the *why*. Availability of alcohol, family and subculture's attitudes toward alcohol, personality makeup, aspirations, and numerous significant life history events are among the relevant variables.

General Systems Model

General systems theory is having considerable impact today on group and family therapy. The systems approach conceives of the individual as a dynamic system in constant interaction with an ever-changing environment.

Altering the family system, and hence the transactions between the persons (subsystems) who are part of the larger system, results in changes in the individual. Thus change at any point in the system may well affect any or all of its components. In other words, transactions within the family system are major determinants of individual behavior. Also, a change in the functioning of one family member is automatically followed by a compensatory change in another family member.

Much of the alcoholic's behavior and symptoms are products of family processes, which influence and are influenced by each family member's intrapsychic dynamics. Accordingly, processes and changes in the family, rather than insights alone, are seen as the major change-producing agents, although techniques for achieving such change vary greatly.

Thus the general systems model considers the alcoholic and his symptoms as part of communication within social systems (like the family or other units). The alcoholic may be seen as playing a symptomatic role that the family needs. Individual diagnosis may be a stigma that once stated or publicized immediately effects a change in family relationships, or it may constitute a self-fulfilling prophecy, thereby becoming part of treatment rather than merely of evaluation.

THERAPY WITH THE FAMILY

Combinations of individual and group therapy—involving many types of therapies—have proven to be effective in the treatment of alcoholics and their families. Space does not permit a discussion of these modalities or the new developments in them as described in books such as *Progress in Group and Family Therapy,* edited by Sager and Kaplan.[6]

If the alcoholic is married and has children, in each stage of recovery the interactions with spouse and children change. At times these interactions become so complex and intense that the members of the family not only expect, but almost seem to wish, that the alcoholic would resume drinking. This phenomenon is more easily understood if one views alcoholism in the conceptual framework of transactional analysis: alcoholism is a game, and a game requires several players in order to be sustained.[7] The spouse and children of the alcoholic, participating at some level in the alcoholic's behavioral patterns, feel a vacuum in their lives when the alcoholic stops drinking, equal to that felt by the alcoholic. Thus alcoholics in families may feel even stronger urges to drink because, in addition to their own internal proclivities, they will feel the pressures applied from the families. Since treatment of married alcoholics requires bringing about change in two or more people, it may appear at times that single alcoholics have better prognoses in treatment. This added burden of treatment by the presence of a family is usually overshadowed, however, by the positive influence that families are able to provide. While thinking at times that a certain alcoholic might profit by a separation or divorce because of the difficulties mentioned above, one usually finds that if this difficulty is worked through, the family is a great adjunct to the patient's health as a source for fulfillment of many needs and as a basis for existential meaning.

Initial Approaches with the Family

The health of each member of the alcoholic's family should be checked. Any member of the family could be physically or emotionally ill.

All family members should make in-depth appraisals of

themselves, their positions in the family, and the character of relationships within the family.

Discuss without delay the family's drinking problem. Find out how it affects each member of the family and how the individual members of the family and the family as a whole affect the alcoholic's drinking.

Try to identify the strengths in the family and help the family mobilize these strengths in a positive direction.

Honestly examine one's own feelings and attitudes about drinking, drunkenness, and the family. The therapist's value system should not dictate the goals for the family, but the therapist can help the family identify and clarify its own goals.

The task of therapy is to create an environment for change, an environment where each family member can make a decision to change his life, to act the part of an autonomous person.

The therapist is an expert in human behavior disturbance and its remedy. With the family in the crisis of alcoholism, the therapist should be *active* in helping all family members discover their problems. (One can overdo the technique of letting patients discover their own problems.) Self-discovery can be awfully slow at times. Why not identify the problems of the family and its members as quickly as possible and get to work on them.

Therapy with the Family Unit

Since the patient's illness is often symptomatic of family psychopathology, some of the problems are more easily worked through with the total family unit rather than on an individual or couple basis. Family therapy is a growing area for exploration. Many clinicians have found that individual therapy can be accelerated by complementary conjoint family therapy. Although the members of the family indicate that they want the patient to get well, "well" means different things to the patient, to the relatives, and to the staff. Often the concept of being well on the part of the relatives means that the patient is to function much like a puppet, carrying out both the expressed and the unexpressed wishes of the family members without observable behavioral eructation. The family may see the hospital or clinic role to solidify and replaster the quality of relative–patient fusion as it was prior to the alcoholic disorder. Also, there may exist a common delusion, shared by both the patient and the family and reinforced by years of living together, that emotional separation and growth can lead only to eventual destruction.

In the treatment of the alcoholic and family, the therapist must not forget the axiom about family dynamics mentioned above: "A family is an autocracy ruled by its sickest member." The situations in which one family member is put forth as the ostensible patient are really special cases in which the real patient may be reluctant to ask for help or to face what is bothering him. Thus the patient seeks help in a disguised and more acceptable way. While the request or call for help is the essential feature of a person's becoming a patient, it is a call that is often muted, disguised, or alloyed with ambivalence. One of the oldest techniques for a family to get help is to choose, and offer as the patient a family scapegoat, with the hope, often unconscious, that the scapegoat will lead the therapist back to the sick family.

Treatment of Couples

Because of the factors previously emphasized, group therapy with married couples has proven to be quite an effective treatment modality.[8] In such treatment programs the goals are (1) penetration of the patient's severe denial mechanism in association with the goal of abstinence, and (2) helping the couple to develop a satisfactory living experience in their marriage. In group meetings the "here and now" approach to treatment is greatly emphasized. Honest, direct impressions of other patients in the group are consistently requested of the couples. These involve opinions regarding improvement, attitudes toward spouse, identification of destructive or constructive behavior, and so on.

Group therapy involving married couples is usually successful because of a number of factors. The spouse of the patient helps in "pulling" the patient back to treatment, and the dropout rate is lower as a result of the spouse's cooperation. (Neither the patient nor the spouse can say, "I am the only one who is trying in the marriage.") There is a common goal of abstinence to unify the group. (After abstinence, the next goal is to have the couples work on their marital problems.) Both therapists and group members get a more realistic view of the home life of each participant by observing the marital interactions, verbal and nonverbal communications as well as feelings and mood. The therapists and group can refuse to accept the distortions of both husband and wife and thereby aid in the correction of the neurotic interaction. The initial neurotic needs that may have attracted the partners to each other in the hope of gratifying dependent or narcissistic tendencies can now be faced and treated in an open manner. With both marital partners present, minor bickering is eliminated and the crucial and urgent problems of the couple are directly faced. In individual therapy, minor bickering can consume the greater part of therapy, consisting usually of perpetual complaints about the spouse. All of the expected problems assocaited with recovery emerge in the group discussions and can be dealt with effectively and together.

In the group one often sees the psychodynamics of the spouse unfold in dramatic self-relevation. One gets a new appreciation of the spouse types such as the parental type or "mama or papa with sex," the managerial type, the martyr, the child type, the rescuer, etc. Let us look at some of these types as manifested by female partners, although they apply equally well to males.

The motherly type is competitive with her own mother and guilty about her femininity and about expressing it. This probably grows out of an old oedipal conflict in which she competed with her mother for the love and attention of the father. At the same time, she can offer sex plus what every mother usually offers. The motherly type is a controlling type who creates exactly the kind of home she wants, although it may be quite different from what her husband or children want. In the novel *The Pleasure of His Company* by Samuel Taylor and Cornelia Otis Skinner, Mackenzie Savage, the father, is quizzed by his daughter: "You were never very happy with Mother, were you?" He replies, "Your mother was a saint, who made our home an outpost of heaven. It's why I spent so much time in saloons."

The managerial type dominates every aspect of the marriage. (At other times she is forced to be managerial because of her husband's alcoholism.) The marriage may be only a vehicle for expressing the wife's distrustful, resentful attitudes toward men in general. In her view of life, men have the advantages. Why risk marrying one over whom you do not have some advantage? Therefore her husband's ineptitude is not only acceptable but even gratifying—up to a point. This type of woman often marries a person she perceives as inadequate, a cripple. She tends to be coldly angry in presenting her complaints about her husband's problems, and there is a quality of hardness and unforgivingness in her manner of expressing criticisms. Such a woman rejects her femininity, is distrustful of human relationships, and grasps for advantage or superior position in all her dealings with the world around her. When a therapist looks beneath the surface of this type of woman, he sees her fearfulness, her anxiety, and her strong dependency needs. When she feels secure with the therapist, she musters the courage to examine her feelings.

The martyr type is actually a sadomasochistic person. The masochistic side of the wife suffers the spouse's alcoholism. The sadistic tendencies in the same type of wife cause her to strike out at the alcoholic when he is drunk. Thus the wife is someone to scold him when he is bad, to think and plan for him when he is puzzled, to extricate him from his binges, and, above all, to worry and suffer over him.

The child-wife may be young chronologically or emotionally. Since both partners may be children emotionally, they cannot fulfill one another's needs.

The rescuer type of wife will be found among those women who repeatedly choose alcoholic, impotent, or unfaithful husbands. In many of these women, there is the history of an alcoholic father. On analysis it becomes clear that the unconscious goal of the marriage was to cure the father's alcoholism in effigy, thus winning back the lost affection of the alcoholic father, while proving at the same time that she could do a better job than the mother. The need to rescue may have other dimensions, as seen in the play *Brigadoon*.[9] Two friends are wandering in an enchanted wood where a lost city appears on one night each 100 years. They pause to rest, and a conversation ensues:

Jeff: Maybe we took the high road instead of the low road. *(Takes a flask from his inside pocket.)* Would you like a drink?

Tommy: No thanks.

Jeff: Good. That leaves more for me. *(He unscrews the top.)*

Tommy: Didn't you tell me you were going to-cut down on that stuff?

Jeff: Yes, I did. But I'm a terrible liar. Besides it doesn't pay. I remember one time I was going with a wonderful girl and she used to plead with me and plead with me to give it up. So one day I did. Then we discovered we had nothing more to talk about, so we broke up.*

The game was over, the game that supplied him with care and attention, and her with a maternal gratification without the problems of intimacy. Both roles, rescuer and rescued, are required. It has been observed that the recovery of the alcoholic may herald the onset of a depressive or psychotic illness in the nonalcoholic spouse, thus reversing the roles of rescuer and rescued. Since a rescuer usually does not have overwhelming numbers to rescue, the subject must be rescued over and over again—like a child with an only toy, or the overprotective mother with an only child.

Just as revealing is the marital game playing of the addicted person, as discussed in Scott's *Struggles in an Alcoholic Family*.[10] Scott writes of the Bitter-Sweet Masquerade, the Egyptian Sphinx, Blue Ribbon Robert, the Bedroom Adult, the Scorekeeper, and the Babe in the Woods. A few words about each of these types are indicated.

In the Bitter-Sweet Masquerade, the person offers a sweet disposition to the outside world but a bitter one to the family. This puts the spouse in an awkward position.

The Egyptian Sphinx is calm and unperturbed amid the storm of problems he creates. Only when the spouse issues an ultimatum does the sphinx come to life.

Blue Ribbon Robert has given up drinking. Now the spouse had better get busy and get rid of his neuroses, or Robert will begin drinking again. This person uses sobriety as a club to beat down the mate. Having won a blue ribbon, Robert assumes no responsibility for restoring harmony to the household.

The Bedroom Adult establishes claim to adulthood principally through sex. The spouse's feelings are ignored. Denial of sex is an excuse for more drinking.

Babes in the Woods refer to very immature partners in a marriage. Although both husband and wife are adults from the physical point of view, each is an immature, pouting, stubborn, frightened child expecting to be supported by the other.

*Reprinted from Lerner AJ, Loewe F: *Brigadoon*. New York, Coward, McCann & Geohegan, Inc, 1974, p 5. By permission of Alan Jay Lerner.

The Scorekeeper in the marital game keeps score on the other partner and seems never to forget the endless number of injustices each partner inflicts on the other.

A special word is in order at this point about the resistances related to sexual matters in the home. In the typical marriage undergoing stress, sex is frequently not the focal point of disagreement—rather it is the bargaining table. The typical husband may say, "Let's jump into bed, and this will help us solve our problems." The wife may respond, "Let's solve our problems, and then jump into bed." The alcoholic husband may complain about the lack of the wife's response to his sexual overtures. Her reply may be, "How can I be romantic and responsive to your advances when awakened at 3:00 A.M. on your return home from a drinking bout?" Furthermore, the alcoholic confuses priorities in sexual as well as other matters, as illustrated by the statement of a member of Alcoholics Anonymous: "When I sat down at the table I wanted to make love, and when I went to bed I was hungry and wanted to eat."

Special Problem Areas with the Spouse

Although many of the relationships and attitudes of the spouse have already been discussed, a few other areas deserve mentioning. The physician ought to have ground rules worked out for relating to the alcoholic's spouse and may prefer to work only with the alcoholic in a confidential relationship, as long as the alcoholic accepts responsibility for himself. The treatment covenant thereby exists between the physician and the alcoholic, and nothing is shared with a "significant other" as long as the agreements between therapist and patient are kept. When alcoholics demonstrate that they cannot accept responsibility for themselves, then the physician brings the spouses into the treatment picture. The physician must make known the treatment approach to both alcoholic and spouse at the beginning of therapy and let each know how relationships with the spouse will differ when the alcoholic is responsible and when the alcoholic is drinking. Another physician, equally successful in treating alcoholism, may include the spouse in many facets of the therapy from the beginning irrespective of the level of responsibility assumed by the alcoholic.

A problem seen not infrequently is a spouse's "theft" from the alcoholic of A.A. activities. The spouse attends with the alcoholic all A.A. meetings, instead of those of Al-Anon, and never lets the alcoholic really become involved in the A.A. process. The spouse gradually emerges as a competitor with A.A., thereby depriving the alcoholic of the benefits of A.A. participation. In most situations of this type, the alcoholic eventually drops out of A.A.

The physician's relationship to the spouse may be complicated at times by overt or covert attempts at seduction of the physician. Furthermore, the spouse may accuse the physician of attempting seduction, and this may relate to efforts to bolster waning self-esteem. Of course, when the alcoholic is of the opposite sex from the physician, the spouse may accuse the physician of trying to seduce the alcoholic. How and why such accusations arise in the treatment situation relate to the nature of the treatment process and emotional needs of all parties involved, including the physician.

The enabler, the spouse who takes care of the alcoholic time and time again and who seems to need this type of sick relationship, has contributed much to the psychodynamic understanding of alcoholism. A few of the spouse types discussed earlier share some similar characteristics with the enabler.

The question is often asked, should abstinence of the spouse be insisted upon? The only truly successful approach is total abstinence for alcoholic and spouse, and both should accept this goal and work toward it. Attainment of this goal means no alcohol in the house and that the nonalcoholic spouse must give up drinking entirely. The couple must be helped to plan a social and family life that encourages abstinence.

The Healing Fellowship of Al-Anon

Alcoholism is recognized as a family disease, capable of impairing the emotional and physical health of any member in the family. Al-Anon is a fellowship of spouses, relatives, and friends of alcoholics—mostly the people who are affected by living with an alcoholic. The Al-Anon Family Groups exist to help restore the family of the alcoholic to a measure of stability. Al-Anon can supplement profoundly the family's own efforts in helping each member of a family.

The physician and any other professional working with alcoholics should be aware of Al-Anon's aims, methods of operation, and accomplishments. The best way to become acquainted with the teachings of Al-Anon and the different facets of its program is to attend some of its meetings. In fact, the physician cannot comprehend the impact of Al-Anon's workings without such attendance. Furthermore, the meetings will furnish the physician an opportunity to gather some insights about alcoholism that may not be available from any other source—insights that will be gripping both intellectually and emotionally.

Al-Anon emerged from its early stages as an adjunct of Alcoholics Anonymous and incorporated in 1952 as a separate fellowship known as the Al-Anon Family Group Headquarters, Inc. The only requirement for membership is that the person has been, or is being, deeply affected by close contact with an alcoholic. Members pay no dues, and contributions are voluntary.

Local Al-Anon groups are active in educational and public relations work within their communities, cooperating with all agencies or resources involved in the treatment of alcoholism. Also, the Al-Anon groups, through regular meetings and personal contact, help the relatives of alcoholics to (1) learn the facts about alcoholism as a disease and about the treatment process, (2) benefit from the therapeutic experience of personal contact with other members who have the same problem, and (3) improve their own attitudes and personalities by the study and practice of the suggested "Twelve Steps," adopted from Alcoholics Anonymous.[11]

The basic ideas of Al-Anon, like those of Alcoholics Anonymous, are the concepts on which all spiritual philosophies are based. The working philosophy of Al-Anon forms a pattern for right living, for overcoming difficulties, and for helping persons achieve their aspirations. People come to Al-Anon to solve the specific problem of alcoholism and its disastrous effect on their lives. They apply the basic spiritual ideas by means of the "Twelve Steps." These are augmented or reinforced by the "Twelve Traditions," the "Serenity Prayer," and the concepts known simply as the "Slogans."

From experience with an Al-Anon group, the members learn about improving their own thinking and attitudes. What they need to learn varies from person to person. A woman expressed it this way:[12]

The first thing I really learned was that I must bring myself to release my husband and my children from my direction and domination.

. . . The second important thing I learned was to release myself from the need for my husband's approval and fear of his disapproval. I do what I do for free, with no strings attached; I have to be myself, and do the best I can with what I have. . . . I have learned to live by the Twelve Steps. The Fourth suggests an inventory of ourselves, and this is certainly of vital importance. There is some danger, however, of concentrating too much on digging for defects of character. Perhaps it would be more constructive to regard our defects as character traits channeled in the wrong direction. . . . I found that working the Twelve Steps helped me to rechannel those traits into constructive rather than destructive attitudes.*

This is a vivid testimony to the effectiveness of Al-Anon in helping its members learn to live through living with Al-Anon.

CHILDREN AND PARENTAL ALCOHOLISM

Probably the greatest cost of alcoholism relates to the disruption and disorganization of the family. Frightening to contemplate is the price children must pay in bewilderment, humiliation, physical neglect or abuse, and emotional deprivation. Alcoholism takes a toll in another way in the alarming frequency with which alcoholism tends to recur within families. Some authorities estimate that as many as 50 percent of alcoholics come from families where alcoholism was a problem. While a particular percentage figure may be hard to substantiate with firm data, at least it can be said that the children of alcoholics are much more likely to become alcoholics than the children of nonalcoholics. With conflicting customs and feelings about alcohol in their family and society in general, the children of an alcoholic parent have a good chance of growing up either in a broken home or in one in which they experience profound inconsistencies in their relationships with both parents. Children of an alcoholic are vulnerable to the influence of a poor or inadequate model—an alcoholic who is their parent. They see a parent coping with stress by using alcohol.

It is difficult for children of alcoholics to escape emotional problems. The severity of these will depend on factors such as the

*Reprinted from *Al-Anon Faces Alcoholism.* New York, Al-Anon Family Group Headquarters, 1965, p 179.

age of the children at the onset of parental alcoholism, the social class level of the parent, the sex of the alcoholic parent (emotional scarring is usually greater if the mother is the alcoholic), the quality of the relationship with the alcoholic parent, and the strength of the nonalcoholic parent. Other factors to consider in measuring the crippling impact of parental alcoholism are the inherited temperament and intelligence of the children, level of education and economic security of the family, the personality and maturity of the nonalcoholic parent, and whether or not the alcoholic parent has brought the drinking under control.

Some of the family situations that are quite disturbing to the children of alcoholics include the following:

1. The shift in or reversal of parental roles. When the alcoholic parent is drinking, the nonalcoholic parent takes over his or her family responsibilities, regardless of what they may be.
2. Inconsistencies in the affection, support, and security offered by one or both parents. These inconsistencies can have a profound impact on the children's own sense of security and self-worth. The alcoholic who is often kind and considerate, sometimes overbearingly affectionate, when sober may become cruel or withdrawn when drinking. The nonalcoholic parent, responding to contrasting mood swings in the alcoholic spouse, may appear equally inconsistent and disturbed to the children while conveying to them that it is only because of her that the family is able to survive. Children may be unable to evaluate the situation in their home and unwilling to blame either parent. They often withdraw into a noncommital attitude that makes it difficult to communicate. Exposed to a fluctuating conversational level at home, ranging from morose silence to wild ravings in their parents, the children become more and more withdrawn, with a breakdown in verbal communication.
3. A disturbed nonalcoholic parent who is inadequate with the children. This parent is obsessed with the drinking of the spouse, lonely and frustrated in not having personal needs met in the marital relationship, and therefore unable to meet the emotional needs of the children.
4. Increased social isolation of the family and a sense of personal alienation. The children stop bringing friends home because of the embarrassment and humilitation when their

visitors are confronted by a drunken parent. As the family turns in upon itself and feeds on the problems, the children are cut off from the support and healing of their peers.

Some children may not withdraw into their sick home setting but use a variety of methods to remove themselves from an alcoholic parent. An adolescent seen at juvenile court had been breaking into boats at the waterfront and also setting fires. Once he left his wallet, containing his name and address—in order to be caught, it must be assumed. His father had deserted the family, and the mother had begun drinking heavily. He often had to put his mother to bed or bathe her. Once when she admonished him about repeatedly getting into trouble, he replied, "Mom, I'll make a deal with you. If you stop drinking, I promise to behave and get into no more trouble." This adolescent found his home so unbearable that his antisocial behavior was a way of getting out of the family and into an institution. Nobody would interpret his removal from the family in this way as his really wanting to leave. Actually wanting to leave would carry implications of being disloyal to his family, of abandoning them in a time of great trouble.

Children of alcoholics frequently suffer from a behavior disorder with neurotic traits.   The alcoholic parent is usually not a psychopath but has a conscience and feelings and shows them. After an alcoholic spree, guilt motivates the alcoholic parent to try to do better toward the children, giving them hope that he will change. The frequent swing from high hopes to shattering disappointments, owing to the inconsistent behavior of the alcoholic, may build up in the children such a basic distrust that all their later intimate relationships will be colored or distorted.

In spite of the inconsistency of the parent's overall behavior, during the periods of sobriety the children have strong feelings of identification with the alcoholic parent. This identification helps the children develop consciences. At the point at which they have to hate the parent because of the alcoholic sprees, they become guilty. They react strongly to this ambivalence and handle it by acting out. Such children do a great deal of acting out and at the same time show considerable hypochondriasis and other neurotic symptoms.

The end result in these children is a psychologic disturbance composed of a reactive disorder (reactive to physical and emotional neglect) and of guilt-ridden feelings in terms of their hate of the alcoholic parent that they also love. This blend of reactive behavior and of internal conflict with guilt is diagnosed as a behavior disorder with neurotic traits.

Such a disorder will express itself in many ways. Children may cower in a corner, outwardly conforming, or they may rebel and become defiant or delinquent. Combined with their acting out, they may express the classic symptoms of the hypochondriac, as well as other neurotic symptoms. Feeding the neurotic symptoms will be the ambivalent feelings of love and hate, the sense of deep personal rejection (for example, "If my father really loved me, he would not drink"), neglect or sudden withdrawals of love produced by liquor, and so on. Guilt in its rawest form may come from what appears to the children as a betrayal of the parent. When children become old enough to be aware of persons outside their immediate family, they have also become aware of the condemnation of the alcoholic by society, and they react with shame and humiliation. They feel isolated, estranged, and different. When their alcoholic parent is jeered or laughed at, they may try to defend him out of love. Usually, however, they cannot bring themselves to make such defense, and they feel guilty over what seems to them a betrayal of their parent.

The neurotic traits of the children of the alcoholic parent often bring the children into profound conflict with the alcoholic parent. Not infrequently, the alcoholic parent goes into psychotherapy because of inability to tolerate the neurotic children.

Treatment of the Children of the Alcoholic

In the treatment of such children, the goal is to help them find a long-term relationship in order for them to develop trust and rid themselves of their acting out. Through this sustained relationship, the children are helped to work through their conflicts and guilt. This is accomplished first in relation to the therapist and in group experiences such as that afforded by Alateen or Al-Anon. Then through such therapeutic experiences, conflicts and guilt are resolved regarding the alcoholic parent.

In treatment of the children who live in an alcoholic family situation, the therapist should not forget Alateen. Alateen is for the 12–20 year-old age group and is an outgrowth of Al-Anon, the worldwide fellowship for relatives and friends of alcoholics. The first Alateen group was started in 1957 by a youth in California whose father was an alcoholic, but sober and active in Alcoholics Anonymous. His mother was a member of an Al-Anon family group, and he modeled Alateen after the Al-Anon ideas and principles. Each Alateen group is sponsored by a member of Al-Anon (at times co-sponsored by a member of A.A.) who is present at meetings but who does not participate unless invited to express an opinion or answer a question.

The purpose of Alateen is to discuss the difficulties teenagers face when they live in the destructive environment of alcoholism. The teenagers exchange experiences, encourage and help each other understand the principles of Alateen, and learn effective ways of coping with their own problems. Alateen's group therapy, like that of Alcoholics Anonymous and Al-Anon, is based on the well-known A.A. "Twelve Steps," which the teenagers discuss and apply to their own attitudes and relationships with others. The members of the group receive from each other understanding of their problems and feelings and emotional support, which facilitates change of attitude and behavior. They also receive basic information about alcoholism as a disease and the recovery process. As they gain perspective on their common problems, they change their way of thinking, and their behavior becomes more realistic. They develop feelings of security, in part because of the structuring that Alateen has brought to what had been a chaotic life situation.

In the treatment process, the therapist must remember that it is not easy to help the children unless the family cooperates in a total rehabilitation program. Assistance obtained from outside the family can be neutralized and rendered ineffectual by a continuing state of insecurity at home. Thus it is imperative that the alcoholic problem itself be tackled first, if at all possible.

In serious cases where the alcoholic is chronically drunk and repeatedly refuses to seek help, removal of the children from the home may be advisable. Drastic steps such as removal of the children from the home, separation, or divorce may be needed to awaken the alcoholic to the "eleventh hour" of the situation.

Children tolerate the family crisis better if they understand and accept the concept of alcoholism as a disease. When children understand their parent's struggle or "the dark journey of the soul," their shame can turn to pride and admiration, their defiance to obedience, their resentment to love. The feeling of hopelessness and isolation is replaced by a feeling of being needed and useful. Furthermore, upon learning of the nature of alcoholism, they may play a crucial role in persuading a parent to seek treatment. Such is the testimony of many children who have gone through this experience. For those just beginning in the work with alcoholics and their families, it is imperative to read the literature from Alateen, Al-Anon, and Alcoholics Anonymous and to attend their meetings. Also, the alcoholic, the family, and the therapist may be encouraged by the words of Francis Fenelon, 17th century French writer and cleric: "As light increases we see ourselves to be worse that we thought. . . . Bear in mind, for your comfort, that we only perceive our malady when the cure begins."

CONCLUSION

Recently, in a class in medical ethics, I asked the medical students to identify some ethical problems that are often overlooked or not identified as ethical problems in the practice of medicine. One medical student responded by saying that before coming to and during medical school he had worked, on numerous occasions, in the admission and emergency rooms of several hospitals and had noted a common response to the alcoholic—overt or covert hostility—that influenced profoundly the treatment given or not given. He also noted that if the alcoholic's family, or what appeared to be the family, brought the patient in, the response and the treatment were much better and often as humane and professional as if the problem had been other than alcoholism.

One can draw from this story many implications. It is another testimony to the value of the alcoholic's family in the alcoholic's treatment and recovery. The story also calls for a reassessment of our values in regard to our fellow humans in both sickness and health. The alcoholic is a person, belonging to a specific family and in broader terms to the family of humankind.

This kinship, this relationship has been especially illuminated by John Steinbeck's *Burning Bright*.[13]

Burning Bright concerns Joe Saul, who desperately wanted a child but who did not know that his seed was dead. The desire that was strongest in him—would it go forever unfulfilled? His wife Mordeen knew he was sterile but loved him deeply, and out of her great love and without his knowledge, she turned to another man to give her husband the child he wanted. About the time Mordeen was going into labor, Joe discovered through a physician's examination of his sperm that he was sterile and unable to father a child. At that moment his joy turned to ashes, and he walked into the darkest night of his life. Then he found himself at the hospital where Mordeen had delivered. He was given a surgical mask and gown and allowed to enter the room. In the conversation that took place between them, she, although half asleep, realized that he knew the secret and understood. Her eyes were clearing now as she came from under the influence of the anesthetic. Follow carefully what took place between the two:

"I know," he said. "I had to walk into the black to know—to know that every man is father to all children and every child must have all men as father. This is not a little piece of private property, registered and fenced and separated. Mordeen! This is *the Child*."

Mordeen said, "It is very dark. Turn up the light. Let me have light. I cannot see your face."

"Light," he said. "You want light? I will give you light." He tore the mask from his face, and his face was shining and his eyes were shining. "Mordeen," he said, "I love the child." His voice swelled and he spoke loudly. "Mordeen, I love our child." And he raised his head and cried in triumph, "Mordeen, *I love my son*."*

This sense of family, of kinship, of community, of belonging as expressed by John Steinbeck, is the tie that binds us to alcoholics and holds them in the family of humankind. And each of us can say: my mother, my father the alcoholic; my brother, my sister the alcoholic; my husband, my wife the alcoholic; my son, my daughter the alcoholic. This is the basis of our responsibility to the alcoholic.

*Reprinted from Steinbeck J: *Burning Bright*. New York, Bantam Books, 1950, pp 129–130. By permission of Viking Penguin, Inc. Copyright, 1950, by John Steinbeck.

REFERENCES

1. McClelland D, Davis WN, Kalin R, Wanner E. *The Drinking Man: Alcohol and Human Motivation.* New York, Free Press, 1972
2. Pearson, MM, Little RB: The addictive process in unusual addictions: A further elaboration of etiology. *Am J Psychiatry* 125:8, 1969
3. Rado S: Narcotic bondage—A general theory of the dependence on narcotic drugs. *Am J Psychiatry* 114:165–170, 1957
4. Framo JL: Symptoms from a family transactional viewpoint, in Sager CJ, Kaplan HS (eds): *Progress in Group and Family Therapy.* New York, Brunner-Mazel, 1972, pp 277–284
5. Karpman SB: Fairy tales and script analysis. *Transact Anal Bull* 7:39–43, 1968
6. Sager CJ, Kaplan HS (eds): *Progress in Group and Family Therapy.* New York, Brunner-Mazel, 1972
7. Steiner C. *Games Alcoholics Play.* New York, Grove Press, 1971
8. Gallant DM, Rich A, Bey E, Terranova L: Group psychotherapy with married couples: A successful technique in New Orleans alcoholism clinic patients. *J La State Med Soc* 122:41–44, 1970
9. Lerner AJ, Loewe F: *Brigadoon.* New York, Coward, McCann & Geohegan, Inc, 1947, p 5
10. Scott EM: *Struggles in an Alcoholic Family.* Springfield, Ill., Charles C. Thomas, 1970, pp 94–97
11. *Al-Anon–Family Treatment Tool in Alcoholism.* New York, Al-Anon Family Group Headquarters, 1971
12. *Al-Anon Faces Alcoholism.* New York, Al-Anon Family Group Headquarters, 1965, p 179
13. Steinbeck J. *Burning Bright.* New York, Bantam Books, 1950

Herbert S. Peyser

12
The Roles of the Psychiatrist, Psychologist, Social Worker, and Alcoholism Counselor

This book is intended for medical students, for residents and practicing physicians in all specialties (particularly internal medicine, general practice, and psychiatry), for psychologists, social workers, nurses, alcoholism counselors, and, in general, all who have to do with treating these patients and their illness. It espouses a fundamental medical model of alcoholism as a disease yet supports as a treatment a form of psychotherapy and group therapy. The treatment program eschews the use of medication unless absolutely necessary. Instead, following the short detoxification period, it concentrates on attacking the addiction itself. Whether as inpatient or outpatient, whether in an office situation and the one-to-one relationship or in group therapy, whether with A.A. and Al-Anon or without—and usually involving all of these modalities—it concentrates its attack on the symptom itself, on the urge to drink.

The therapeutic program tends to avoid attention to whatever physiological or psychological basis there may be for the alcoholism or sedative addiction, and it regards discussion of inner conflicts as quite secondary to the problem of stopping drinking. It utilizes all the weapons it can (encouragement, acceptance, direction, common sense, conscience, morality, religion, a kind of conversion experience, the support of a sort of surrogate family of

229

ALCOHOLISM
ISBN 0-8089-1227-5

Copyright © 1980 by Grune & Stratton
All rights of reproduction in any form reserved.

others who have suffered similarly and have been through the
therapeutic process, their experiences, advice, and example, etc.)
to combat the addiction—permanently and continuously.

This model of the illness and the therapeutic approach may
embody certain problems for two groups of physicians and
therapists.

The first group affected includes the more organically or
biochemically oriented physicians and psychiatrists. Recent advances in the chemotherapy of psychiatric disorders and developments in research on the role of the brain monoamines and
endorphins and their receptors have supplied theories and, more
important, treatments for disorders up to now more or less refrac-
tory to psychotherapy. In the light of this, these physicians and
psychiatrists have found support for a strict medical model of
psychiatric illness. They have therefore tended to extend the use
of lithium, the tricyclics, and MAO-inhibiting antidepressants
and the butyrophenones, phenothiazines, and thioxanthenes to
symptom pictures that are not classically bipolar or unipolar affective disorders or schizophrenia. Small wonder they have seen
at least some cases of alcoholism in this light, conceiving of the
use of alcohol as a symptom of an underlying organically based
disorder (e.g., Winokur's notion of depression spectrum disease
with depressions in female family members and alcoholism in
male family members; he claims even to have found genetic
markers in serum proteins[1]).

There is danger in this, however, from the clinical point of
view. After removing the 2−5 percent (or possibly 10 percent or
even slightly more) of clearly psychotic alcoholics, one is left with
a large group on which one can try the above medications but for
whom it is as yet unproven that any of them will respond to such
medications. It is known, however, that most of them can respond
to the psychotherapeutic and group therapeutic approaches described in this book.

The essence of these approaches is, as noted, the engaging of
the patient in a therapeutic alliance, in a cooperative effort
against the urge (need? drive? compulsion?) to drink and to use
chemicals to solve life's problems. In light of this, it is indeed
dangerous to suggest that a different chemical, even though it not
be alcohol or another sedative−hypnotic, can solve a problem. It
can encourage the patient to avoid the necessary intensive and
continuing personal work of combating the urge, becoming "dry,"

and ultimately changing his life and achieving true sobriety. In this respect, the alcoholic will be much like the cardiac patient who, taking faithfully the seemingly magical medication given by the physician, neglects the hard work of dietary restrictions, the regular exercise program, and the changes in living habits that are perhaps even more important in treating the condition. It is as if the patient said, "If I take the pill, I need not do the work."

The second group of physicians and other therapists that might find difficulty with the model and the therapeutic approach consists of the more psychologically and dynamically oriented practitioners, including, in particular, psychoanalytically trained therapists. The medical model itself and, particularly, the disease concept may not be thoroughly agreeable to them.

First, then, a word about the idea of alcoholism as a disease. In certain ways it is clearly a most useful concept, repudiating notions of alcoholism as a weakness, a "badness," a sin, or a crime. In this it is akin to Pinel's revolution in psychiatry at the end of the 18th century, when he struck the chains off the inmates of the madhouses in Paris. With this act he converted the inmates into patients, the madhouses into hospitals, and the keepers into therapists. The mentally ill were no longer mad beasts or possessed people. They were sick. They were to be studied and treated. Medicalization of alcoholism and the disease concept does the same for the alcoholic now.

Yet dynamically oriented psychiatrists and other therapists have been further influenced by Freud's subsequent revolution, seeing meaning and motivation in symptoms, seeing in psychological illness a search for solutions to life's problems, although aberrant and maladaptive solutions. They look askance at what might seem to them a return to purely biological, Kraepelinian concepts as reductionistic, mechanistic, and incomplete. There is much to be said for this, but the disease concept itself is really quite broad. No one any longer believes that the urge to drink is simply analogous to the cells of the body needing insulin in diabetes. A.A. itself, for all its espousal of the disease concept, recognizes implicitly that one can psychologically substitute one addiction for another. "If you feel like drinking, go out and eat something, preferably something sweet." Anyone who attends A.A. meetings cannot help but notice the clouds of cigarette smoke hovering over the group and the crowd around the coffee machine.

The notion of alcoholism as a disease is more complicated than that. It understands the disorder as containing sociologic loading (many of the Irish drink; first generation Jews and Chinese, for the most part, didn't), genetic loading (not absolutely proven but very strongly suggested), and psychological loading. The predisposition lies latent until the disorder appears openly. It may come on insidiously and progressively (e.g., the patient discovers that alcohol disinhibits and thereby eases social, sexual, and interpersonal relationships and even work tasks, particularly those requiring appearance in a "test" situation before some group of supervisors or even peers), or it may appear abruptly (e.g., on losing a beloved or a job, or, paradoxically, on receiving a promotion or achieving some success). Whatever triggers it off, once the alcoholism appears it stamps its mark, its pattern on it as a cookie cutter does on dough. Then the patient's course follows a predictable pattern with a unitary set of symptoms and consequences and an inevitable prognosis. If this is what is meant by a disease, most people will be able to ascribe to it.

The second problem the dynamically oriented physicians and therapists might have is that the therapeutic approach seems symptomatic rather than etiological (in the psychological sense of etiology). In general, in psychoanalytically oriented psychotherapy one tends to look *behind* the symptom rather than to concentrate on the symptom itself as the primary cause of difficulty. In so doing, as Freud noted, there is induced "a certain tolerance for the state of being ill." He goes on to say that "the resistance, however, may exploit the situation for its own ends and abuse the license to be ill. It seems to say: 'See what happens if I really give way to such things. Was I not right to consign them to repression?' " Such people "are inclined to make the necessity imposed by the treatment for their illness a welcome excuse for luxuriating in their symptoms."[2]

This is the case with those symptoms that are directly gratifying. In contradistinction to the ego-alien symptoms (phobias, compulsion, hysterias, etc.) and even to the more difficult to treat ego-syntonic disturbances (traits of character, etc.), the group of directly gratifying symptoms (perversions, addictions, and symptoms where secondary gain is especially prominent, etc.) are close to impossible to treat by orthodox psychoanalytic procedures or psychotherapeutic procedures closely aligned to them.

In the case of this last category, certain parameters enter the treatment of these people, and attention must be paid first and foremost to the symptom (in this case, the drug or alcohol dependence). Only when *it* has become truly the enemy and when the patient is solidly (not merely transiently) engaged in an alliance with the therapist against it can deeper treatment occur. One must always be on guard for the reappearance of the addiction, because when it recurs all other treatment disappears until further therapy of the addiction has returned it to its previous state—which is manifested by abstinence. When alcoholics are drinking, all insight is used to defend, shore up, rationalize, and "enable" the drinking and to postpone their really doing anything about the problem. All they want to do is to drink and to solve problems by avoiding them and anesthetizing themselves.

Therefore one can say that the approach outlined in this book is in accord with good principles of psychoanalytic and dynamic psychotherapy. In fact, perusal of the "Twelve Steps" of A.A. (see Chapter 7) will show how they resemble a psychological (or religious or secular) conversion experience, and they too are therefore in accord with dynamic principles. To abandon the old self and the old ways (alcoholism) and to develop a new self and new ways (sobriety), one must go through an "identity crisis," "take a second chance," just as one may well do in one's adolescence or in one's psychotherapy. One admits the failure of the old ways, admits and faces one's smallness and helplessness, gives up one's grandiosity and sense of omnipotence, curbs one's narcissism and tendencies to wishful denial, faces reality, gives up the belief in magical solutions (in this case, drugs and alcohol), and surrenders to (not merely submits to and complies with) the need for interpersonal relationships (of one-to-one and/or group type). It is to these relationships and the experiences of others that one will look for one's further growth and change. One must search in one's self for one's defects and faults, admit them, and then make amends. Then one must utilize all this by carrying the message to others.

In this one can see the outlines of specific roles for the psychiatrist, psychoanalyst, psychologist, social worker, and other therapists in the treatment of alcoholism.

First, therapists must be aware of the possibility of alcoholism or sedative addiction in the patients they are seeing. They must keep in mind that agitation may not be psychogenic anxiety but the physiological agitation of "withdrawal," present even while the patient is drinking or on drugs, as described in Chapter 2. The interpersonal and marital difficulties they see, the automobile accidents and the falls they hear reported, the angry outbursts, the depressed moods, the isolation and withdrawn behavior may all be secondary to the alcohol or the drugs, as well, too, may be the business and financial difficulties that are developing in the life of their patients. Therapists must remember that patients may turn to alcohol or sedatives as solutions to problems that are not being solved immediately in therapy. They must keep on top of the situation where the occasional drink is developing into needed relief and then progressing to outright alcoholism. It is the same for sleeping pills for the insomniac. Some symptoms may be due to alcohol and pills; some may lead to alcohol and pills; and some may move the physician to prescribing sedatives and so-called "minor tranquilizers" that will set the patient on to the road to addiction.

The psychiatrist or other therapist must also be on the lookout to make the diagnosis of a major psychiatric disorder (unipolar or bipolar affective disorders, schizophrenia or other paranoid psychiatric state, or organic mental syndrome) that requires psychiatric intervention in order to enable the patient to participate in such an alcoholic program as that described in this book. After all, for example, the paranoid who believes that there are spies and "plants" in the A.A. group or rehabilitation center will not be able to remain there or to cooperate in the appropriate therapeutic regimen, and the manic–depressive's mood swings will push him into alcoholism too strongly for the alcohol program to combat such a push all by itself. These are a small number of patients (somewhere between 2 and perhaps 10 percent), but one must be on the watch for them. At the same time one must be aware that many depressive symptoms and some paranoid or other thought disturbances may be secondary to the alcohol or sedative intake. They will clear up in 2–6 weeks of sobriety (perhaps a month or two longer in the case of solid sedatives). Of course, regardless of its origin, any truly suicidal depression or severely agitated psychotic state is a psychiatric emergency whenever it presents itself.

The physician, psychiatrist, or other therapist who makes the diagnosis of alcoholism must then recognize that regardless of what other psychiatric condition exists (with the above-noted exceptions), he must pay primary attention to the alcoholism or sedativism. This becomes the first thing to be attacked, and there is no treatment for the other conditions until this is under control. In psychodynamic terms it may be seen as a symptom of an underlying problem, but once it appears, the symptom (alcoholism) becomes *the* problem.

The therapist is then concerned with motivating the patient to enter some alcoholism treatment program, of which the physician or therapist may be more or less a part. Motivation requires, essentially, poking about for the therapist's leverage with the patient—the loss of a spouse or lover, of a job or career, of health, even of life, or of control over some forbidden or dangerous sexual or aggressive impulse. This is discussed in Chapter 3 at length.

Some deep psychological problems emanating from the unconscious can present themselves this early in the course of the therapy and can interfere with the motivation to go into treatment in the first place. Should a male patient, for example, have no sexual life except for some perverse, masochistic "game" acted out with a prostitute, a "game" permissable for him only under the disinhibiting influence of alcohol, and should he have no gratifications elsewhere and be impotent otherwise, then to take away his alcoholism is to take away his sexual life and the only gratifications in his life. Such a patient may well be quite resistant to treatment. It will require some deeper and longer psychotherapeutic work at this point to get him into an alcoholism program in the first place. This kind of problem is not common, but when it appears it requires the skilled attention of a trained psychotherapist who must nevertheless regard all psychotherapeutic work as aimed primarily at getting the patient into alcoholism treatment and sobriety.

The therapist may then continue working with the patient in conjunction with the alcohol program, particularly if the patient is one of those relatively few who require psychotropic medication or psychological help as noted above. The psychotropic drugs must never be other members of the sedative–hypnotic group (see Appendix A) and should probably not include amitriptyline (Elavil) or its derivatives because of the sedative effect and potential for abuse. (Even the anti-Parkinsonian drugs used with the phenothiazines, etc., have been abused, trihexyphenidyl [Artane] in particular.[3]) For these and other reasons, A.A. groups are often very distrustful of and even opposed to the use of what they call "mood-altering" drugs and may oppose even necessary ones. Working this out with one's patient who is attending A.A. and the A.A. groups themselves is a necessary practice, also discussed in this book (Chapter 7).

The therapist may work along with patients, in part to keep them in the program and to supplement the program psychotherapeutically, even if the patients are not on drugs. The therapist must work with the resistances as they arise. The therapist who cannot get a patient to attend a program may have to see other members of the family and work with them along the lines discussed in Chapters 3 and 11 and may have to work with the family while the patient is in the rehabilitation facility or refer the family members to Al-Anon and/or to another therapist to help them to "detach with love" (not punitively), a process so necessary for the alcoholic's recovery. Certainly, as the alcoholic grows and develops towards sobriety, a certain kind of maturity and emotional separateness (not necessarily physical or geographic separateness) will appear as the dependency diminishes. The family's therapist then will have to be a different one from the patient's at that time.

This leads to the problem discussed in Chapter 7. To be "dry" is not enough. One must be "sober." By this we mean that patients must assume responsibility for their lives, face rather than disavow or minimize feelings and conflicts at work or at home, and work out some other way of dealing with them rather than the ways they had been utilizing in the past. They could conceivably achieve this on their own, but this is unlikely, and their protests that they can do so almost always represent resistance to change. A.A. or other aspects of an alcohol program can help, as can counseling and psychotherapy, particularly if there are deeper difficulties.

At times one may see deeper factors interfering with progress, psychological factors emerging from the presence of unconscious conflict. It is interesting to note that the concept of the unconscious in the psychoanalytic sense tends not to play a significant role in the psychotherapeutic techniques discussed in the book. This arises out of some bad experiences with the incorrect utilization of the concept, a problem not merely specific to the treatment of alcoholism but involving all psychotherapies as well.

It does not matter that the concept of unconscious mental activity is a valid concept, supplying connections and psychic continuity and therefore meaning to many human actions, thoughts, feelings, and experiences. Despite peoples' statements to the contrary, the very concept itself has a feeling of "place," separate from the sense of true self, the "I." Indeed, this is the very essence of repression, which is a kind of disavowal. Thus the very notion of the unconscious is embraced as a disavowal of responsibility, and is used as a resistance in itself, particularly in obsessional neuroses but also in addicted persons. This is what Freud had in mind in the quote from his writings given earlier in this chapter. It is as though the patient is saying, "It stems from my unconscious; it is not my fault, and therefore I need do nothing about it. More than that, because it comes from the unconscious, I therefore cannot help it."

This refusal to accept the responsibility for that which is in one's unconscious is incorrect. In a paper entitled "Moral Responsibility for the Content of Dreams," Freud states, "Obviously one must hold oneself responsible for the evil impulses of one's dreams. In what other way can one deal with them?"[4]

Nevertheless, this idea of the unconscious seems to encourage such a sense of not being responsible for one's actions (as, for example, in the law, where one is punished only for what one *consciously* intended and is innocent if one didn't consciously intend to perform the criminal act). Attempts have been made in psychoanalysis to deal with this problem by altering the concept (e.g., Roy Schafer[5]), but then another important notion may be interfered with—the emphasis on work, on struggle, on forces to be overcome by one's own efforts continued over a period of time. No magic pill and no magic process (whether medication, exhortation, or even correct psychoanalytic understanding and interpretations) can substitute for the persistent work and effort to be expended.[6]

It therefore is simpler to ignore the whole idea of the unconscious, and for the most part the writers in this book have let it go. From a clinical and therapeutic point of view it is just as well. The vast majority of alcoholics, it seems, will not recover from their alcoholism if one pays attention to their unconscious and will get better if one ignores it. It is not that it is not there; it is just that the patients make their compromises between sickness and health in the psychoanalytic sense and for all intents and purposes are well satisfied. These compromises are common enough in life and in all psychotherapies.

A case demonstrating these matters follows.

A highly talented musician struggled upward and finally achieved success. He opened at Philharmonic Hall, New York City, to rave notices and promptly went to pieces. He felt anxious and tense, began having trouble sleeping, began to drink heavily, and seemed in all respects to be following a pathway described by Freud as demonstrating a character "wrecked by success".[7] As the alcoholism took over, the manifestations of the disease appeared, and the course progressed along the predictable paths described in this book. He suffered agitation, depression, irritability, blackouts, accidents, misbehavior, including hitting his wife, etc. He had to give up his career. He went to several psychiatrists, to no avail, and finally came to the office of an internist–addictionist who hospitalized and detoxified him and then sent him to A.A. and an alcoholism counselor. The latter continued treating him as he resolved certain interpersonal difficulties and entered another field, a commercial one, in which he made a considerable financial success.

In A.A. he became a very useful sponsor and "Twelve Stepper," helping many others. He himself became restless, though, and went in for different types of more magical activities hoping they would help— transcendental meditation, est, etc. The conflict and the dilemma remained, now unobscured by the alcoholism. His deeply cherished desire to be a successful musician was psychologically forbidden to him for some reason. If he tried to carry it out in the face of his internal taboo, anxiety would result and drive him into some symptom formation—in this case the disease of alcoholism to which he was predisposed. If he tried to renounce the wish, he would suffer a terrible discontent. He therefore found himself looking for some magical solution to this problem, but each one, of course, failed him.

Finally he landed on what he was really seeking all the time and made a contract to reappear in a concert performance. As he did so, he became increasingly anxious and tense again, began smoking again, and finally wound up with an equivocal alcoholic "slip"—he devoured half of a coffee cake soaked in whiskey that had been sent to him as a gift. At the point that his counselor was considering hospitalizing him, he tore up his contract and gave up the concert performance. His anxiety disappeared with this action, but after a while he became restless again and went after another fad, this time a dietary fad. But he remained then and since secure in his sobriety. He had made his compromise between sickness and health.

Whether or not to go into these concerns more deeply is a matter for the most sensitive clinical judgment. One must *not* return the patient to alcoholism. But where—and when—the patient is able to tolerate the tension and work with the physician, and where the problems seem deeply rooted in the unconscious, one may begin to work with the patient in deeper therapy to continue the process of developing and consolidating sobriety in its fullest sense.

An example of such a situation follows.

A distinguished mathematician, a man with great psychological knowledge as well, had worked closely and collaborated on some papers with psychologists of his university, with people in the nearby psychoanalytic institute, and with practicing psychiatrists. He had even seen some patients and had had himself a personal analysis (thus demonstrating that reason and intellectual knowledge are no more protection against alcoholism than against neurosis or psychosis).

The patient had written many important papers and two highly thought of books. When his wife became psychologically ill and began to make many false and delusional accustations against him, he became increasingly upset. He had an extremely strict and overly scrupulous conscience and felt responsible for her illness (as he had felt responsible for his mother's illness in his childhood). A writing block developed, and he could no longer produce any papers. In an effort to overcome this he began to take amphetamines and other stimulants, and then to take sedatives to counteract the stimulants, but the severe manifestations of the disease process did not begin until his wife died suddenly, a possible suicide, following an argument with him. Guilty, even accused by a member of her family of being responsible for her death, he began drinking alcohol heavily and taking drugs indiscriminately. Various symptoms developed, and after several hospitalizations they were attributed vaguely to some kind of diffuse demyelinating neurological disorder (not an uncommon misdiagnosis in these conditions). This went on for several years until he reached the hands of a physician who recognized, despite the patient's denials, his alcoholism and sedativism.

He was hospitalized and detoxified and then went through an inpatient rehabilitation facility for 2 months. Immediately after discharge, and without giving another class or facing again any of his students or fellow teachers, he resigned his post at the internationally renowned university and took a position at a small, second-rate college in a rural area a considerable distance away. He never took any sedatives or stimulants again, but he did, half a year later, have a short slip with alcohol. Proper treatment helped, and he developed over the next few years a strong and solid sobriety.

He remained chronically depressed and retiring in behavior, however, felt no real joy in life, never wrote any papers, never attended conferences in his field, and refused requests to appear on panels, but in general seemed to be getting along. He lived comfortably with a woman, gratefully if not enthusiastically, and then married her, but he seemed to look forward to nothing. He attended A.A. meetings regularly, was a useful A.A. member himself, and was living a life of useful duty and sober responsibility but without pleasure. After a few years a true, deep depression slowly developed and increased with terminal insomnia, anorexia, and weight loss. He came to a psychiatrist, one trained in alcohol work as well, fearing he might slip again. He was hospitalized and started on imipramine, but the depression deepened greatly, agitation and suicidal thoughts appeared, and he had to be given a course of ECT. He recovered from the depression and returned to his previous state as just described.

It was not enough, and continued meetings with a psychotherapist brought out how terrible he felt in this rural area and this not very good college, how unstimulating it was for this highly cultured and sophisticated man. He suffered from chronic tension headaches apparently related to this. Yet it developed further that he feared to return to the great university he had been part of, not so much because of a danger to his sobriety but because of a deep sense of guilt and of shame before his former students and, more importantly, his colleagues. It was shame over his alcoholism, and further work revealed earlier origins for this sense of shame. As he continued the work of therapy and began to feel he might be able to work through both this shame and the irrational guilt over his wife's illness and death, his mood improved, he made plans to return to his university, and he began for the first time in a long while to enjoy life and to look forward to the future.

This case history is reported to illustrate certain problems in alcoholism and to give therapists some idea of the course of the illness and the further role for the therapist in the handling of alcoholic patients. Once the alcohol is given up, other symptoms or symptomatic actions may take their place. The sense of guilt, in this case, that became overt first with his wife's accusations, and for which he expiated by developing his writing block, worsened with her death and found atonement and expression in his alcoholism and drug misuse. After he ceased punishing and destroying himself that way, he then had to flee his university and continue his expiation by exile, so to speak, to the rural area and the lesser college. Thus, later on, there was further work for the therapist, since now the guilt was contaminated by shame over his alcoholic behavior before his colleagues and students. Full sobriety required a return to the status quo ante, to a life of achievement and enjoyment.

Except for relatively rare instances, as mentioned earlier, in general the psychotherapist should wait at least 6 months, perhaps a year, maybe even more, after sobriety begins before getting really involved in deep treatment with a patient. This is true even if one has started treatment, helped such a patient as in the example above get involved in an alcoholism treatment program, and continued alcoholism treatment during this time, working on the symptom itself. One should wait and move but slowly into deeper issues, or else one risks a return to the addiction. It was years after his last slip that the mathematician was able to go into his difficulties without again menacing his sobriety. He had to expiate for a while.

Even then, when one can go into deeper matters, it is questionable whether an orthodox psychoanalysis is in order. It is certainly improper earlier. Analysis, without considerable alteration of parameters, at which point probably it can no longer properly be called psychoanalysis, throws the patient into a degree of aloneness that is very dangerous for the alcoholic. It is always best to preserve some of the traditional medical role, with its ambience of parental benevolence and even some degree of parental support. This can be diminished slowly as time goes on and as the patient takes over more and more responsibility for himself ("takes charge of his own life"). It is a process of nurturing and growth.

In this respect, one can quote Henri Bergson: "To exist is to change, to change is to mature, to mature is to go on creating oneself endlessly."[8]

There are a few other considerations in the treatment of the alcoholic. One must keep in mind that all alcoholics are not the same even though the alcoholism itself tends to present a more or less unitary picture. In addition to the many personal and psychological differences among alcoholics and the presence or absence of other psychiatric disorders, there are significant socioeconomic considerations as well.

In this regard there are a number of groups of alcoholics that deserve special attention, and the groups fall into two categories. One category consists of those groups separated, excluded, and alienated from the mainstream of the middle class culture of this country and who therefore adhere to something different from the middle class ideology and values out of which A.A. and most alcohol programs have grown. These are, among others, blacks, chicanos, Puerto Ricans, Native Americans and certain poor white groups. They present special problems in terms of social relocation, the development of language and occupational skills, job opportunities, housing, health care, and even nutrition. What can it mean to these people if they hear advice to "take charge of their lives" when they cannot even exist without welfare and Medicaid? What is their pathway to self-esteem, so essential a part of sobriety? These problems are discussed in depth in Chapter 10.

A second general category is basically part of the middle class culture, yet presents unique problems because of a specialness within that culture and a more subtle kind of exclusion and alienation. Less oppressed, not educationally or economically deprived, they nevertheless present certain problems of their own. This category would include, among others, women, homosexuals, and the aged. The first group is covered in Chapter 9. Much of what they have to say can be applied with modifications to the other subgroups. But a few additional statements about homosexual alcoholics are necessary.

First, the incidence of alcoholism among male homosexuals and, to a lesser degree female homosexuals, is very high. Then again, the very structure of the social contact among certain types of homosexuals is that they meet at special homosexual bars and clubs. To give up alcohol may mean that they must avoid the temptation of the bar situation, but this may also then seriously interfere with their meeting with lovers and friends. (This is less true of the homosexuals who "pass" and the others who are settled down in relatively stable relationships.)

A substitute place of contact must be found, and it is present in the same urban areas where those bars are, in the form of gay A.A. groups or analogous gay alcohol treatment groups. Here a nonalcoholic environment substitutes completely for the gay bar and provides almost everything the bar provides. It is therefore a good idea for the physician, therapist, counselor, etc., to have contacts among alcoholics in the community (usually through A.A.) to find a recovering alcoholic who is homosexual and can help bridge the gap and lead the homosexual alcoholic to the proper group.

A word of caution, though. It is probably best, in most instances, to discourage much involvement in sexuality in the very
early phases of recovery (and this is true of the heterosexual as
well) where the sexuality is anxiety producing or even where it is
highly charged. Alcohol and sobriety have the first and overrid-
ing priority, and sexuality, and even love and duty, must intially
take a considerable back seat to the main problem. The only question is whether sexuality *aids* or *interferes* with the task of sobriety, and all questions about it must be viewed in this light. At
first, then, it is best for the homosexual to avoid gay A.A. groups
where there may be active "cruising" and solicitation.

When one has the more difficult problem of the alcoholic who
is unclear about his sexual choice, one must have him put off all
consideration of this until sobriety is clearly established. For
example, the married man who, when drunk, engages for the
most part in homosexual acts will ultimately have to face this
problem. He may, with sobriety, "seal over" the homosexuality
and return to heterosexuality exclusively. He is, for all intents
and purposes, most probably a true heterosexual who might, for
example, be enmeshed in a most difficult situation with a spouse
or lover. Separation from that person may, in the long run, be
necessary to preserve his sobriety by diminishing the push in the
direction of a disavowed homosexuality, a push that would compel
him to drink in order to disinhibit and enjoy his otherwise re-
pudiated homosexual tendencies.

On the other hand, he may truly be a homosexual. Then the
doctor, therapist or counselor must—in time—work with him to
confront and accept this fact. Unresolved issues and unsettled
conflicts such as this are festering sores, so to speak. Sobriety may
not be solid until they are worked out and resolved. Many workers in the field feel that, as part of this acceptance and resolution,
the homosexual must eventually bring up his homosexuality and
discuss it in the A.A. or treatment groups of which he is a
member.

But such decision-making, as noted, awaits the establish-
ment first of a good sobriety, and as the homosexual moves in the
direction of his sexual object choice, exploring the ground, as it
were, the therapist must keep his eyes and ears on the anxiety
level and the tendencies to recidivism and slips.

Several other points: The therapist must not permit the
homosexual to use this problem of his conflicts and worries over

his homosexuality as an excuse to drink or even to direct the therapeutic attention away from the primary task at hand. Furthermore, the therapist must be prepared for the possibility in homosexuals (and heterosexuals, too, for that matter) that the existing level of sexual activity prior to sobriety may change, temporarily or permanently, in either direction after sobriety. Usually, as the illness of alcoholism progresses, sexuality diminishes, especially in terms of the ability to perform. Sobriety can, but may not, restore that. Indeed, it may even take away the ability to perform sexually (which had been allowed only after the disinhibiting effect of alcohol). Frequently, for a short time after sobriety begins—a matter of months—sexual passions disappear, but will reappear later as the recovery process continues. One can make no promises to the patient, but one can also assure him that continued intake of alcohol usually leads to sexual hypofunction sooner or later.

The very essence of sobriety is the development of the capacity for love and work, for achievement and enjoyment, without resorting to alcohol or other such chemicals. All psychotherapy must be conducted in light of this.

REFERENCES

1. Winokur G: Unipolar depression. *Arch Gen Psychiatry* 36:47–52, 1979
2. Freud S: Remembering, Repeating and Working Through. [Strachey J (ed)] vol 12: London, Hogarth Press, 1958, pp 152–153
3. Goggin DA, Solomon GF: Trihexyphenidyl abuse for euphorigenic effect. *Am J Psychiatry* 136:459–460, 1979
4. Freud S: Some additional notes upon dream interpretation as a whole: (B) Moral responsibility for the content of dreams, in Strachey J (ed): *Collected Papers,* vol 5. London, Hogarth Press, 1950, pp 156–159
5. Schafer R: *A New Language for Psychoanalysis.* New York, Yale University Press, 1976
6. Ricoeur P: The question of proof in Freud's psychoanalytic writings. *J Am Psychoanal Assoc* 25:835–871, 1977
7. Freud S: Some Character Types Met with in Psychoanalytic Work: (II) Those Wrecked By Success [Strachey J (ed)] vol 14. London, Hogarth Press, 1958, pp 316–331
8. Bergson H: *Creative Evolution.* New York, Modern Library, 1944

Appendix A:
Sedative–Hypnotic Drugs

Barbiturates Phenobarbital (Luminal), Amobarbital (Amytal), Pentobarbital (Nembutal), Secobarbital (Seconal), Butabarbital (Butisol), Aprobarbital (Alurate), etc.; also combinations of these (Tuinal = Seconal + Amytal) or barbiturates with other drugs (e.g., Fiorinal, Dexamyl, etc.).

Benzadiazepines ("minor tranquilizers"): Diazepam (Valium), chlordiazepoxide (Librium), flurazepam (Dalmane); lorazepam (Ativan), chlorazepate (Tranzene), prazepam (Verstran), oxazepam (Serax), and mixtures of these with non soporific drugs (Librax).

Others: Meprobamate (Miltown, Equanil), Chloral Hydrate (Noctec, Somnor), Glutethimide (Doriden), Methaqualone (Quaalude, Sopor, Parest, Somnafac), Methyprylon (Noludar), Ethchlorvynol (Placidyl), paraldehyde, bromides, and such anesthetics as nitrous oxide, ether, chloroform, etc., and mixtures of these with non soporific drugs (Milpath, Deprol).

Ethyl alcohol, other alcohols and organic solvents.

Appendix B:
Criteria for the Diagnosis
of Alcoholism

These criteria were compiled by a committee of medical authorities from the National Council on Alcoholism to establish guidelines for the proper diagnosis and evaluation of this disease. Criteria are weighted for diagnostic significance and assembled according to types: Physiological and Clinical (including major alcohol-associated illnesses) and Behavioral, Psychological, and Attitudinal. Because early diagnosis is helpful in treatment and recovery, manifestations are separated into their earlier and later phases. There are brief discussions of recurrent and arrested alcoholism, cross-dependence, and the types of persons at high risk of alcoholism.

The problem of alcoholism has been receiving increasing interest in the past few years. Extensive treatment programs are being mounted, hospitals are beginning to accept patients for treatment, labor-management programs are attempting to identify alcoholic employees to give them special benefits and rehabilitation, third-party payments are being afforded by insurance

---

This article by the Criteria Committee, National Council on Alcoholism, is reprinted with permission from the *American Journal of Psychiatry* 129:127–135, 1972, copyright American Psychiatric Association 1972; and *Annals of Internal Medicine* 17:249–258, 1972, copyright Annals of Internal Medicine 1972. Reprints of the "Criteria for the Diagnosis of Alcoholism" are available from The National Council on Alcoholism, 733 Third Avenue, New York, N.Y. 10017.

carriers, and courts are making special disposition for rehabilitation. Therefore, it is important to establish a set of criteria for the diagnosis of alcoholism. To this end, the National Council on Alcoholism established a committee to prepare a set of criteria, to submit it for criticism and documentation by other experts, and to publish it for the guidance of those involved in the diagnosis of alcoholism.

At the outset, it became apparent that we had undertaken a formidable task, for, despite a great deal of work in the past, much of the literature is burdened by anecdotal material and special assumptions made a priori, and there is a dearth of scientifically controlled observations on the natural course of the disease. In addition, people of many disciplines have made observations from their own points of view, which may be hard to reconcile, and there are not a few who, by their definition of disease, have eliminated alcoholism from the category of disease. But any tendency to withdraw from the field was overcome by the urgency of the task, and the committee herewith presents the results of its deliberations.

Diagnostic criteria may serve several purposes. They may be used *to ascertain the nature of a disease* from a cluster of symptoms. This was not the main goal of the committee. They may be used to promote *early detection* and provide *uniform nomenclature* , both objects of this endeavor. Criteria may be used to *prevent overdiagnosis*. This is important because of the psychological, finanial, legal, and therapeutic implications in a diagnosis of alcoholism for the life of the patient. Criteria may be set for *treatment* purposes. Beyond indicating that a need for treatment exists, the committee believes that any indication of different modalities of treatment, except in broad terms, is beyond the scope of its mandate. Criteria may be set for *prognosis*, at present the prognosis for alcoholism is obscure.

Mainly, the committee expects the criteria to be used to identify individuals at multiple levels of dependence. The committee has endeavored to use objectively reproducible data that are obtainable from the patient, his immediate family, or his associates. These data have been weighted for their diagnostic significance. We have included material that would differentiate degrees of severity and that would allow for progression of the disease, where that exists, without prejudging the possibility that cases of alcoholism may exist in which progression is not a factor. All but one consultant believed that, in alcoholism, there generally is a progression of the disease, although this might not necessarily be reflected by continually increasing drinking. Many consultants have exhorted us to concentrate more on "early manifestations." The reader will note a separation into early, middle, and late effects, which is a general guide. Our first intent, however, is that the person who is diagnosed as having alcoholism surely fits into that category.

THE NATURE OF ALCOHOLISM

The committee was unanimous in defining the disease of alcoholism as a pathological dependence on ethanol, as it is classified under Section 303.2 in the *Diagnostic and Statistical Manual of Mental Disorders,* second edition, of the American Psychiatric Association.

Aside from the legal difference between the distribution of alcohol and that of other drugs, there are important scientific differences. A drug is defined in two senses: it is a substance of use in medicine, and it is a habit-forming substance. It generally produces its effect in small quantities. Although alcohol does produce an effect with small quantities, it differs from other drugs in both senses in that large quantities over a long period of time are necessary for it to become habit-forming.

Another difference between alcohol and other drugs particularly those of the optiate class, is the relative risk of addiction. Many people drink, but less than ten percent develop the psychological and physiological dependency on alcohol that can be categorized as alcoholism. With opiates, the risk of pharmacological addiction is considerably higher. Many alcoholics believe that they were alcoholics from their first drink, that their reaction to alcohol was different from that of others. These retrospective data are suspect until and unless a clear difference is established between these individuals and others. Family incidence of alcoholism and other factors may indicate a portion of the population at high risk.

Whether *anyone* who drinks a sufficient quantity over a sufficient period of time will develop alcoholism, whether a specific biochemical or psychological difference leads to alcoholism, or whether both conditions (with other as yet undetermined factors possibly turning the balance) are necessary to cause alcoholism has not yet been established. Thus, whether there is continuous or discontinuous progression from drinking alcoholic beverages to dependence on alcohol has not yet been clearly decided. Animal data suggest that anyone who drinks enough over a sufficiently long period of time will develop the signs of alcoholism. In the free state, however, neither all humans nor all animals choose the paths that lead to this condition. In establishing criteria for diagnosis, the committee wishes to avoid prejudging these issues of etiology.

On the other hand, once alcoholism is established, there is general consensus on its manifestations, and the committee thus feels it is appropriate to describe it as a disease, in agreement with the American College of Physicians, the American Medicial Association, the American Psychiatric Association, and other bodies. Alcoholism fits the definition of disease given in *Dorland's Illustrated Medicial Dictionary,* 24th edition:

A definite morbid process having a characteristic train of symptoms, it may affect the whole body or any of its parts, and its etiology, pathology, and prognosis may be known or unknown.

Partial and intermittent forms of alcoholism pose some problems that will be treated separately. Isolated episodes of inebriation, even if they generate unfortunate consequences, are eliminated.

DIVISIONS OF DATA

Data are assembled according to the type of material they represent. Therefore, there are separate data "tracks"—Track I: Physiological and Clinical, and Track II: Behavioral, Psychological, and Attitudinal. The Track II data are grouped together because behavioral manifestations, the easiest to determine and most objective to recognize, imply attitudinal and psychological manifestations.

There is no rigid uniformity in the progress of the disease, but, since early diagnosis seems to be helpful in treatment and recovery, manifestations are separated into "early," "middle," and "late." In addition to identifying early and late symptoms and signs, each datum was graded according to its degree of implication for the presence of alcoholism. Of course, some of the more definite signs occur later in the course of the illness. But this does not mean that people with earlier signs may not also have alcoholism.

Various terminologies for these signs have been suggested; we propose to weight them and group them into three "diagnostic levels," with those weighted as "1" being the most significant.

Diagnostic Level 1. Classical, definite, obligatory. This criterion is clearly associated with alcoholism.

Diagnostic Level 2. Probable, frequent, indicative. This criterion lends strong suspicion of alcoholism; other corroborative evidence should be obtained.

Diagnostic Level 3. Potential, possible, incidental. These manifestations are common in people with alcoholism, but do not by themselves give a strong indication of its existence. They may arouse suspicion, but significant other evidence is needed before the diagnosis is made.

DIAGNOSIS

It is sufficient for the diagnosis of alcoholism that one or more of the major criteria of diagnostic level 1 are satisfied, or that several of the minor criteria in Tracks I and II are present; see Tables B-1 and B-2. If one is making the diagnosis because of major criteria in one of the tracks, he should also make a strong search for evidence in the other track. A purely mechanical selection of items is not enough; the history, physical examination, and other observations, plus laboratory evidence, must fit into a consistent whole to ensure a proper diagnosis. Minor criteria in the physical and clinical tracks alone are not sufficient, nor are minor criteria in behavioral and psychological trakcs. There must be several in *both* Track I and Track II areas.

Table B-1
Major Criteria for the Diagnosis of Alcoholism

Criterion	Diagnostic Level
TRACK I. PHYSIOLOGICAL AND CLINICAL	
A. Physiological Dependency	
1. Physiological dependence as manifested by evidence of a *withdrawal syndrome** when the intake of alcohol is interrupted or decreased without subtitution of other sedation**** it must be remembered that overuse of other sedative drugs can produce a similar withdrawal state, which should be differentiated from withdrawal from alcohol.	
a) Gross tremor (differentiated from other causes of tremor)	1
b) Hallucinosis (differentiated from schizophrenic hallucinations or other psychoses)	1
c) Withdrawal seizures (differentiated from epilepsy and other seizure disorders)	1
d) Delirium tremens. Usually starts between the first and third day after withdrawal and minimally includes tremors, disorientation, and hallucinations.*	1
2. Evidence of *tolerance* to the effects of alcohol. (There may be a decrease in previously high levels of tolerance late in the course). Although the degree of tolerance to alcohol in no way matches the degree of tolerance to other psychotropic drugs, the behavioral effects of a given amount of alcohol vary greatly between alcoholic and nonalcoholic subjects.	

*See Seixas.[1]
**Some authorities term this "pharmacological addiction."

Table B-1
(Continued)

Criterion	Diagnostic Level
A. Physiological Dependency (*continued*)	
2. Evidence of *tolerance* to the effects of alcohol (*continued*)	
a) A blood alcohol level of more than 150 mg/100 ml without gross evidence of intoxication.	1
b) The consumption of one-fifth of a gallon of whiskey or an equivalent amount of wine or beer daily for a period of two or more consecutive days, by a 180-lb individual.	1
3. Alcoholic "blackout" periods. (Differential diagnosis from purely psychological fugue states and psychomotor seizures.)	2
B. Clinical: Major Alcohol-Associated Illnesses. Alcoholism can be assumed to exist if major alcohol-associated illnesses develop in a person who drinks regularly. In such individuals evidence of physiological and psychological dependence should be searched for.	
Fatty degeneration in absence of other known cause	2
Alcoholic hepatitis	1
Laennec's cirrhosis	2
Pancreatitis in the absence of cholelithiasis	2
Chronic gastritis	3
Hematological disorders:	
Anemia: hypochromic, normocytic, macrocytic, hemolytic, with stomatocytosis, low folic acid	3
Clotting disorders: prothrombin elevation, thrombocytopenia	3

Criterion	Diagnostic Level
B. Clinical (*continued*)	
Wernicke-Korsakoff syndrome	2
Alcoholic cerebellar degeneration	1
Cerebral degeneration in absence of Alzheimer's disease or arteriosclerosis	2
Central pontine myelinolysis ⎫ diagnosis only	2
Marchiafava Biomini's disease ⎬ possible postmortem	2
Peripheral neuropathy (see also beri-beri)	2
Toxic amblyopia	3
Alcoholic myopathy	2
Alcoholic cardiomyopathy	2
Beri-beri	3
Pellagra	3

TRACK II. BEHAVIORAL,
PSYCHOLOGICAL, AND ATTITUDINAL

All chronic conditions of psychological dependence occur in dynamic equilibrium with intrapsychic and interpersonal consequences. In alcoholism, similarly, there are varied effects on character and family. Like other chronic relapsing diseases, alcoholism produces vocational, social and physical impairments. Therefore, the implications of these disruptions must be evaluated and related to the individual and his pattern of alcoholism. The following behavior patterns show psychological dependence on alcohol in alcoholism:

1. Drinking despite strong medical contraindication known to patient — 1

2. Drinking despite strong, identified, social contraindications (job loss for intoxication, marriage disruption because of drinking, arrest for intoxication, driving while intoxicated) — 1

3. Patient's subjective complaint of loss of control of alcohol consumption — 2

Table B-2

Minor Criteria for the Diagnosis of Alcoholism

Criterion	Diagnostic Level
TRACK I. PHYSIOLOGICAL AND CLINICAL.	
A. Direct Effects (ascertained by examination)	
1. Early:	
Odor of alcohol on breath at time of medical appointment	2
2. Middle:	
Alcoholic facies	2
Vascular engorgement of face	2
Toxic ambloyopia	3
Increased incidence of infections	3
Cardiac arrhythmias	3
Peripheral neuropathy (see also Major Criteria Track I, B)	2
3. Late (see Major Criteria, Track I, B)	
B. Indirect Effects	
1. Early:	
Tachycardia	3
Flushed face	3
Nocturnal diaphoresis	3
2. Middle:	
Ecchymoses on lower extremities, arms, or chest	3
Cigarette or other burns on hands or chest	3
Hyperreflexia, or, if drinking heavily, hyporeflexia (permanent hyporeflexia may be a residuum of alcoholic polyneuritis)	3
3. Late:	
Decreased tolerance	3
C. Laboratory Tests	
1. Major—Direct	
Blood alcohol level at any time or more than 300 mg/100 ml	1
Level of more than 100 mg/100 ml in routine examination	1

Table B-2
(Continued)

Criterion	Diagnostic Level
C. Laboratory Tests (*continued*)	
2. Major—Indirect	
Serum osmolality (reflects blood alcohol levels): every 22.4 increase over 200 mOsm/liter reflects 50 mg/100 ml/alcohol)	2
3. Minor—Indirect	
Results of alcohol ingestion:	
Hypoglycemia	3
Hypochloremic alkalosis	3
Low magnesium level	2
Lactic acid elevation	3
Transient uric acid elevation	3
Potassium depletion	3
Indications of liver abnormality:	
SGPT elevation	2
SGOT elevation	3
BSP elevation	3
Bilirubin elevation	2
Urinary urobilinogen elevation	2
Serum A/G ration reversal	2
Blood and blood clotting	
Anemia: hypochromic, normocytic, macrocytic, hemolytic with stomatocytosis, low folic acid	3
Clotting disorders: prothrombin elevation, thrombocytopenia	3
ECG abnormalities:	
Cardiac arrhythmias, tachycardia, T waves dimpled, cloven or spinous atrial fibrillation, ventricular premature contractions, abnormal P waves	2
EEG abnormalities:	
Decreased or increased REM sleep depending on phase	3
Loss of delta sleep	3
Other reported findings:	3
Decreased immune response	3

Criterion	Diagnostic Level
C. Laboratory Tests (*continued*)	
3. Minor—Indirect (*continued*)	
Decreased response to Synacthen test	3
Chromosomal damage from alcoholism	3
TRACK II. BEHAVIORAL, PSYCHOLOGICAL, AND ATTITUDINAL	
A. Behavioral	
1. Direct effects	
Early:	
Gulping drinks	3
Surreptitious drinking	2
Morning drinking (assess nature of peer group behavior)	2
Middle:	
Repeated conscious attempts at abstinence	2
Late:	
Blatant indiscriminate use of alcohol	2
Skid Row or equivalent social level	2
2. Indirect effects	
Early:	
Medical excuses from work for variety of reasons	2
Shifting from one alcoholic beverage to another	2
Preference for drinking companions, bars, and taverns	2
Loss of interest in activities not directly associated with drinking	2
Late:	
Chooses employment that facilitates drinking	3
Frequent automobile accidents	3
History of family members undergoing psychiatric treatment; school and behavioral problems in children	3

Table B-2
(Continued)

Criterion	Diagnostic Level
A. Behavioral (*continued*)	
2. Indirect effects, Late (*continued*)	
Frequent change of residence for poorly defined reasons	3
Anxiety-relieving mechanisms, such as telephone calls, inappropriate in time, distance, person or motive, (telephonitis)	2
Outbursts of rage and suicidal gestures while drinking	2
B. Psychological and Attitudinal	
1. Direct effects	
Early:	
When talking freely, makes frequent reference to drinking alcohol, people being "bombed," "stoned", etc. or admits drinking more than peer group	2
Middle:	
Drinking to relieve anger, insomnia, fatigue, depression, social discomfort	2
Late:	
Psychological symptoms consistent with permanent ongoing brain syndrome (see also Major Criteria, Track I, B)	2
2. Indirect effects	
Early:	
Unexplained changes in family, social, and business relationships complaints about wife, job, and friends	3
Spouse makes complaints about drinking behavior, reported by patient or spouse	2
Major family disruptions: separation, divorce, threat of divorce	3
Job loss due to increasing interpersonal difficulties, frequent job changes, financial difficulties	3

Table B-2
(Continued)

Criterion	Diagnostic Level
B. Psychological and Attitudinal (*continued*)	
2. Indirect effects (*continued*)	
Late:	
Overt expression of more regressive defense mechanisms: denial, projection, etc.	3
Resentment, jealousy, paranoid attitudes	3
Symptoms of depression: isolation, crying, suicidal preoccupation	3
Feelings that he is "losing his mind"	2

PSYCHIATRIC DIAGNOSIS

After a suitable evaluation, a separate psychiatric diagnosis should be made on every patient, apart from the diagnosis of alcoholism. Patients may suffer from schizophrenia, latent or overt; from manic-depressive psychosis, obsessive-compulsive neurosis, recurrent depression, anxiety neurosis, or psychopathic personality; or have no psychiatric constellation differing from normal. The diagnosis should be made after treatment for withdrawal is complete, since alcohol is anxiety-producing and can also bring out psychological mechanisms and traits that are not apparent without alcohol. In particular, the hallucinatory behavior induced by alcohol withdrawal is not to be equated with schizophrenic hallucinatory behavior.

ALCOHOLISM WITH INTERMITTENT OR RECURRENT DRINKING

Intermittent or recurrent drinking may represent a phase in the course of alcoholism. This pattern should be noted separately. The same criteria control the diagnosis. In some individuals there are recurring episodes of inebriation that become more frequent over a period of years until a daily drinking pattern emerges. In many individuals daily drinking increases until the individual himself slowly becomes aware that physiological and psychological dependence exist. At this point periods of "going on the wagon" may occur, with a resulting intermittent or recurrent pattern of drinking. For most drinkers, there are lesser or greater periods of time when, because of circumstances or the acute effects of alcohol, drinking is not possible. This pattern is not inconsistent with other drug dependence situations, in which interruptions of use, are commonplace and have been accepted without the necessity of making a separate category for them.

Even with a "steady" pattern of alcohol use, there are marked fluctuations in the blood alcohol level during each day. The patient with an alcohol problem, given free choice, does not, as one might assume, keep drinking to maintain a steady blood level of alcohol. It has been observed that men who were incarcerated for public intoxication for three-month periods had a total yearly alcohol intake and a total time available for drinking that may have been less than that of the "normal" drinker. Yet these men reported withdrawal signs and symptoms upon cessation of each drinking spree. There is also good experimental evidence for a withdrawal syndrome upon cessation of relatively short periods of heavy drinking.

Thus, where the practitioner has a patient whose drinking pattern consists of intermittent or recurrent drinking and in whom the appropriate diagnostic criteria are satisfied, the condition should be diagnosed as alcoholism (with the qualification as to pattern added if it seems important).

ALCOHOLISM: RECOVERED, ARRESTED, OR IN REMISSION

Since alcoholism is relapsing and chronic, there are very few authorities who claim a complete cure. But there are many patients who, after a time of complete sobriety, have reordered their lives in a rehabilitative way and are completely able to perform complex and responsible tasks. There are also a few patients who have returned to "social" drinking, or who have infrequent "slips" but who still function as rehabilitated persons.

Although these diagnostic criteria are not devised as a guide to prognosis, it is the opinion of the committee that a history of alcoholism in the past, followed by a significant recovery, should be taken into account as a guide to treatment, employment, and restoration of rights and privileges previously denied because of active alcoholism. Some members of the committee believed that total abstinence would not, in the future, turn out to be an absolute, final necessity for recovery from alcoholism. However, it was agreed that total abstinence, as a measure of recovery, arrest, or remission, was usually more easily measurable, definitive, and generally accepted that a change from dependence to "social" drinking. Thus, the committee agreed that the following considerations should determine the diagnosis of recovered, arrested, or remitted alcoholism:

—Duration of abstinence
—Concurrent active treatment program
—Concurrent A.A. attendance with full participation
—Concurrent self-administered and professionally guided deterrent medication
—Resumption or continuation of work without absenteeism
—No traffic violations
—No substitution of other drugs

Although the committee did not choose at this time to assign definitive time values for any of these considerations, the recovery or remission gains in its validity with a progressively longer time. For abstinence alone to be the criterion, without other therapeutic activity, there needs to be a longer time period than if abstinence is combined with other criteria.

ALCOHOL USE

Diagnostic terms that define conditions that fall short of alcoholism are necessary because of the effects of alcohol on behavior. Although the term *alcohol abuse* has wide currency, we prefer *alcohol use*, accompanying this term with a description of effect.

This leaves the term "abuse" for such situations as child abuse, animal abuse, or self-abuse, where there is an animate object of the abuse, and does not anthropomorphize alcohol, which, after all, is a chemical (the "neutral spirit"). The term *misuse,* we believe, also carries an unnecessary moral implication.

Alcohol Use with Inebriation

Intoxication may be mild, moderate, or severe, or may lead to coma. Although alcoholics are frequently obviously intoxicated, mere intoxication is not sufficient for the diagnosis of alcoholism. Indeed the physician should be cautious in making a diagnosis of alcohol intoxication on the basis of a staggering gain, slurred speech, other neurological signs, and an odor of alcohol on the breath. In such cases, one must be sure to rule out diabetic acidosis, hypoglycemia, uremia, impending or completed stroke, and other cases of cerebral impairment. An alcohol breath test, determination of blood alcohol level, or serum osmolality measurement may assist in making a diagnosis of alcohol intoxication. A history from the patient and from family members or friends is usually helpful but must in itself be subject to evaluation. Alcohol intoxication must be thought of in any person in coma; *in addition,* barbiturate and other sedative intoxication must be investigated: cross-dependence and cross-tolerance are common.

Alcohol Use with Pathological Intoxication

In some individuals a small amount of alcohol will evoke violent, aberrant behavior. Pathological intoxication is an idiosyncratic response to alcohol and is separate from alcoholism.

Alcohol Use: Reactive, Secondary, or Symptomatic

Reactive, secondary, or symptomatic alcohol use should be separated from other forms of alcoholism. Alcohol as a psychoactive drug may be used for varying periods of time to mask or alleviate psychiatric or situationally induced symptoms. This may often mimic a prodromal stage of alcoholism and is difficult to differentiate from it. If the other criteria of alcoholism are not present, this diagnosis must be given. A clear relationship between the psychiatric symptom or event must be present; the period of heavy alcohol use should clearly not antedate the precipitating situational event (for example, an object loss). The patient may require treatment as for alcoholism, in addition to treatment for the precipitating psychiatric event: one may be able to confirm the diagnosis only in retrospect.

Alcohol and Anxiety

The effects of alcohol on the rising slope of the absorption curve parallel the four stages of anesthesia, and thus excited or uninhibited behavior may be shown with mild inebriation. But it also has been documented that, with large doses over a prolonged period of time, alcohol produces anxiety. Whether this bimodal effect occurs as a regular result of any amount of alcohol is currently being investigated. The progressive rise of anxiety with continued heavy drinking is responsible for many of the effects listed as minor criteria.

CROSS-DEPENDENCE

Cross-dependence (or "cross-addiction") may begin iatrogenically or spontaneously with the use of any of the sedative class of drugs, barbiturates, or "minor" tranquilizers, in an attempt to control the anxiety generated by heavy alcohol use or in the mistaken impression that pharmacological control of the anxiety will stop the alcohol use. Such cross-dependence is so common that it must be investigated in any person suspected of alcoholism.

In addition, the life-style of persons who seek pharmacological "highs" is associated with heavy alcohol use *pari passu* with other psychoactive chemical materials. Such persons are at risk of alcoholism, and patients being investigated for the diagnosis of alcoholism should also be evaluated for use of these materials.

Treatment programs for the use of other drugs engender a

significant proportion of "instant alcoholics" who, having relinquished the other drugs, turn to alcohol and experience an unusually rapid onset of dependence. Thus, patients in this category should also be screened for alcoholism, and attempts should be made to prevent its onset.

PERSONS AT HIGH RISK OF ALCOHOLISM

Epidemiological and sociological studies show that the following factors indicate high risk for the development of alcoholism. There is not complete agreement on the extent of risk for each factor.

- A family history of alcoholism, including parents, siblings, grandparents, uncles, and aunts.[2]
- A history of teetotalism in the family, particularly where strong moral overtones were present and, most particularly, where the social environment of the patient has changed to associations in which drinking is encouraged or required.[2]
- A history of alcoholism or teetoalism in the spouse[2] or in the family of the spouse.[3]
- Coming from a broken home or home with much parental discord, particularly where the father was absent or rejecting but not punitive.[4]
- Being the last child of a large family or in the last half of the sibship in a large family.[3]
- Although some cultural groups (for example, the Irish and Scandinavians) have been recorded as having a higher incidence of alcoholism than others (Jews, Chinese, and Italians) the physician should be aware that alcoholism can occur in people of any cultural derivation.[5-7]
- Having female relatives of more than one generation who have had a high incidence of recurrent depressions.[8]
- Heavy smoking; heavy drinking is often associated with heavy smoking, but the reverse need not be true.[9]

RECORDING THE DIAGNOSIS

If alcoholism as defined above is present, the diagnoses should be stated in this order:

—Alcoholism: intermittent use, recurrent use, steady use (early, moderately advanced, far advanced)
—Psychiatric diagnosis
—Physical diagnosis

If major criteria or a sufficient number of minor criteria are not met, the diagnosis should be:

—Suspected alcoholism; psychiatric diagnosis, physical diagnosis

Other diagnoses that can be made:

—Alcohol use: reactive, secondary, or symptomatic; psychiatric diagnosis; physical diagnosis.
—Alcohol use with inebriation

A description of the physical diseases associated with alcoholism and their diagnosis will be the subject of a separate communication.

REFERENCES

1. Seixas FA (ed): Treatment of the Alcohol Withdrawal Syndrome. New York, National Council on Alcoholism, 1971
2. Guze SB, Tuason VB, Gatfield P, et al: Psychiatric illness and crime with particular reference to alcoholism: a study of 223 criminals. *J Nerv Ment Dis* 134:512–521, 1962
3. Barry H, Blame HT: Birth order as a method of studying environmental influences in alcoholism. *Ann NY Acad Sci* 197:172–178, 1972
4. McCord W, McCord J: *Origins of Alcoholism.* Stanford, Calif. Stanford University Press, 1960
5. Perceval R: Alcoholism in Ireland. *J Alcoholism* 4:251–257, 1969

6.   Whitney ED (ed): *World Dialogue on Alcohol and Drug Dependence.* Boston, Beacon Press, 1970
7.   Snyder CR: *Alcohol and the Jews.* Glencoe,, Ill. Free Press, 1958
8.   Winokur G: Genetic findings and methodological considerations in manic-depressive disease. *Brit J Psychiat* 117:267–274, 1970
9.   Pollack S: Drinking Driver and Traffic Safety Project, vol I. Los Angles, Public Systems Research Institute, University of Southern California, 1969

Appendix C:
AMA Guidelines for Alcoholism: Diagnosis, Treatment and Referral

GUIDELINES	EXPLANATORY NOTES

I. For All Physicians With Clinical Responsibility: Diagnosis and Referral

A. Recognize as early as possible alcohol-caused dysfunction in the biological, psychological and social areas.	A. Manual on Alcoholism (AMA); Criteria for the diagnosis of alcoholism. *(Am J Psychiatry* 129 (2): 127 – 135, 1972; or *An Int Med* 77: 249 – 253, 1972); and Keller, M: Definition of alcoholism, in *Quart J Stud on Alcohol* 21: 125 – 134, 1960.
B. Be aware of those medical conditions that are frequently caused by, attributed to, or aggravated by alcohol abuse.	B. Chronic tension states, vague somatic complaints, depression, cardiovascular and gastrointestinal disorders.

This article is as adopted by the American Medical Association Council on Scientific Affairs, October 8 – 9, 1979. Copyright 1978, American Medical Association.

GUIDELINES	EXPLANATORY NOTES

C. Insure that any complete health examination includes an in-depth history of alcohol and other drug use.

D. Evaluate patient requirements and community resources so that an adequate level of care can be prescribed, with patient needs matched to appropriate resources.

D. Information usually available from county medical societies, local Council on Alcoholism, and state or local Divisions on Alcoholism and Drug Abuse.

E. If there are medical needs, including severe withdrawal, make referral to a resource that provides adequate medical care.

E. Another physician, hospital or alcoholism program featuring integrated medical services.

II. *For Physicians Accepting Limited Treatment Responsibility (To Restore the Individual Patient to the Point of Being Capable of Participating in a Long-Term Treatment Program)*

A. Assist the patient in achieving a state free of alcohol and other sedative-hypnotic drugs, including management of acute withdrawal syndrome, which is commonly referred to as detoxification.

A. Office, hospital or clinic may be used depending on patient's condition.

B. Recognize and treat or refer all associated or complicating illnesses.

B. Both physical and psychiatric conditions.

GUIDELINES

EXPLANATORY NOTES

C. Apprise the patient of the nature of his disease and the requirements for recovery.

C. Discuss issues relating to onset, nature and course of illness, as well as prognosis, if treated or untreated.

D. Evaluate resources—physical health, economic, interpersonal and social—to the degree necessary to formulate an initial recovery plan.

E. Determine the need for involving significant other persons in the initial recovery plan.

E. Determine clinical appropriateness, depending on ethical codes, state laws and HEW rules and regulations concerning confidentiality. Significant other persons may include families, (parents, sisters/brothers) and sexual partners.

F. Develop an initial long-term recovery plan in consideration of the above standards and with the patient's participation.

F. This long-term recovery plan would address those factors listed in the following section entitled "For Physicians Accepting Responsibility for Long-Term Treatment." At this point, the physician can assume the responsibilities delineated in the next section, or refer to another physician.

GUIDELINES   **EXPLANATORY NOTES**

III.   For Physicians Accepting Responsibility for Long-Term Treatment

A.   Acquire knowledge, by   A.   Specialized programs:
     training and/or   abstracts of scientific
     experience, in the   literature available from
     treatment of alcoholism.   NIAAA, NCA, AMA, *J Stud*
                                      on Alcohol; visitation to
                                      alcoholism treatment centers
                                      and Alcoholics Anonymous.

B.   The following
     responsibilities should be
     conducted or supervised
     by the physician:

     1. Establish a   1. This is the vehicle whereby
         supportive,   the physician directs,
         therapeutic and   supports, and monitors the
         nonjudgmental   patient over a period of
         relationship.   years. Attempt to modify
                                      the patient's isolation, grief
                                      and guilt, and deal with
                                      other significant
                                      psychotherapeutic issues.

     2. Within the confines of   2. Physician and patient
         this relationship,   responsibilities should be
         establish specific   clearly defined.
         conditions and limits
         under which the
         therapy will be
         conducted, and
         carefully explain
         them to the patient.

     3. Periodically evaluate
         and update the
         recovery plan with the
         patient's
         participation.

GUIDELINES

4. Involve the patient with an abstinent peer group when appropriate.

5. Become knowledgeable about and be able to utilize various health, social, vocational and spiritual support systems.

6. Evaluate directly or indirectly significant other persons and, unless clearly contraindicated, involve them in treatment.

C. Continually monitor the patient's medication needs. After treatment of acute withdrawal, use psychoactive drugs *only* if there is a clear cut and specific psychiatric indication in addition to alcoholism.

D. Be knowledgeable about the proper use of deterrent drugs.

EXPLANATORY NOTES

4. At this point it is critical that referral to professionally guided or self-help groups, such as Alcoholics Anonymous, is specific and appropriate to the patient's needs.

5. i.e., vocational rehabilitation, educational advancement, skills training, halfway and recovery houses, recreational facilities.

6. Treatment may be provided by the physician, another professional, Al-Anon or a comprehensive treatment program.

C. Schizophrenia or major affective disorders may be treated with psychoactive substances that are not ordinarily dependence producing or subject to abuse. However, special care should be exercised in the administration or prescribing of anti-anxiety agents, or barbiturates and barbiturate-like drugs.

D. Specifically, disulfiram (Antabuse) in this country.

GUIDELINES	**EXPLANATORY NOTES**
E. Throughout the course of treatment, continually monitor and treat or refer for any complicating illness or relapse.	E. Check for organic and psychiatric complications, as well as for inappropriate use of alcohol or other sedative—hypnotic drugs
F. Be available to the patient as needed or for an indefinite period of recovery.	

Stanley E. Gitlow

Appendix D:
Antabuse

Almost 40 years ago, an adverse physical reaction to ingested ethanol was observed in workers whose aldehyde dehydrogenase had been inhibited incidentally by disulfiram (Antabuse). Earliest clinical thought appeared to concentrate on the possible use of this drug for aversive conditioning, a technique later abandoned by all but the most sanguine. Since 1950, knowledgeable clinicians have used disulfiram in order to achieve temporary or prolonged abstinence. Although a significant ethical change in association with improved self-understanding undoubtedly improves the likelihood of definitive or long-term recovery from alcoholism, a substantive period of abstinence (12–24 months) may, in and of itself, induce a salutory change in many patients. Since clinical experience has shown that the recommendation and use of any drug therapy—especially psychoactive substances—increases recidivism, a preferred therapeutic approach might consist of an initial opportunity to achieve sobriety by other than medicinal means. Indeed, the avoidance of any drug therapy permits patients to assume greater responsibility for their own recovery. Occasionally, disulfiram therapy may even be used by a patient to avoid commitment to group or individual psychotherapeutic involvement. On the other hand, the appropriate use of disulfiram may improve the effectiveness of an already sound treatment program. In the role of such a therapeutic adjuvant, the clinical effectiveness of disulfiram far exceeds its modest value as a sole treatment modality.

The inhibition of aldehyde dehydrogenase results in little, if any, adverse effect in the absence of ethanol ingestion. Within minutes of drinking as little as 5–10 gm of alcohol, however, such a patient may begin to accumulate enough acetaldehyde to initiate a reaction which might eventually include a flush, headache, bounding pulse, diaphoresis, nausea, vomiting, and vasomotor collapse with orthostatic hypotension. This reaction rarely persists for more than a few hours and commonly requires no therapeutic intervention other than bed rest. Occasionally, parenteral phenothiazines or even support of vital functions might be needed. The amount of disulfiram needed to inhibit aldehyde dehydrogenase rarely exceeds 250 mg/day, but is dependent upon body size, age, general health (especially hepatic function), and other drug use, especially those drugs which are metabolized by the SER system (including certain sedatives, dilantin, coumadin, oral hypoglycemics, and various antirheumatic agents). A slightly higher dose of disulfiram, 500–750 mg/day, may be given during the first few days in order to achieve earlier enzyme inhibition. The drug should not be started earlier than 12–24 hours after the last drink of alcohol. Since the enzyme remains inhibited for at least 4–5 days after the last daily dose of disulfiram, even modest doses of ethanol are likely to result in some untoward reaction if ingested prior to that time. By taking disulfiram each day, the patient is continuously protected, at least partially, against a return to drinking for 4–5 days. Although few physicians still use a test dose of ethanol after initiating disulfiram therapy, it is necessary to acquaint the patient with the pharmacologic information concerning disulfiram use. Patients may even be offered an identification card which would serve to alert a physician that disulfiram is being used. Patients need to know that the alcohol used in cooking fails to achieve a high enough concentration to elicit untoward symptoms. On the other hand, a few ounces of wine or beer, or even a smaller quantity of an elixir, might be adequate to result in such a reaction.

Rarely, disulfiram may result in adverse effects without the concomitant use of ethanol. The most frequent of these are somnolence and a subtle garlic-like odor on the breath. A reduction in dosage may alleviate such side effects but rarely will it relieve the patient who experiences a hypersensitivity reaction to the drug. Disulfiram may infrequently induce hepatic, gastrointestinal, or central nervous system dysfunction, but fortunately discontinuation of therapy usually results in prompt clearing of symptoms. It is most important to emphasize that the safety of administering Antabuse is such that the author has observed more frequent adverse reactions from salicylates than from this drug. The ratio of benefits to risk (untoward reactions) is so high that the only absolute contraindications to the use of disulfiram are: (1) hypersensitivity, and (2) the inability to understand the use of the drug (i.e., psychosis). *Relative* contraindications might include: (1) arteriosclerotic heart disease, especially with recent myocardial infarction or angina pectoris; (2) any severe, life-threatening illness unrelated to recent ethanol ingestion (especially cerebrovascular insufficiency); (3) pregnancy (the author used disulfiram during pregnancy on two occasions, each of which resulted in a normal fetus); and (4) the use of drugs such as dilantin or anticoagulants which complicate disulfiram administration.

In judging the wisdom of administering disulfiram, based on the above circumstances, the balance between an ethanol–disulfiram reaction versus the increased likelihood of a return to active drinking must be evaluated. If such a return to drinking would carry with it an immediate and grave prognostic import, the physician would do well to use the disulfiram in order to lessen the possibility of relapse (i.e., the patient with episodes of bleeding varices following each bout of drinking).

More important than emphasizing those rare instances in which disulfiram may *not* be used, let us turn to the clinical indications for its use:

1. For early evaluation of patient motivation. Those patients whose level of motivation is unknown to the physician may be offered Antabuse to assist their recovery program. When the patient replies negatively and with somewhat irrational obstinency, the physician can be fairly secure in estimating a substantive likelihood for early relapse.
2. For parole or probation. Contrary to some early impressions, prolonged enforcement of abstinence may result in an increased likelihood of recovery from alcoholism.

3. For assistance for the impulsive drinker. That patient who apparently fails to plan drinking episodes, but whose resistance to imbibing is low enough to be overcome repetitively under casual circumstances, may be significantly assisted by the use of disulfiram.
4. For the patient preoccupied with the issue of drinking. Certain patients spend most of their working hours determining whether or not to drink. The use of disulfiram each morning relieves this onerous burden and often results in considerable diminution of the associated depression. Unfortunately, such relief rarely persists for more than a matter of weeks or months.
5. For temporary assistance with critical circumstances during otherwise successful abstinence. This might result from the death of a family member or disruption of routine (i.e., travel).
6. For relief of a consort's anxiety regarding the possibility of the patient drinking. The spouse's anxiety is often poorly tolerated by the alcoholic. Disulfiram therefore may reduce the tension within the family unit.
7. As an adjuvant for the patient whose continuous or periodic drinking has persisted despite the professed desire to desist and despite the use of all other modalities of therapy.
8. For increasing the duration of sobriety for the patient leaving the hospital on a pass or a discharge earlier than the physician would have preferred.
9. For assistance in a psychotherapeutic program for the patient unable to develop insight into the mechanism of his slips.

The author has found the use of Antabuse noted in point nine to be one of the most valuable to the physician conducting definitive treatment of the alcoholic. It is not uncommon for a patient to announce that he drank a few days previously. When asked for the details of this circumstance, the patient can offer no more than that he drank for only a few hours and is no longer imbibing. The patient is then offered the opportunity of taking Antabuse, and if, after the usual explanation of the mechanism by which this drug works, the patient accepts such treatment, he is informed that, during the first year of treatment, discontinuation of the Antabuse for any reason whatever will result in uncontrolled drinking within a matter of weeks or at most within three months. The patient is also informed that he might well use one of the following six rationalizations for stopping the Antabuse: (1) "I forgot to take it"; (2) "I went on a trip and forgot to take it with me"; (3) "I ran out and forgot to get the prescription renewed"; (4) "I was doing so well that I didn't think I needed it any more"; (5) "I wanted to demonstrate that I could handle it on my own"; and (6) "My daughter was getting married and I wished to be able to toast the bride." The patient is politely told that all of these rationalizations are lies and that since he would have to discontinue the Antabuse at least five days prior to drinking, the act of discontinuation would repesent a determined plan to return to the use of alcohol.

During the ensuing therapy, it is expected that a dialogue will develop concerning the psychodynamic basis supporting the decision to return to the use of alcohol. Thus, Antabuse could be used as an integral part of a psychotherapeutic program. It may soon become apparent to the patient that alcoholic slips occur in three stages:

1. Withdrawal or reisolation. The patient stops going to A.A. meetings, fails to contact close cohorts within the recovery community, and misses appointments with the physician or clinic.
2. The patient begins to feel compromised and ill-used in the confines of a relationship which he feels powerless to change. This is usually with the consort, other family member, or employer.
3. The actual moment of drinking (the least important aspect of the slip).

Discussion of the first stage often helps to emphasize the critical nature of those empirical mechanisms whereby a return to drinking may be made less likely. Point two will commonly keynote specific psychodynamic factors with which the patient has difficulty. Recurrent review of all such aspects of slips leads to early appreciation of the compelling and self-destructive behavior patterns inherent in the drinking.

Antabuse, an adjuvant for the treatment of alcoholism, has been examined through the perspective of almost 30 years of clinical experience. It must be emphasized that viewpoints vary even

among physicians with extensive experience with this drug.
Moreover, no effort has been made to review the voluminous disulfiram literature; adequate reference articles are available for
that purpose.

REFERENCES

Disulfiram in the treatment of alcoholism: An annotated bibliography.
    Addictions Research Foundation, Bibliographic Series, No. 14, 346
    pp, 1978
Fried R: *Alcoholism* 1:257, 1977
Fuller RK, Roth HP: Disulfiram for the treatment of alcoholism. *Ann Int
    Med* 90:901–904, 1979
Nora AH, Nora JJ, Blu J: Limb-reduction anomalies in infants born to
    disulfiram-treated alcoholic mothers. Letters to the Editor. *The Lan-
    cet* 2:664, 1977
Ritchie JM, in Goodman LS, Gilman A (eds): *Pharmacological Basis of
    Therapeutics,* ed 5. New York, Macmillan, 1975

Index

Page numbers followed by *t* indicate tables.